Managing Evaluation and
Innovation in Language Teaching

APPLIED LINGUISTICS AND LANGUAGE STUDY

GENERAL EDITOR
CHRISTOPHER N. CANDLIN
Chair Professor of Applied Linguistics
City University of Hong Kong
Hong Kong

For a complete list of books in this series see pages v and vi

Managing Evaluation and Innovation in Language Teaching: Building Bridges

Edited by

Pauline Rea-Dickins and
Kevin P. Germaine

Longman

London and New York

Addison Wesley Longman Limited
Edinburgh Gate
Harlow, Essex   CM20 2JE
England

and Associated Companies throughout the world

Published in the United States of America
by Addison Wesley Longman Inc., New York

© Addison Wesley Longman Limited 1998

First published 1998

ISBN 0 582 30373-7 Paper

Visit Addison Wesley Longman on the world wide web at http://www.awl-he.com

British Library Cataloguing-in-Publication Data
A catalogue record for this book is
available from the British Library

Library of Congress Cataloging-in-Publication Data

Managing evaluation and innovation in language teaching : building
   bridges / edited by Pauline Rea-Dickins and Kevin P. Germaine.
       p.   cm. — (Applied linguistics and language study)
   Includes bibliographical references (p.   ) and index.
   ISBN 0–582–30373–7 (pbk.)
   1. Language and languages—Study and teaching—Evaluation.
   2. Educational innovations.   I. Rea-Dickins, Pauline.
   II. Germaine, Kevin P., 1953–   .   III. Series.
   P53.63.M36   1998
   407—dc21   98–24975
                                                           CIP

Set by 35 in 10/12 pt Baskerville
Printed in Malaysia, PP

APPLIED LINGUISTICS AND LANGUAGE STUDY

GENERAL EDITOR
CHRISTOPHER N. CANDLIN
Chair Professor of Applied Linguistics
City University of Hong Kong
Hong Kong

Error Analysis:
Perspectives on Second Language
Acquisition
JACK C. RICHARDS (ED.)

Stylistics and the Teaching of
Literature
H.G. WIDDOWSON

Contrastive Analysis
CARL JAMES

Learning to Write:
First Language/Second Language
AVIVA FREEDMAN, IAN PRINGLE
and JANICE YALDEN (EDS)

Language and Communication
JACK C. RICHARDS and
RICHARD W. SCHMIDT (EDS)

Reading in a Foreign Language
J. CHARLES ALDERSON and
A.H. URQUHART (EDS)

An Introduction to Discourse
Analysis
Second Edition
MALCOLM COULTHARD

Bilingualism in Education: Aspects
of theory, research and practice
JIM CUMMINS and MERRILL SWAIN

Second Language Grammar:
Learning and Teaching
WILLIAM E. RUTHERFORD

Vocabulary and Language
Teaching
RONALD CARTER and
MICHAEL MCCARTHY

The Classroom and the Language
Learner: Ethnography and second-
language classroom research
LEO VAN LIER

Observation in the Language
Classroom
DICK ALLWRIGHT

Listening in Language Learning
MICHAEL ROST

Listening to Spoken English
Second edition
GILLIAN BROWN

An Introduction to Second
Language Acquisition Research
DIANE LARSEN-FREEMAN and
MICHAEL H. LONG

Process and Experience in the
Language Classroom
MICHAEL LEGUTKE and
HOWARD THOMAS

Translation and Translating:
Theory and Practice
ROGER T. BELL

Language Awareness in the
Classroom
CARL JAMES and PETER GARRETT
(EDS)

Rediscovering Interlanguage
LARRY SELINKER

Language and Discrimination:
A Study of Communication in
Multi-ethnic Workplaces
CELIA ROBERTS, EVELYN DAVIES
and TOM JUPP

Analysing Genre:
Language Use in Professional Settings
VIJAY K. BHATIA

Language as Discourse:
Perspectives for Language Teaching
MICHAEL MCCARTHY and
RONALD CARTER

Second Language Learning:
Theoretical Foundations
MICHAEL SHARWOOD SMITH

From Testing to Assessment:
English as an International Language
CLIFFORD HILL and KATE PARRY
(EDS)

Interaction in the Language
Curriculum: Awareness, Autonomy
and Authenticity
LEO VAN LIER

Phonology in English Language
Teaching: An International
Language
MARTHA C. PENNINGTON

Measuring Second Language
Performance
TIM MCNAMARA

Literacy in Society
RUQAIYA HASAN and
GEOFF WILLIAMS (EDS)

Theory and Practice of Writing:
An Applied Linguistic Perspective
WILLIAM GRABE and
ROBERT B. KAPLAN

Autonomy and Independence in
Language Learning
PHIL BENSON and PETER VOLLER
(EDS)

Language, Literature and the
Learner: Creative Classroom Practice
RONALD CARTER and JOHN MCRAE
(EDS)

Language and Development:
Teachers in a Changing World
BRIAN KENNY and
WILLIAM SAVAGE (EDS)

Communication Strategies:
Psycholinguistic and Sociolinguistic
Perspectives
GABRIELE KASPER and
ERIC KELLERMAN (EDS)

Teaching and Language Corpora
ANNE WICHMANN, STEVEN
FLIGELSTONE, TONY MCENERY
and GERRY KNOWLES (EDS)

Errors in Language Learning and
Use: Exploring Error Analysis
CARL JAMES

Translation into the Second
Language
STUART CAMPBELL

Strategies in Learning and Using
a Second Language
ANDREW D. COHEN

Managing Evaluation and
Innovation in Language Teaching:
Building Bridges
PAULINE REA-DICKINS and
KEVIN P. GERMAINE (EDS)

Reading in a Second Language:
Process, Product and Practice
A.H. URQUHART and C.J. WEIR

To our parents

Contents

List of contributors   xi
Editors' acknowledgements   xiii
General editor's preface   xiv

Introduction   1

1   The price of everything and the value of nothing:
    trends in language programme evaluation   3
    P. Rea-Dickins and K.P. Germaine

Part I   Evaluating innovation in language education   21
Introduction   23

2   Evaluating the implementation of educational
    innovations: lessons from the past   25
    Kia Karavas-Doukas
3   Language and cultural issues in innovation:
    the European dimension   51
    Celia Roberts
4   Programme evaluation by teachers: issues of
    policy and practice   78
    Richard Kiely

Part II   Managing evaluation and innovation   105
Introduction   107

5   Using institutional self-evaluation to promote the
    quality of language and communication training
    programmes   111
    R. Mackay, S. Wellesley, D. Tasman and E. Bazergan

6 Managing developmental evaluation activities in
   teacher education: empowering teachers in a new
   mode of learning   132
   Tricia Hedge
7 Managing and evaluating change:
   the case of teacher appraisal   159
   Jane Anderson

   Part III   Views from the bridge   187
   Introduction   189

8 Evaluating the discourse: the role of applied
   linguistics in the management of evaluation and
   innovation   195
   Adrian Holliday
9 Evaluating and researching grammar
   consciousness-raising tasks   220
   Rod Ellis
10 Linking change and assessment   253
   Michael Fullan
11 Eavesdropping on debates in language education
   and learning   263
   Elliot Stern

   Bibliography   269
   Index   291

List of contributors

Jane Anderson Personal Skills Section Head, The Training Centre, Petroleum Development Oman, Muscat, Sultanate of Oman

Etty Bazergan Lecturer, Faculty of Letters, Hasanuddin University, Ujung Pandang, Indonesia

Rod Ellis Professor, Institute of Language Teaching and Learning, University of Auckland, New Zealand

Michael Fullan Dean, Ontario Institute for Studies in Education of the University of Toronto, Canada

Patricia A. Hedge Lecturer, Centre for English Language Teacher Education, University of Warwick, Coventry, England

Adrian Holliday Principal Lecturer, Department of Language Studies, Canterbury Christ Church College, Canterbury, England

Kia Karavas-Doukas Lecturer, Centre for English Language Teacher Education, University of Warwick, Coventry, England

Richard Kiely Senior Lecturer, Centre for International Education and Management, Chichester Institute of Higher Education, West Sussex, England

Ronald Mackay Professor of Education, Concordia University, Montreal, and Senior Fellow, The International Service for International Agricultural Research, The Hague

Celia Roberts Senior Research Fellow, Centre for Applied Linguistic Research, Thames Valley University, London, England

Elliot Stern Director EDRU, The Tavistock Institute, London, England

Djasminar Tasman Director LEMIGAS English Language Centre, Research and Development Centre for Oil and Gas Technology, Jakarta, Indonesia

Sally Wellesley Editor and translator, Legal information project, Jakarta, Indonesia

Editors' acknowledgements

We have a number of people to thank for supporting this publication. First of all we thank all the contributors to this edited collection for agreeing to prepare a chapter. We also thank them for responding so positively to our editorial comments and for keeping to the timescales we imposed. The staff at Addison Wesley Longman carefully and diplomatically steered us through the twists and turns that the volume at times faced. Finally, we wish to express our immense gratitude to Professor Christopher Candlin, the Series Editor, for his timely, insightful and steering comments which have, without a doubt, made for a better volume.

Pauline Rea-Dickins
Kevin P. Germaine

General editor's preface

As the editors of this the most recent contribution to the *Applied Linguistics and Language Study Series* convincingly demonstrate, evaluation bids fair to be the greatest growth industry in education – and not only in education – since the invention of printing. Its aims, procedures, tools and techniques also provide, reflexively, one of the most significant objects for critical review in education that one might conceive, precisely because of their pervasiveness, their effects, their potential for affecting directions of change, and, above all, their costs. Not only the processes themselves, but also its practitioners, their roles and their actions offer themselves equally for appraisal. *Quis custodiel ipsos custodies* – who guards the guards themselves – is as pertinent an axiom now as it was in classical antiquity. Further, these practitioners, from car smash assessors, systems analysts, art connoisseurs through to juries and language programme evaluators, invest a spectrum of contexts that encompasses contemporary society. As such we are all engaged in the evaluative process. Indeed, it is hard, on reflection, to imagine a context that does not have evaluation as a key defining factor, in many of which the authors and agents of the evaluative processes are professionally guilded and articled. Beyond this, the discourses of evaluation – though as yet not much studied – themselves offer a rich field of research, especially as they exhibit a fascinating propensity to colonise each other across these contexts, and often to coalesce.

Again, in terms of the methodologies of evaluation research, although there has been traditionally a significant preference for the more positivistic and quantitative types of evidence, this is by no means always the case, indeed much recent work has lent towards the qualitative and the ethnographic. However, it is also the case that evaluation research and practice often inhabits an uncomfortable no-mans-land between both broad methodological traditions, frequently displaying both submissiveness and contestation towards either paradigm, and often self-contradictorily, as for example where art critics struggle between price and painterliness, and language programme evaluators, often using the same or similar terms, weigh up end-of-course test scores against classroom accounts and juggle both against an assessment of the long term impact of a teaching programme on learners' communicative capacities. Is there life after the course, in Alderson's memorable phrase, is then not only a language tester's and language programme evaluator's nightmare question but one that has a quite general haunting value.

It is no accident either that this proliferating of evaluative activity is coupled with that other pervasive metaphor of the late twentieth century, that of *accountability*, or that one should be surprised at all to discover that an increasingly large amount of educational resource worldwide is being diverted towards the discipline of discovering whether what is being done is what some think is what ought to be being done, rather than being more profitably directed towards new activities. Or, indeed, to be surprised that the costs of mounting such often elaborate evaluation and accounting exercises is increasingly being put into question as the gremlins hint that such exercises may not only not tell us how things are, or even how they have been, but may work in fact to stifle innovative and imaginative enterprises bent on exploring how things might become.

But this is to run a little ahead of this rich and varied book, and to bias the picture. It is nonetheless important to display these tendencies towards uniformity and towards contestation amid the apparent diversity of evaluation practices. As fifteen years ago at a notable TESOL Summer Institute in Toronto, Lyle Bachman tellingly displayed in an imaginative plenary on the topic, where like a Victorian chapeaugraphist he appeared and reappeared on stage in a range of guises, as detective, as policeman and as counsellor, evaluation places its professionals in a range of roles, but there's no escaping the judgement day. I don't recall his appearing as *clairvoyant*, which given the theme of this book, linking evaluation to innovation and change, was certainly not prescient. I am not sure if anyone at that time noticed. But this is once again to jump the gun; after all evaluation does not have to be future-focused at all. It can and has been happily engaged with retro-spective accounting, associated with the meeting of targets, the recording of actions taken and not taken, sponsoring a legion of assessors, outputting a library of educational accounts, many of which, once catalogued, may not even be referred to subsequently, as the exigencies of circumstances, the presence of people, and the currency of programmes, change. It has often happily assumed consensus on goals, on causes and effects, on variables, certainly on criteria and standards, and context for context has assembled a formidable array of research tools and techniques ranging from quantitative cost-benefit analyses, achievements tests, surveys and questionnaires, log-frames, critical reviews and focus groups, panels, case studies and just plain free-flow talk, in the search for evidence that can be marshalled and displayed in the evaluative cause, though often with considerable difficulty. Questions, too, regularly repeat themselves inter-contextually and interdiscursively: Are the planned-for effects achieved? Can they be achieved more economically? What are the most efficient ways of reaching the goals? Is the programme/service/effective? Do different partici-pant investments alter perceptions of what is to be evaluated, how, and against what degree of anticipated success? Like maps, evalu-ations have different projections; micro-studies share elements of the evaluation processes of macro studies but are not the same as them, not only in terms of the scope of expected outcomes but also in terms of their focus, their degree of commitment to participation by stakeholders, the insiderness or outsiderness of their participants, their design features, their data and modes of collection. What they all share, however, and this is the key critical point to make, is the essential questionability of their constructs.

As the papers in this valuable collection by Pauline Rea-Dickins and Kevin Germaine illustrate, evaluation can be directed at a range of objects in the domain of language education; at plan-ning and policy decision-making, at programmes, products, re-sources, activities, participants and their interactions, curricula and at the organisational structures themselves within which the eva-luation takes place. So much is in a sense straightforward. The questionability lies in the critical questions one needs to ask of the constructs, as many of the authors do in the papers here: how to focus the evaluation, how discrete are the targets to be, what in-deed are the targets: the purposes and processes of language learning, the products and the outcomes or, much more speculatively and ambivalently, what the impacts are of the programmes and their component and contributing factors, and how they can be displayed. Such a focus on *objects* implies (though it may not be accompanied by) an evaluative focus on *purposes*. To take as an example programme evaluation, one might legitimately ask why the evaluation is being conducted. To improve the programme? To illuminate it to its own participant-stakeholders and to others? To develop the programme further? To provide an account for programme sponsors? A combination of these? Here again, taking a critical stance is helpful to deeper understanding of the issues: in what terms is the evaluation to be conducted? What requirements are being set upon the programme and by whom? For which stakeholders is the evaluation intended, and to what ends is it being provided and, more hard to answer, to what ends will the evaluation be put?

All evaluation is like a theatre, it has a stage, it has players and these have roles and they play to scripts. Unlike the theatre, however, the scripts are not pre-determined; for the most part they unfold, frequently subject to local exigency and always ideologically motivated. A focus on the *players* in any evaluation raises critical questions about who these sponsors, who these end-users are, indeed, who the evaluators themselves are and from what positions they come at the task in hand. The frequently pre-existing relationships of these players are usually opaque, if not actually concealed, to others, and their own agendas and needs only rarely and always gradually uncovered as the evaluative process takes shape. Crucial to these relationships, as Owen (1993) has pointed out, is the insider or outsider status of the evaluators. Exploring this single variable is, in his view, and that of many papers here, the central way to unpacking and understanding issues of the objectivity and credibility, validity and relevance of the evaluation process. It also assists in grasping the nature of the real threat to self always present in any such activity. Of course, these issues of potential bias, special interests and hegemony among the evaluating players can not only be acknowledged, proposals can be made to regulate them.

In one proposal for the evaluation of the National (English Language) Curriculum Project of the Australian Adult Migrant Education Service in 1988, Bartlett argued as follows:

1. No participant in the project will have privileged access to the data of the evaluation
2. No participant will have an unilateral right to, or power of veto over, the content of the report
3. The evaluation will attempt to represent the range of viewpoints encountered
4. Explicit and implicit recommendations made by the evaluators will not be regarded as prescriptive. As far as possible, recommendations will reflect the views of the participants, not those of the evaluators
5. The evaluators will assume that they can approach any individuals involved in the project to collect data. Those approached should feel free to discuss any matter they see fit, and all such discussion will be treated as confidential by the evaluator
6. The release of specific information likely to identify informants will be subject to negotiation with these informants
7. The criteria of fairness, relevance and accuracy form the basis for the negotiations between the evaluators and the participants in the study. Where accounts of the work of participants can be shown to be unfair, irrelevant or inaccurate, the report will be amended. Once draft reports have been negotiated with the participants on the basis of these criteria, they will be regarded as having the endorsement of those involved in the negotiations with regard to fairness, relevance and accuracy
8. There will be no secret reporting. Reports will be made available first to those whose work they represent
9. Interviews and meetings will not be considered 'off-the-record', but those involved will be free, both before and after, to restrict parts of such exchanges, or to correct or improve their statements
10. The evaluators are responsible for the confidentiality of the data collected by them.

I have cited this valuable quasi Code of Practice at some length because its clauses go to the heart of the problematising of evaluation that I take to be important. However, it is itself, of course, open to question, especially from those involved in language education programmes where routinely issues of the degree of shared inter-cultural understanding, shared presuppositions and beliefs, mutualities of interest cannot be taken-for-granted. Perhaps such issues which classically arise in contexts of evaluation in aid and development settings, as Bill Savage and Brian Kenny in another recent book in the *Applied Linguistics and Language Study Series* amply illustrate, merely highlight what is routinely the case, though elsewhere naturalised. Certainly, there is much to critique (not criticise) in Bartlett's stance, however sympathetically drawn one may be to its inherent sensibleness and fairness.

If the objects, products, purposes, players of evaluation lay themselves open to critical evaluation, so much do also the *procedures*, and the choice of *tools* and *techniques* in the evaluative process. Pauline Rea-Dickins and Kevin Germaine rightly devote a good deal of their introductory paper to this issue, as do many of the contributors. What is essential to recognise here, as all papers in this collection do and several quite explicitly, is that these evaluative practices are discoursed and mediated in a variety of ideologically-invested ways and, like all discourse, are subject to questions about indeterminacies and partisanships of meaning-making, the influence from overriding agendas and (il)legitimate interests. Further, as with all discourse-based research, the tools and techniques of evaluation and in particular the data they produce, are open to debate about their comprehensiveness, their representativeness, in short, their reliability. Such questioning does not end with data collection and analysis; the communication of findings from evaluation is equally susceptible to bias and partiality, not only because the use to which such findings are to be put is often unclear but also because such vested uses materially constrain the extent and nature of the presentation of reports. There is no telling it as it is, in Stenhouse's famous dictum about classroom research, and this still holds true, but there is still plenty of opportunity for creatively reconstructing how it was thought to have been.

Central to the approach taken in this book is that to address this questionability surrounding evaluation practices and constructs and the contests such critique can give rise to, these discourses of evaluation need themselves to be subject to collaborative and integrative negotiation. In short, they need the *bridge-building* of the sub-title. For the editors and the contributors this requirement is as much necessary for the determining of the outcomes of evaluation as it is for the analysis of processes, the contribution of different but complementary disciplinary knowledge and methodology, and for the reporting of results. The book, however, does more than this; it directs such bridge-building negotiation of the constructs and partnerships of evaluation squarely at the introduction of innovation and change. It makes this very plain. In particular, readers may note the extent to which the contributors consistently embrace this critical dimension, not just about evaluation, but about innovation and, incidentally, the ways in which they test the robustness of the bridges.

One embracing way in which they do this, and entirely appropriately in the light of what has been said so far in this Preface, is to focus on the description, interpretation and explanation of discourse as way of understanding evaluation and as a way of appraising the likelihood of some consequent innovation and change. It is as if they had taken as some governing axioms the following proposed by Owen (1993), all of which emphasis this discursive mediation between evaluation and subsequent action:

- the more the evaluator consults with audiences during the planning phase, the more the findings will be used;
- the more the evaluator pursues questions of importance to the audiences, the more the findings will be used;
- the more 'proximate' the evaluator is to the audiences during the evaluation, the more likely the findings will be used;
- the more interactive the form of the reporting, the more the findings will be used;
- the less complex the 'mix' of audiences, the more the findings will be used;
- the more assistance the evaluator provides with implementation of the findings the more the findings will be used;

Note how each of the above directly or indirectly calls on the facilitating discourse as a means of assuring the take-up of innovation. These processes are explicitly discursive. They resonate with Bachman's evaluator's guises alluded to earlier: *consult, pursue questions of importance, establish proximity to audience, report interactively, assist with implementation.* Indeed the final axiom proposed by Owen:

- any evaluator who thinks her study will have an exclusive impact on change in the program or organisation concerned is under a delusion.

explicitly warns against a *monologic* stance.

Now what is striking about the contributors to this volume is the way all, in different ways and with different audiences and contexts in mind, emphasise the importance of mediated interaction in their evaluation processes. Whether it be an emphasis on dialogue among the stakeholders in general, or more specifically among researchers from different paradigms, between teachers and researchers, or by encouraging teacher-teacher collaboration in in-house evaluation, every paper returns to the central concern with dialogue. Not that engendering such dialogue is necessarily easy; several papers warn against traps and snares that only programmes of professional development and critical awareness can guard against, especially when seeking to manage those insider-outsider tensions I raised earlier which can rapidly coalesce into resistance and dissent, as some contributors here warn. Whether the search is for Fullen's 'silver bullet' or some other magic wand, mixing metaphors only compounds the communicative problematic inherent in the link between evaluation and innovation. As in Miller's play, views from the bridge are always deeply disturbing; looking backward while looking forward not only produces a crick in the neck, it runs the ever-present risk of some catatonic impasse. To circumvent that, there is only one recipe, as Miller unerringly prescribes, and that is to *relate* and to *talk*. After all, as Stern points out in the concluding paper in this stimulating collection, what is conversation if it isn't simultaneously retrospective and prospective, essentially evaluative *and* innovative at one and the same time.

Professor Christopher N. Candlin
General Editor
City University of Hong Kong

References:
L. Bartlett (1988): *Proposal for the evaluation of the National Curriculum Project. Adult Migrant Education Service.* Sydney. NCELTR
J.M. Owen (1993): *Program Evaluation: Forms and Approaches.* Sydney. Allen & Unwin
W. Savage & B. Kenny (eds) (1997): *Language and Development: Teachers in a Changing World.* London. Addison Wesley Longman

Introduction

1

The price of everything and the value of nothing: trends in language programme evaluation

P. REA-DICKINS AND K.P. GERMAINE

Introduction

Evaluation has become something of a hot topic in recent years, with numerous books and articles devoted to its different aspects. A quick survey of recent publications demonstrates the continuing topicality of evaluation in language education, in education and, more generally, in the social sciences. Accountability in one form or another has been a primary motivation for much evaluation practice although, as we demonstrate in this volume through a range of case studies, the purposes for evaluation extend well beyond the concerns of 'value for money' (VFM). These purposes affect the way the evaluation process is conceived and implemented in relation to innovation, the role of the 'evaluator', the participation of stakeholder groups, and how and what decisions are made on the basis of evaluation results, and with what effects.

In this chapter we first identify some of the main trends and emergent issues in language programme evaluation through a brief review of some of the more recent publications and evaluation initiatives; we then analyse some of the dynamics shaping language programme evaluation in the 1990s which are further exemplified by the contributors to *Managing Evaluation and Innovation in Language Teaching*, thereby building understanding of the parameters and potential of evaluation in a range of curricular contexts in language education.

Trends in language programme evaluation

Visibility of evaluation

In 1992 Beretta wrote 'To date very few books have appeared on the evaluation of language teaching programs in general' (p. 5). He goes on to say that this compares unfavourably with the field of educational evaluation 'where dozens of titles appear annually'. The situation in the latter half of the 1990s is rather different. Since Alderson and Beretta produced their edited collection in 1992, several other publications have appeared, including Anivan (1991; edited collection), Rea-Dickins and Germaine (1992), Weir and Roberts (1994), Rea-Dickins and Lwaitama (1995; edited collection), Lynch (1996). An evaluation-focused issue of *Language Culture and Curriculum* appeared in 1991 (Vol. 3/1), as well as a survey article on 'Evaluation and English Language Teaching' (Rea-Dickins 1994). Recent journal articles also reveal a growing concern with evaluation (e.g. Blue and Grundy 1996, Ellis 1996a, Pacek 1996, Chambers 1997). Details of funded programme evaluations include Low *et al.* (1993), Walsh *et al.* (1990) and the PRODESS Scheme of The British Council (The British Council 1994, 1995). The upsurge of interest in evaluation evidenced by the number of recent publications indicates a change in the position documented in the early 1990s for language education.

The evaluation community itself is very active with the founding of several societies since 1993. This includes the European Evaluation Society, the UK Evaluation Society, the Australasian Evaluation Society with branches across Australia and New Zealand, a network in Sweden and, more recently (1996), the establishment of the Swiss Evaluation Society. In connection with the first meeting of the International Evaluation Society in Canada in 1995, Chelimsky (1997: 1) comments that this 'marked the first time that five evaluation associations and more than 1600 evaluators from 66 countries and five continents had come together'. Thus, activity in evaluation has been maintained, if not increased, in a range of discipline areas.

Evaluation is also more conspicuous in other ways in our professional lives as we become increasingly accountable not only to those in the institutions within which we work but also to external bodies. These may be national schemes such as the Higher Education Funding Council for England (HEFCE) in the UK university sector, or OFSTED, the Inspection Scheme for English state schools. In addition there are now a number of professional accreditation organisations from whom British language schools, colleges and universities seek approval. In the UK, these include BALEAP, EQUALS, BASCELT,[1] and The British Council Accreditation Scheme. The emergence of IELTDHE, BATQI[2] and the proposals to establish a British Institute of ELT have all developed within the evaluation and accountability climate of the last decade. Within such schemes, accountability is largely defined in terms of identifying and upholding standards; in some it has strong links with professional learning and development.

At this point we may ask: What are the emerging trends from all of the above?

Recent studies

In Table 1.1 below we analyse a small sample of evaluation studies selected primarily for the range of views they represent in terms of current evaluation practice in different language education contexts.

Here we make four main points in relation to these studies, which are not intended as a comprehensive listing. Firstly, and predictably, we identify a range of motivations for the evaluations, from the need to provide information on issues of impact and the effects of language intervention, with the underlying intention of findings feeding into policy (e.g. Low *et al.* 1993) to those which are concerned with the role of evaluation in furthering quality and development in professional practice (e.g. Alderson and Scott 1992), or a combination of both (e.g. Lynch 1996). Secondly, the aims of an evaluation influence the role of the external evaluator, affecting the relationships with and between programme staff. In the study by Alderson and Scott the evaluation expert functions as a facilitator for the evaluation work and takes on a collaborative role. In turn, the aims and nature of stakeholder involvement shape the selection of methodology and have implications for evaluation training for project staff (see also Murphy 1995, 1996). Concerned only with identifying impact from a teacher training programme on the classroom and learners' level of language proficiency, Weir and Roberts function in the traditional role of external evaluator as expert. The training they provided was for technical staff who were

Table 1.1 Some recent macro-evaluation studies

Study	Purpose	Focus	Evaluator role	Stakeholder involvement	Stakeholder training	Design features	Data
Weir & Roberts (1991)	Impact VFM Retrospective	Impact from teacher training programme on students' language proficiency	External evaluator as expert	None	None Training for contracted technical staff in preparation for data gathering	Outsiders as evaluators Non-participatory Non-equivalent control group design with pre- & post-test	Product & process data Quantitative: student & teacher language assessment test results Qualitative data: ■ systematic classroom observation ■ teacher self-reports Samples of students' written work Teacher interviews
Mitchell (1992)	Impact & Effects Retrospective Policy shaping	Implementation of bilingual primary education Bilingual proficiency: Gaelic & English	External evaluator as expert	None	None Training for field workers	Outsiders as evaluators Preliminary survey to narrow down sample Sample: high and low uptake schools Two classes in each of 10 schools for detailed classroom-based study	Product & process data Quantitative: systematic classroom observation (teacher & pupil focused) Interviews Assessment tasks: spoken and written in both Gaelic & English Parental attitudes Triangulation

Table 1.1 *continued*

Study	Purpose	Focus	Evaluator role	Stakeholder involvement	Stakeholder training	Design features	Data
Alderson & Scott (1992)	VFM & review Developmental Policy shaping	National ESP project: e.g. methodology, materials, attitude to project	Consultant, facilitator, collaborator	Yes: project staff as evaluators mainly at data collection & analysis stages Insiders & outsiders	Yes	Participant evaluation	Qualitative & quantitative, e.g. survey questionnaires, student & teacher reports; no test data or classroom observation Triangulation
Low *et al.* (1993)	Impact & effects Policy shaping	Foreign language learning in Primary Schools: e.g. learners' linguistic attainment, programmes & methodology	External evaluator as expert	Some teachers' assistance with assessment tasks	None	Outsiders as evaluators Largely non-participatory Some 'project' & 'non-project' school comparisons	Product & process data Quantitative: test scores Qualitative: classroom observation, language samples, interviews with all stakeholder groups

to assist in the data collection; also the case for the field workers in the Mitchell evaluation. Thus, the extent to which an evaluation is, or can be, participatory is largely dependent upon the aims of the project articulated at the outset. Further, we note influences from the empiricist paradigm for evaluation, with some attempt to control variables. Weir and Roberts use a non-equivalent control group design with pre- and post-tests; Low *et al.* also attempt to make 'project' and 'non-project' school comparisons. Overall, however, we observe a shift towards multiple methods in evaluation, away from sole reliance on test results to triangulation of data sources via tests, performance tasks, classroom observation, questionnaires and interviews.

These points also arise in relation to smaller scale evaluation studies, as reported in Table 1.2, which provides an overview of recently reported micro-evaluations, indicative of another trend in English language education (see also Ellis, Chapter 9 in this volume). It is noticeable that all the evaluations reported demonstrate the awareness of integrating evaluation with professional practice and the importance of having systematic evaluation at the heart of a programme of learning. Although there may be a reluctance to accommodate external (and extrinsic) evaluation of language programmes geared towards accountability and review, there is growing recognition of the need to integrate evaluation practice at a micro level as a means of contributing directly to curriculum and individual professional development. This should not be surprising in a profession which is oriented towards the practical and immediate concerns of the curriculum, pedagogy and the classroom. Another dimension evident from these accounts of evaluation is that the design and the intention of the authors is to be inclusive and collaborative, involving stakeholders wherever possible (see below). Blue and Grundy (1996) have an interest in intrinsic team evaluation by checklist, which may subsequently contribute to external evaluation. Pacek's focus (1996) is more summative but indicates that formative (and presumably) collaborative evaluation took place during the INSET programme itself. However, even the summative evaluation is oriented towards future developments in the programme reported. Collaboration and consensus between teachers evaluating coursebooks is at the centre of Chambers' account (1997) and, like the others, has a practical orientation (and in this case a decision to be made about selection of materials).

Table 1.2 Recent micro-evaluation studies

Study	Purpose	Focus	Evaluator role	Stakeholder involvement	Stakeholder training	Design features	Data
Blue and Grundy (1996)	Accountability Review Developmental: curriculum and professional	EAP: programme resources, organization, professional activities	Internal facilitator	Yes: self-evaluation	None	Participatory in implementation	Checklist Group discussion (team)
Pacek (1996)	Developmental Impact Formative Retrospective	ELT INSET: effects on practice in the classroom	Facilitator (distance)	Some presumed in ongoing evaluation None in questionnaire	None reported	Outsiders as evaluators	Focus group discussions Questionnaires
Chambers (1997)	Decision-making	ELT coursebook	Internal 'expert'	Yes: teachers	Integrated	Internal evaluator following a systematic and principled set of evaluation stages	Checklist

A few other examples are noteworthy. Murphy's work (e.g. 1995, 1996) arises from his role as an evaluator in English language projects where he has been involved in training teachers to carry out their own evaluations. Focusing on the process of learning to do evaluation and on 'how the practitioners become proficient users of the techniques and methods described', he documents the training of participant evaluators 'to introduce developmental uses of evaluation, and to involve a sector of the profession that had not normally used evaluation before' (1996: 321).

Also promoting evaluation as a developmental, awareness-raising and management tool is the example of the Project Development Support Scheme (PRODESS) introduced to promote programme-based evaluation in ELT projects managed by The British Council in Central and East Europe (see, for example, Rea-Dickins and Potter 1994, Kiely *et al.* 1993, 1995, 1996). In particular the scheme has encouraged the use of evaluation activities as a catalyst in the management of change and process of reform in English language education and as an essential tool in ELT project management. PRODESS did not conduct external evaluations. It was about information exchange, communication, stimulating and supporting professionals in their own use of developmental evaluation. The newsletter in support of this scheme, *PRODESS News*, provided a forum for reports and discussions of project evaluation over a three-year period (The British Council 1992–1995).

Returning to the accountability and value-for-money functions, numerous commissioned evaluation studies are also regularly conducted in overseas aid contexts, e.g. for the World Bank, The British Council and the Department for International Development, formerly ODA (e.g. Cracknell 1996). By their very nature, circulation is more often than not restricted and, thus, in the words of Beretta (1992: 6) 'it is virtually impossible to know if any of these evaluations are scholarly or disciplined studies'. In this respect there is no significant change. On the other hand, the perception of Rea-Dickins, who is regularly commissioned to undertake such studies, is that change is taking place. There is an increase in inviting tenders for this work, terms of reference which call for a more rigorous evaluation design and which require the active involvement of and evaluation training for different stakeholder groups in relation to the project, as well as a focus in evaluation aims beyond immediate project objectives and extended to evidence of impact through unintended outcomes.

From the foregoing, we have identified a change in evaluation practice in language education over the last decade, not only in terms of its enhanced profile and an increase in activity, but changes are also observed in the way in which evaluation is currently defined, with a paradigm shift evidenced by greater participation of stakeholder groups, an extended range of functions for evaluation, and the use of multiple methods with triangulation of data sources: informants and elicitation techniques. Evaluation is portrayed not only as a tool for determining impact and value for money but is also about stimulating learning and understanding. This has led, overall, to a greater democratising of knowledge about evaluation.

The dynamics shaping language programme evaluation in the 1990s

In this section we take forward some of the issues raised above. First of all, we examine further the changing nature of evaluation which then leads into the identification of the different functions for evaluation in language education programmes. We also examine stakeholder roles in the evaluation process before briefly considering the concepts of bridge building and knowledge in evaluation.

What is evaluation?

A book on evaluation needs to define the term *evaluation*. How is it shaped? What are its aims? What are its methods? How is evaluation different from research?

Evaluation should be principled, systematic and ask relevant questions. It is about forming a judgement, and providing evidence, about the worth of something. The responsive dimension of evaluation, in addressing the needs of stakeholder requirements, highlights the *utilisation* function of evaluation in professional practice, with evaluation feeding into decision making. Evaluation is thus intended to have immediate utility for policy shaping and is expected to be influential in short-term decision making.

A narrow judgemental definition presents evaluation as a largely objectives-driven undertaking, associated with the conventions of experimental design (cf. Pawson and Tilley 1997). Many in the educational evaluation literature have eschewed this perspective and promoted a view of evaluation as a curriculum-focused inquiry grounded in professional practice of an illuminative, responsive and developmental rather than recommendatory nature (e.g. Stenhouse 1975, Parlett and Hamilton 1977). This developmental position is clearly captured by Cronbach and colleagues (1980, cited in Nevo 1986: 16) who describe an evaluator as 'an educator (whose) success is to be judged by what others learn' (p. 11) rather than a 'referee (for) a basketball game' (p. 18) who is hired to decide who is 'right' or 'wrong'. Analysing different evaluation models and approaches – for example, goal-free evaluation (Scriven 1967), the objectives model (Tyler 1986a, Weiss 1972), the illuminative approach (Parlett and Hamilton 1977), responsive evaluation (Stake 1975, Guba and Lincoln 1981), and the connoisseurship approach (Eisner 1985) – we arrive at a view of evaluation as multifaceted, with the *potential* to make judgements and recommend, to evaluate effectiveness and efficiency and to contribute to curriculum improvement and development. The blending of the distinction between curriculum development and evaluation brings a clearer focus on professional practice and action, a theme taken up throughout this volume (see in particular Chapters 4 and 6).

Early evaluation tradition focused on measurable outcomes in relation to pre-ordained objectives and implied a positivistic approach (see also discussion in Lynch 1996). Changes in goals for evaluation have also been accompanied by a shift in methodology away from the empiricist tradition towards 'a paradigm of choices emphasising multiple methods, alternative approaches and . . . the matching of evaluation methods to specific evaluation situations and questions'. (Patton 1981, cited in Norris 1993: 51). The emergence of 'naturalistic', 'responsive' and 'utilization-focused' evaluation advocated flexibility in methodology with choice of paradigm sensitive to the particular information requirements of the stakeholders. Thus the influences evident in educational evaluation in the 1970s and 1980s now regularly permeate current language education evaluation practice, emerging clearly in Chapter 3 by Roberts.

Evaluation, in our view, is grounded in professional practice and is expected to provide information that will feed into decision making, planning, action and change, defined in our professional context in very practical curricular terms. Evaluation, too, has contributions to make to theory but to a theory of *implementation* to inform pedagogical practice and practitioner decision making.

Functions of evaluation

Whether we like it or not the *judgemental* dimension of evaluation is here to stay. Educational administrators and other professionals are forced into 'accountability bonding' either linked to issues of funding or mechanisms for quality assurance. This dimension of accountability is seen most directly in sponsored programmes and project-based work (see Weir and Roberts 1994), the area in which many evaluations in English language education have been grounded. Harrison (1996b) writes of the complexities of accountability in relation to ODA projects and programmes and outlines different levels of responsibility from project officers to government, which is accountable to taxpayers. Accountability is still very much on the agenda but there is some evidence in the ELT profession, at least, of a move from 'fiscal responsibility' (Sanders *et al.* 1994), very much a product of our age, and its schemata of economics and money, to a broader consideration of accountability. This is especially noticeable within the 'project' context which recognises that 'Running a project is not a neat linear process' (Chambers 1996: 27), that there will be 'unintended outcomes' (*ibid.*: 26), that formative evaluation undertaken by project stakeholders should be integrated within projects for 'external . . . accountability demands as well as for the more usual developmental purposes' (Weir 1996: 20).

Developmental evaluation represents the concerns of teachers and a curriculum management team who share a common ownership of current and future curriculum development. There are now many examples of evaluation used as a developmental tool (e.g. Marpaung and Kirk, also Hall, all cited in Kenny and Savage 1997). To serve this purpose, specific tasks and feedback mechanisms need to be introduced to facilitate curricular improvements. A central feature of this type of evaluation is stakeholder participation, i.e. the engagement of professionals, in the critique of the curricular practices leading to action in the form of collaboratively refining classroom procedures (see Hedge, Chapter 6 in this volume). Evaluation may thus be action-oriented and supportive of programme and curriculum development goals.

It has long been argued that development within the curriculum is contingent upon an *awareness* in the profession of the workings of the classroom (Stenhouse 1975; see also van Lier 1988). As the basis for contributing to curricular improvement, professionals need to be provided with opportunities to develop a deeper under-standing of the tasks in which they are involved. The goal here is to develop, through evaluation activity, a personal knowledge base. Evaluation has therefore the potential to stimulate profes-sional involvement and development (see Chapters 6 and 9 in this volume).

Evaluation is also a *management* activity, and takes up the con-cerns of managers and key staff for regular information and know-ledge in order to plan strategically, with data from evaluation activities feeding into this process. A corollary of this is the need for clear frameworks for evaluation data to feed into. Chapter 5 Mackay *et al.* in this volume is a significant example in this re-spect). This management function for evaluation is also much in evidence in several of the contributions to Kenny and Savage (1997).

Dialogue and engagement with stakeholders

Curriculum evaluation, it is suggested, is to be viewed holistically and as a series of contextualised events. One implication of this position is the need to integrate the contributions (views, inter-pretations, etc.) of the different participants in an evaluation at different stages of the evaluation process, as in the Alderson and Scott (1992) and Lynch (1996) studies. Evaluators with all their pre-acquired knowledge, experience and skills (and ethically they need to have these) may view an evaluation as a two-way learning bridge between themselves and the stakeholders. The evaluator and stakeholders build a bridge from past experience, knowledge, education and training to the present reality of the actual evalua-tion being undertaken. From this perspective, all participants are involved in a learning cycle (Kolb 1984, cited in Aitchison 1993), enhancing their knowledge not only of the evaluation itself but also that of the innovation, programme or project, and its context. Experiential knowledge is thus seen as important to enhancing the validity of evaluations, and is derived through dialogue with, and the involvement of, stakeholders in the evaluation process.

From this it becomes clear that evaluators are not autonomous in their functioning, in opposition to earlier rather restricted views of stakeholder contributions, and it is interesting to reflect how over the last ten years the range of participants in evaluation has broadened (see, e.g., Denham 1997). The gathering of information via a small number of interviews with 'key informants' identified by the sponsoring agency was, especially in the 1970s and into the 1980s, a typical approach practised in ELT project evaluation work, thus reflecting a limited understanding of the range of potential contributions to the evaluation process. As seen in Alderson and Beretta (1992), Weir and Roberts (1994), and in the way that some of the terms of reference for evaluations are now being framed by sponsoring agencies, the evidence is that practice is changing towards a greater and more influential role of stakeholders in evaluation processes. In summary, we find a greater democratisation in evaluation and the more active involvement of many of those who are affected by the innovation being evaluated.

The concept of bridge building in evaluation

Evaluation is about innovation, planning and change and is characterised in different ways. Evaluation is not unique to applied linguistics or to language education. As we have seen, in relation to the different purposes for evaluation, the different roles that evaluators may take, the wide range of stakeholders who may be involved, as well as the nature of the educational change process itself, the 'roots' of evaluation are not clear. As Stern states (Chapter 11, this volume): 'To be an evaluator . . . today inevitably requires the building of many bridges across many disciplinary divides.' Evaluation cuts across domains, e.g. education, health, social welfare, business, public policy development, etc., although, by the nature of the work of applied linguists within the field of language education, our first encounters will usually be within educational contexts.

In addition to 'domains', we have also seen that there are choices in terms of methodological frames. Much early evaluation practice was firmly rooted in the positivist tradition, representing a bridge between the natural sciences, psychometrics and educational evaluation. In the early 1970s the emergence of the 'new wave' evaluation (e.g. Parlett and Hamilton 1977, Parlett 1984) was associated with, among other things, more naturalistic approaches to evaluation 'suggestive of a social movement drawing strength from more humanistic research traditions outside of psychometrics, experimentalism and the social survey' (Norris 1993: 48). The influences in this case are reflective of the social sciences. Bridge building is therefore nothing new and, as Stern points out, is indeed inevitable.

But what else do we mean by 'building bridges'? We can readily identify the more global influences on the way we perceive, think, and are expected to implement evaluations with, for example, the influence of economics on our outlook on the value of things, and hence accountability from a VFM perspective. But in what other ways can bridge building be useful? And, why is it important to do this? Fullan (Chapter 10, this volume) is very clear on the relationships between change processes and evaluation and argues persuasively for strong bridges to be built between innovation and evaluation processes: 'as long as change and evaluation are detached from each other we cannot mobilise the data and motivation to make improvements'. Integration in this way is a theme running throughout this volume and, it is suggested, is key to educational change and impact. Communication is also important and evaluation is a powerful means of opening up dialogue. For example, it can be said that one of the strengths of gatherings such as the Dunford House Seminar[3] (see, e.g., Bullough and Webber 1996) is the building of bridges between the different players in language education overseas: development field officers, academics, government civil servants and others with a stake in language education in development contexts. At events of this kind, systematic attempts are made to evaluate and explore new ideas in relation to ongoing problems or situations, and to create a better understanding between these different stakeholder groups. Thus, within the ELT profession (and other academic disciplines) there is an implicit acknowledgement of this need to build bridges in order to promote professional development and validity. The articles in this volume provide evidence for the usefulness of bridge building.

There is, of course, the danger, as rightly cautioned by Roberts (Chapter 3, this volume) of jumping into an 'atheoretical ditch', by merely importing ideas or methods from other disciplines. Another danger of uncritically importing ideas and practices from other closely allied disciplines lies in the shared common-sense assumptions between them. Similar discourse communities explain reality in similar ways and often share perspectives on how to engage and deal with that reality. The inherent danger here may be that ideas and practices merely reinforce rather than challenge the shared outlooks. Our intention in this volume is not only to affirm positively but also to challenge assumptions.

Bridge building implies issues of knowledge and an extension to our knowledge base. In this volume knowledge is defined in different ways. There is knowledge from the perspective of a discipline and content base. Unsurprisingly education is one domain providing knowledge for much evaluation practice in English language education – see Anderson (Chapter 7) and Karavas-Doukas (Chapter 2). Inputs from management theory and managing change from outside the educational context are also seen as influential across a number of contributions – see Hedge (Chapter 6) and Anderson (Chapter 7). Knowledge in relation to methodology is discussed by Roberts in Chapter 3 from an ethnographic and anthropological position. It is argued that these examples are to be seen as direct links in the move towards achieving greater validity in evaluation through a wider and more informed knowledge base.

However important domain knowledge may be, we also assert the importance of experiential knowledge, generated within the context of an evaluation and with which evaluators engage through reflection on the experience of evaluating. This is seen as key to the validity of evaluations and enhanced by contributions from stakeholder groups.

The status quo

In our view many changes have taken place in the theory and practice of evaluation in language education. As we have seen above, there is a sharper focus on the different functions of evaluation constructed around the *accountability* dimension (identified with providing results and judging programme effectiveness against results and costs), *developmental* evaluation (functioning as a means for stimulating curricular improvements) and closely linked to the concept of *awareness raising* and the professional development of those individuals invested with the responsibility for the implementation of educational programmes. Further, evaluation provides data for *managing* developments of different kinds within the curriculum, and it also informs decision making.

We also observe a concern to find an appropriate evaluation methodology and one that reflects the developing trends in ELT teaching and learning methodology (see Kiely, Chapter 4 in this volume). This is expressed in three general directions.

Firstly, there is the need to find and operationalise an evaluation that is systematic. In other words, an evaluation plan must have some sort of framework based on the kind of knowledge it seeks to find. This plan must also reflect both a theory of knowledge and of action consistent with what is being evaluated. This means that the methods used to evaluate a programme or project must reflect what the programme or project does, or is supposed to do. Evaluators in language education contexts are attempting to find coherent ways to carry out evaluation consistent with their own outlook.

Secondly, we identify the need to develop an evaluation plan of action that is collaborative and involves stakeholders to a fuller degree. As language teaching has developed towards learner-centredness, it has inspired evaluators dealing with micro-evaluations to find ways of actively involving participants in this process (see Hedge, Chapter 6 in this volume). A tension may therefore exist between the demands of clients who are focused on accountability purposes for evaluation and evaluators who want to broaden the scope of evaluation with a developmental and awareness-raising aim in mind.

Thirdly, there is the need to implement an evaluation which yields results. Language teaching, by its nature, is pragmatic. Evaluators in this area seem to want the findings of evaluation to be of practical use to learners, teachers and course leaders – e.g. coursebook evaluation, appraisal to address staff development needs, and so forth.

These trends seem to reflect the debates taking place in the wider evaluation community (Adelman 1996, Pawson 1996, Chelimsky 1997, Kushner 1997). For some time there has been debate between *positivists* who view objective empirical methodology as generating measurement-driven data for evaluation and *constructivists* who deem that appropriate and often ethnographic methodologies are to be used according to the demands of the context and its participants. The latter lean towards qualitative, naturalistic methods which not only increase democracy and participation in evaluation but also provide information on the full(er) context (or at least more than by partial empirical methods). This methodological diversity is not unique to language education and is mirrored in the profession of evaluation more generally.

Evaluation needs careful identification of relevant questions, and systematic investigation, and may make contributions to developing professional practice. Distinct characteristics of evaluation are its action orientation in terms of shaping decision making, policy and practice; it is grounded in and integral to professional practice; and is about generating educational knowledge. Evaluation, thus, has the potential for contributing theoretical insights constructed experientially. From this perspective, evaluation contributes to a theory of practice, to knowledge about implementation, which is distinguishable from the contributions that research makes to a discipline.

Finally, as the title of this introductory chapter implies, evaluation has both positive and negative sides but is also a professional necessity. We may also wish to take account of the cautionary note from Chelimsky and Shadish (1997: xiii):

> It is often uncomfortable to stir oneself from familiar cultural, topical, conceptual, and methodological niches. But . . . Evaluation in the next century will be far more diverse than it is today. So we must face the discomfort of stirring ourselves if we are to avoid being left behind.

The chapters in this volume portray some of this complexity through deconstructing evaluation processes. By so doing, they articulate some of the competing tensions between the harsh and supporting shades of evaluation. They signal ways in which our knowledge of curriculum implementation may be professionally developed and taken forward through the means of evaluation.

Notes

1. The different accreditation schemes are as follows: The British Association of Lecturers in English for Academic Purposes (BALEAP), The European Association for Quality Language Services (EQUALS); the British Association of State Colleges in English Language Teaching (BASCELT) is administered through The British Council Courses Validation Scheme.
2. The Institute for English Language Teacher Development in Higher Education (IELTDHE); the British Association of TESOL Qualifying Institutions (BATQI).
3. The Dunford House Seminars have been organised since the late 1970s by The British Council on themes topical to English language education and to the implementation of projects and programmes in development contexts worldwide.

Evaluating innovation in language education

Introduction

In the first part of this volume we focus in particular on the relationship between evaluation and innovation in language education. We start with an overview of evaluation of innovation in the first chapter. According to Karavas-Doukas, 'Evaluating the implementation of educational innovations: lessons from the past', the history of educational innovation is not very encouraging. She identifies five influential factors which inhibit the adoption of change: teachers' attitudes, the clarity of the innovation proposal, teacher training, communications and support during the innovation, and the compatibility of the innovation with the contingencies of the classroom and the wider context in which the innovation is placed. She encourages us to take account of these factors in the planning and implementation of educational change. Both in her review of the literature on educational innovation and from her evaluation of an innovation in English language teaching in secondary schools in Greece, she signals a number of key issues with which other professionals can identify and about which Fullan (Chapter 10 in this volume) comments further. Implicit in much of what she finds is the need for a closer integration of evaluation within the implementation of new curricula and programmes. The role of communication and dialogue, of awareness raising, reflection, and the critical engagement of stakeholders in curriculum implementation is a message that comes across clearly in this chapter (see also Markee 1997).

Chapter 3, by Roberts, 'Language and cultural issues in innovation: the European dimension', demonstrates the methodological diversity of evaluation by examining the role of ethnography as an evaluative tool. The evaluation of an innovative programme and way of enhancing the modern language student's year abroad provides the opportunity to explore a range of ideas from those of intercultural learning to the selection of appropriate strategies for conducting an evaluation. Her work shares certain similarities with Kiely (Chapter 4 in this volume) in that her vision of course development and evaluation is an integrated one which examines 'the potential for a symbiotic relationship between the content and method of a language education project and the evaluation of it'. She is concerned with the educational value from evaluation, rather than accountability-driven motivations for evaluation, and amply illustrates the complexities and multidimensional nature of evaluation. The closing of distance between the staff and students working in this innovative programme provides a further dimension to the concept of stakeholder involvement in evaluation with, in this case, the staff becoming part of the community of learners thus mirroring 'the more equal footing between informants (or teachers as Agar 1987 calls them) and ethnographers' (Roberts, this volume, p. 66). In addition, she is concerned with the development of new perspectives and new knowledge on the part of the participants in the process of evaluation. She shows how learning from other disciplines can be integrated within educational evaluation processes – in her case, drawing from anthropology and sociology.

Chapter 4 by Kiely, 'Programme evaluation by teachers: issues of policy and practice', represents a contribution to a greater democratising of knowledge about evaluation processes. His context is the evaluation of an EAP programme by teachers who are concerned not only with programme improvement but also with accountability to institutional managers and the students participating in the course. In his study, Kiely raises important questions of how teachers manage different agendas in doing evaluation, and the role of evaluation in teachers developing professionally from this experience.

Stakeholder participation is considered to be important in strengthening the validity of an evaluation that aims to promote developments in pedagogy. However, this participation should extend beyond 'completing a questionnaire' or 'being interviewed': knowing that an evaluation is being carried out, and providing information or data is not sufficient. For the educational value of an evaluation to be achieved, it requires the active involvement, critical reflection and engagement on the part of all those involved. Taking a qualitative case study approach, and through listening closely to the key participants in the programme – i.e. the teachers and their students – Kiely investigates the relationship between developments in evaluation and classroom pedagogy. He goes beyond the description of evaluation procedures and findings and examines the 'dialogue' of an evaluation, focusing on student and teacher perceptions and subjective representations of the evaluation process, and the impact of the evaluation on the classroom and its participants. He also considers how the form of evaluation he describes might be further researched and developed to improve programme effectiveness as a means of achieving greater validity.

2

Evaluating the implementation of educational innovations: lessons from the past

KIA KARAVAS-DOUKAS

Abstract. The history of educational reform is a rather gloomy one with innovations proposing changes in teachers' practices and beliefs failing many more times than they succeed. In many cases teachers either reject the innovation outright or profess commitment to the innovation but in reality carry on as before. This chapter examines the nature of the change process and identifies those factors that have been found to influence the implementation of educational innovations and ELT projects in particular. A case study of the implementation of an EFL innovation in Greek public secondary schools is presented in order to exemplify the combination of factors that inhibited the educational reform process. It is believed that awareness of and sensitivity to these factors by educational policy makers may prevent duplication of some mistakes of the past and allow for the more successful planning, design and *implementation* of ELT innovations.

Introduction

Within the last forty years, changes in the structure and role distribution of the family, profound changes in economic, organisational and geopolitical spheres, innovations in the production and dissemination of knowledge and technological advancements have prompted governments to invest in the reform of education in order to prepare future generations to cope with and operate within this constantly evolving environment. Innovation has become a fundamental and all-pervasive feature of society and its effects have slowly but steadily trickled down to the classroom, the learner and the teacher (see Hargreaves 1994, Hopkins *et al.* 1994).

Indeed, today one will have difficulty finding a teacher anywhere in the world who has not been faced or threatened with the notion of change. Change and innovation have become words that policy makers seem to love and teachers seem to dread.

The systematic study of educational innovations began in the 1960s when large sums of money were invested in massive curriculum reforms in the USA. Innovations were being planned and introduced haphazardly without rationale or justification. The focus of policy makers was on the object of change rather than the process, i.e. on the *what* of the innovation rather than the *how*. The process of implementation was not of concern to policy makers and had not even been contemplated as a problem; everyone naively expected that something good would result from these reform efforts. Materials and curricula were being produced and disseminated widely with no overall plan or strategy of how these materials would be interpreted and translated by teachers and learners in practice (see Fullan and Steigelbauer 1991, Fullan 1992, 1993, Hopkins *et al.* 1994).

The 1970s were years of shock and brute reality for the educational world when researchers went into schools to see how the innovations were working on the ground. Most innovations had failed: 'Teachers took what they thought was of use from the materials and integrated them into their own teaching. The curriculum as an innovation . . . was consequently subverted' (Hopkins *et al.* 1994: 22). The 1970s thus became the decade which offered the first glimpses into the complexity of the change process. It was the time when the study of change started in earnest, when the process of implementing innovations started to become a concern.

Since the 1970s, innovations continue to dominate every sphere of educational reality. Implementation studies also continue to reveal findings similar to those of the 1970s. Whether in science, history or language teaching, curriculum innovations are seldom actually implemented as intended. Parish and Arrends (1983) estimate that approximately 20 per cent of educational innovations enjoy successful implementation. The others suffer two fates.

One possibility is that teachers exhibit a token adoption (Hurst 1983) whereby they profess to have changed their practices but in reality carry on as before. Case studies in education include: Morris's (1985) study of the implementation of a curriculum emphasising a heuristic style of learning and active student involvement in Hong Kong secondary schools; Olson's (1981) study of the English Schools Council Integrated Science Project, and Brown and McIntyre's (1978) analysis of four innovations in Scottish secondary schools involving mixed ability teaching and guided discovery techniques. Within English as a Second or Foreign Language contexts examples include: (1) in an ESL context, Lawrence's (1990) curriculum evaluation focused on the 'use' of English in Zambian secondary schools; Cumming's (1993) case study of experienced ESL teachers' attempts to implement an innovative writing course for undergraduate students in Canada and (2) in an EFL context, Mitchell's (1988) study of communicative language teaching practices in French language secondary school classrooms in Scotland; Karavas's (1993) study of the implementation of a communicative learner-centred approach in Greek secondary schools; and Harrison's (1996a) account of a large-scale EFL curriculum renewal project in Oman.

A second outcome is where teachers wholly or partly resist or reject or transform the innovation. Examples of such innovations can be found in Fullan and Pomfret (1977), Fullan and Steigelbauer (1991) and Fullan (1993) who review the results of curriculum implementation studies in Canada, the USA and the UK in a variety of areas at all levels of education (e.g. from the introduction of progressive, open education in primary schools to the development of computer literacy skills and to the development of cognitive skills of handicapped children). This finding is also raised in Marsh (1986) in his review of curriculum implementation studies in Australian schools. Accounts of ELT innovations, either partly or wholly rejected, can be found in Holliday (1992b, 1994a) who reviews ESP curriculum innovation projects, in Brindley and Hood's (1990) account of the implementation of the AMEP project in Australia and in Penner's (1995) and D. Kennedy's (1996) accounts of the causes of Chinese teachers' resistance to communicative language teaching practices in their classrooms.

Indeed, in the literature examples of innovations that were implemented as intended are few and far between (but see Verspoor 1989, Fullan 1992, Mitchell 1992, Low *et al.* 1993, Pennington 1995, Hamilton 1996). The stark reality is that innovations fail more times than they succeed mainly because the process of implementing innovations continues to be downplayed or overlooked (Fullan 1992).

The purpose of this chapter is to examine the implementation issues in more depth and to identify key factors that have been influential in the innovation process. This will be followed by an account of an EFL innovation in Greek public secondary schools which was largely not implemented, in order to demonstrate how the factors identified severely impacted on this innovation. It is believed that both knowledge of and sensitivity to these factors by policy makers and initiators of change will prevent the duplication of mistakes of the past and the waste of precious time, money and energy. As Brindley and Hood (1990: 233) argue:

> A better understanding of how curriculum innovation happens 'on the ground' through systematic exploration and documentation of the adoption process would help to put language curriculum development on a more rational footing and allow curriculum developers to plan more effectively for the changes that follow innovation.[1]

What is implementation?

Educational innovations are planned to bring about improvement in classroom practice with the ultimate aim of enhancing student achievement. Whatever the focus of the innovation – e.g. introduction of pair/group work in the classroom, use of discovery techniques, more active involvement of students in the learning process – fundamental innovations[2] involve changes at three levels: (a) change or revision of teaching materials, syllabi or curricula, (b) changes in teacher behaviour, e.g. new techniques, approaches or activities and (c) changes in beliefs and principles underlying new materials and approaches. Change must occur at all three levels if it is to have an effect in the classroom and on students. If changes occur in either of these levels (i.e. use of materials, behaviour *or* beliefs) rather than all three, then the chances of achieving the intended outcomes of the innovation become drastically reduced (Kennedy 1987, Fullan and Park 1981, Fullan and Steigelbauer 1991, Markee 1993, Hopkins *et al.* 1994). An example will make this 'multidimensionality' of innovation clear. In the last ten years many countries – e.g. China (Penner 1995), Greece (Karavas 1993), Zambia (Lawrence 1990), Kuwait (Sawwan 1984) – have introduced a communicative learner-centred approach in the teaching of English as a second or foreign language. These innovations are usually accompanied by a revision of the curriculum and syllabus and the development of new textbooks. Teachers may well use the materials in the classroom, i.e. change at level (a) above, but may transform them or choose activities to suit their existing teaching style and to conform to their existing beliefs of the nature of the teaching/learning process, i.e. no change at levels (b) and (c). Alternatively, they may use the materials in the classroom and alongside the intended techniques and activities (change at levels (a) and (b)) without an in-depth understanding of the principles or the rationale of the innovation (no change at level (c)). In this last case, teachers are not able to rationalise, justify, critically reflect on or improve upon classroom practice.

Implementation thus refers to the extent to which changes have occurred at all three levels in relation to a particular innovation. It refers to the actual use of the innovation in the classroom. It differs from adoption – i.e. teachers' acceptance or decision to use an innovation (see Fullan and Pomfret 1977, Fullan and Steigelbauer 1991, Hopkins *et al.* 1994, Everard and Morris 1996) – because of the multiplicity of factors (see below) that affect and override initial acceptance and positive predisposition towards the innovation. As Waugh and Punch (1987: 241) explain, 'quite often a change may be adopted but not implemented as planned because, for example, the role change required is resisted by many personnel'. Implementation studies focus on the extent to which the teachers' behaviour and beliefs have changed in relation to a particular innovation or on how an innovation has been taken up in practice and the factors that have led to the successful or unsuccessful use of the innovation. Implementation studies, in other words, seek answers to such questions as: What is happening? How far does practice match intention? What is going well and not so well, and why?

Data on programme implementation would include information about the context and critical features of the programme, the process of its initiation coupled with classroom observation data and interviews (or questionnaires) with teachers, students and other relevant stakeholders (King *et al.* 1987).

Why study implementation?

The investigation of programme implementation should form an integral, fundamental part of curriculum evaluation for three reasons:

1. To enable the reliable and accurate interpretation of the outcomes of the innovation. Although initiators of change are mainly concerned with the extent to which programme objectives (i.e. enhanced student achievement) have been achieved, it is impossible to interpret any such results in the absence of implementation data. As Fullan (1992: 22) argues,

   > without knowing what's in the 'black box' of implementation, we do not know how to interpret the outcomes (or absence of outcomes). Is failure due to implementing poor ideas or to the inability to implement good ideas? In short, without implementation data we cannot link particular changes to learning outcomes.

2. As a part of process (Long 1984) or developmental evaluation (Rea-Dickins and Germaine 1992) to help identify strengths and weaknesses within a programme, leading to its continuous improvement and development.

3. To help us understand and identify the ingredients of successful innovations and to 'provide present and future audiences a picture of what good or poor programs look like' (King *et al.* 1987: 10).

The non- or limited implementation of most educational innovations is mainly due to the fact that curriculum developers devote too much time, energy and attention to planning and design issues, ignoring the difficulties and complexities involved in actual implementation. Reading through the literature of ELT projects verifies this emphasis on planning and design to the exclusion of implementation processes. As Holliday (1992b: 415) asserts, 'much of the published material on this subject misses the mark in that it is mainly involved with setting up and planning project action, with little attention to what actually happens in implementation'. There appears a naive assumption on the part of curriculum developers and policy makers that a change in policy automatically leads to a change in practice (Sarason 1990). What is often underscored or even ignored by curriculum developers is that bringing about educational change is a long, complex, anxiety- and conflict-ridden operation with many unforeseeable obstacles and problems (Fullan 1993). Implementation does not happen overnight. It could take as long as ten years for a new idea or practice to become an integral part of an educational system (Verspoor 1989) provided that the idea or practice corresponds to a perceived need and is suitable to the context (Holliday 1994a). Within this long and arduous journey the teachers' contribution to and participation in the innovation are essential; teachers are the instruments of change and without their willingness, co-operation and participation there can be no change (Brown 1980, White 1988).

Factors influencing the implementation of educational innovations

The following lists some of the most salient factors involved in successful innovations, namely (1) teacher's attitudes, (2) clarity of the innovation proposal, (3) teacher training, (4) communications and support during implementation and (5) compatibility of the innovation with the contingencies of the classroom and the wider educational context. The list is necessarily selective; one need only look at the numbers of books written on this issue (e.g. Sarason 1971, Huberman and Miles 1984, Sarason 1990, Dalin and Rolff 1993, Fullan and Steigelbauer 1991, Fullan 1992, 1993, Hargreaves 1994, Hopkins *et al.* 1994) to appreciate that a thorough understanding of the dynamics and complexities of implementation cannot be captured within a few pages. The factors discussed here are among those most commonly examined in the literature and those that, through personal experience, have proved to be most crucial for implementation.

Teachers' existing attitudes and beliefs

Teachers are not atheoretical beings before the introduction of a new idea or practice. They have established, well-entrenched (although, in many cases, unconsciously held) beliefs about the teaching/learning process and the roles of both teacher and learner in the classroom. These beliefs have been found to affect and guide teachers' interpretation, judgement and classroom behaviour (Clark and Peterson 1986, Wright 1987, Grotjahn 1991, Nunan 1990a, Pajares 1992). Teacher attitudes have been identified as context-specific, influenced by the values and philosophy of the educational system of which the teacher is part (Sarason 1990, Dalin *et al.* 1992, Fullan 1993) and by the attitudes and norms held by others in the teacher's working context (i.e. colleagues and head-master, see Kennedy 1993). As Kennedy (1987: 166), writing within the context of ELT innovations, asserts:

views held on theories of language teaching and learning and views on the educational process and what happens or should happen in classrooms between the teacher and students are ultimately context specific and derived from the culture of the society in which learning takes place.

The introduction of a new set of materials or activities will have a direct bearing on the ways students are organised in the classroom and the ways in which students and teachers interact. A new set of materials or a new approach will have implications for the roles the teachers and learners should adopt in the classroom, and how learning and teaching should be carried out, which may be in conflict with the teacher's existing theories of the teaching and learning process. If incompatibilities between the innovation project's philosophy and the teachers' theories exist, teachers will tend to interpret new information in the light of their existing theories and will translate innovatory ideas to conform to their existing practices, as many case studies have revealed (Nunan 1987, Mitchell 1988, Lawrence 1990, Lamb 1995).

As mentioned above, change needs to occur at three levels (use of materials, behaviour and beliefs) if planned outcomes are to be achieved. And changes in beliefs, which are inextricably linked to and guide behaviour, are the most difficult to achieve. Steps must therefore be taken by curriculum developers and related authorities to alleviate conflicts and minimise incompatibilities by making teacher attitude change and refinement important dimensions of teacher training (Fullan and Pomfret 1977, Brown and McIntyre 1978, Brown 1980, Waugh and Punch 1987).

Indeed, some authors (Sarason 1990, Fullan 1993, Hopkins *et al.* 1994) argue that changing teachers' attitudes is only a small minor step towards successful educational reform. It is the culture of schools that first and foremost must change; even if teachers revise their attitudes in line with the spirit of the innovation and become active inquirers and agents of change they still have to operate within a system that may be essentially conservative and intractable to change. Schools must therefore first develop the capacity to deal with, manage and thrive on change. As Fullan (1993: 3) states,

it is simply unrealistic to expect that introducing reforms one by one, even major ones in a situation which is basically not organised to engage in change, will do anything but give reform a bad name.

However promising and even logical this idea seems, it is rather unrealistic to expect the structure and nature of educational systems to change before introducing innovations, particularly in the case of ELT innovations which are, in the majority of cases, single, lone innovations introduced in existing conservative educational structures. On the other hand, as many case studies of language teaching innovations attest (see, for example, Brock 1994, Pennington 1995, Hamilton 1996), teachers can become successful implementors and even innovators within an essentially conservative context provided they are given opportunities to become aware of their attitudes, clarify them and develop the appropriate frame of reference in which to receive new ideas. Attitude awareness and clarification enables teachers to sift through and discern the most effective and appropriate ideas for their students and for their context and puts teachers' decision making and judgement on a more rational footing. Attitude clarification and refinement paves the way towards successful change but does not guarantee it. Clarity and knowledge of the innovation, to which we now turn, is essential if new ideas are to be applied effectively.

Clarity of the innovation

The lack of clarity of innovatory proposals, both on a theoretical and practical level, has been a persistent problem in many reform efforts and has been cited as a major cause for the rejection or limited implementation of innovations (Fullan and Steigelbauer 1991). The literature abounds with examples of innovation case studies which did not clearly articulate the goals of the innovation, did not specify the means of implementation, and used language outside the teachers' frame of reference (see Gross *et al.* 1971, Brown and McIntyre 1978, Brown 1980, Olson 1981, Brindley and Hood 1990, Karavas 1993). As a result, teachers were unable to identify the critical features of the innovation and were unclear about what it was they should be doing differently. This lack of understanding, of the objectives and principles of the innovation and the means of its implementation, may lead to two forms of non-change, as highlighted by Fullan and Steigelbauer (1991).

One is defined as *false clarity* whereby '. . . people think that they have changed but have only assimilated the superficial trappings of the new practice' (*ibid.*: 35). In such cases teachers profess commitment to an innovation and claim to be using it in their classrooms without in essence changing their classroom beliefs and practices. The introduction of communicative language teaching is a case in point. Teachers in various studies (Aziz 1987, Nunan 1987, Mitchell 1988, Burns 1990, Lawrence 1990) have claimed to be following communicative language teaching principles while observations of their classrooms reveal little, if any, evidence of communicative language teaching practices.

Painful unclarity is a second form of non-change whereby teachers are completely confused and unclear about the principles and practical implications of the innovation and eventually reject or misimplement the innovation. An example of this situation can be found in Beretta's (1990a) retrospective evaluation of the Communicational Teaching Project (CTP) in Bangalore, India. He found that the regular teachers (i.e. those not involved in the development of the project and thus representative of the majority of teachers in south Indian schools), despite using activities advocated by the Bangalore project, had great difficulty coming to terms with the demands of this fluency-based innovation. Regular teachers were not fully aware of the theoretical and practical implications of the CTP (see also Gross *et al.*'s 1971 case study).

This lack of clarity is summed up by Brown and McIntyre (1978: 19), based on their study of four innovations in Scottish secondary schools:

> where planners have not made their interpretations explicit and have not developed their concepts there is danger that either teachers will have no idea what was intended and ignore some aspects of the innovation, or they may misunderstand their intentions and react with disfavour . . . explicit detailed descriptions are not enough; the curriculum planners must further negotiate the meanings ensuring that teachers both attend to and understand them.

Curriculum developers must ensure not only that a joint understanding of the meanings of the innovation is achieved but also that the practical implications of the innovation and the means by which it is to be implemented are clearly articulated to teachers. This is an element frequently neglected by curriculum developers in their belief 'that teachers are trained professionals and will, therefore, have acquired any skills that might be called for' (Brown 1980: 36). Teachers need to know what an innovation entails in practice for them and their students, and what it is they will be doing differently after the innovation has been implemented. Teachers, therefore, must be given direct and explicit guidance, in simple and non-technical terms (Macdonald and Rudduck 1971, Doyle and Ponder 1977, Olson 1981, White 1987, Everard and Morris 1996) on what innovative principles entail at classroom level, in terms of, for example, classroom management processes, learning activities and student assessment. Nevertheless, it should not be assumed that clarity and understanding of an innovation can be achieved merely through detailed teachers' guides and project documentation disseminated to schools. Clarity and understanding, like attitude change and refinement, are desiderata, achieved only through experimentation with new ideas, dialogue, questioning, evaluation and constant support – a process in which teacher training has a key role to play.

Teacher education

> Teacher education still has the honour of being simultaneously the worst problem and the best solution in education.
>
> Fullan (1993: 105)

Effective change in practice is synonymous with continuous and systematic teacher education. Although the paramount importance of continuing professional development has been highlighted by many (Fullan and Pomfret 1977, Stern and Keislar 1977, Fullan and Park 1981, Parish and Arrends 1983, Verspoor 1989, Fullan and Steigelbauer 1991, Fullan 1992), innovations are still being introduced, in different parts of the world, with one-off mass training sessions in which teachers are bombarded with theoretical exhortations of the new approach or idea and are then expected to return to their classrooms and manage change. As Brindley and Hood (1990: 245) among others explain, this practice is largely ineffective because,

> if teachers are being asked to change some aspect of their classroom behaviour they need professional development activities which enable them at the same time to use an innovation and to work through the implications of the change with colleagues. This requires an ongoing program in which teachers commit themselves to classroom action followed by reflection and theory as necessary.

More precisely, teacher training programmes (see Fullan and Steigelbauer 1991, Hopkins *et al.* 1994) do little towards effecting sustainable changes in the ways teachers behave and think when some or all of the following features are present:

- focus is on quick-fix solutions
- participation is optional
- training is not related to the individual needs of schools and teachers
- training does not take into account the contingencies of classrooms
- training takes place exclusively outside schools with no follow-up in school
- training fails to take into account the characteristics of change and how teachers change.

Based on the findings of successful innovation projects which invested heavily in teacher education (Verspoor 1989, Fullan 1993), training programmes both prior to and during implementation have been seen to share the following characteristics:

(a)   They are systematic, ongoing and long term

In any innovation, teachers need time to familiarise themselves with new practices and tools, learn to handle them and experiment with them. They need time to come to grips with new ideas and time to reflect individually and with colleagues on the implications of those ideas. They need time and space to understand new ideas and new roles, time to develop the appropriate skills in carrying them out and adapt new ideas to their classroom context (D. Kennedy 1996). In-service teacher training must occur not only before implementation, as is more commonly the case, but, importantly, during the implementation process. It is when theory is put into practice that people have the most specific problems and concerns. It is only when teachers are given extensive opportunities to experiment with new ideas, understand the mechanics of a programme, express and clarify their problems and concerns at the initial stages of implementation that they develop a true understanding of the programme and a commitment to it. It is only when teachers become skilled and confident in using a new idea that a sense of ownership of the new idea develops, as revealed by Huberman and Miles's (1984) study of twelve innovations. Teacher development must therefore take place in the workshop context *and* in the workplace (Hopkins *et al.* 1994). In the former, new ideas will be presented and teachers will be encouraged to try them out in a comfortable and non-threatening environment among peers. In the latter setting, teachers will attempt to transfer skills and ideas from the workshop to their own classroom context, identify problems and, with the support of colleagues and trainers, identify solutions. On-site support and training may thus be seen to alleviate the pressures of change, to facilitate and establish teachers' theoretical and practical understanding of the meanings of the innovation and, eventually, to pave the way towards effective and sustainable change.

(b) Teacher attitude change is a key aspect of the teacher training process

Old habits die hard and teacher attitudes are not easily amenable to change. Developing changed perspectives is a long and arduous process yet it is the first and necessary step towards real change. Teacher training must primarily strive to uncover the knowledge and beliefs teachers hold and make teachers aware of these (Breen *et al.* 1989, Lamb 1995). Both pre-service and in-service training must encourage teachers to clarify their attitudes and, subsequently, accommodate new elements within their existing mental framework (Breen 1991, G. Ellis 1996). When teachers are aware of and have clarified their own attitudes, they are able to develop the appropriate frame of reference in which to receive new ideas and experiment with them.

(c) Training takes into account teachers' existing knowledge and experience

New knowledge about the subject area and the principles of the innovation must be accommodated into the teachers' frame of knowledge and be communicated in simple non-technical terms in order to have meaning to teachers. Training must be geared towards the specific needs of teachers and schools and focus on the practical problems and issues teachers will face during implementation. Verspoor (1989), in his review of 21 case studies of education reform projects in developing countries, found that successful projects were not only those that had allocated three or four times as much of their total resources for in-service training but had also adjusted the content of their training programmes to the teachers' level of knowledge and experience.

(d)   Making teachers change agents and not merely recipients of change

Apart from familiarising teachers with the theoretical and practical implications of a particular innovation, teacher training should ultimately strive to make teachers innovators in their own right. By confining teacher development to the transmission of knowledge of a single programme, an innovation becomes ephemeral and its success short-lived while teachers continue to be recipients of change rather than change agents. This is where the concept of teacher *education* (as opposed to teacher training, i.e. preparing teachers for the demands of a particular programme, see Hopkins 1986) becomes vital. Educating teachers means teachers becoming life-long learners by developing their ability to raise questions, to reflect upon and evaluate their own practice with a view to constantly improving it (Larsen-Freeman 1983). Teacher education should strive to make teachers work collaboratively in identifying and solving problems of their teaching and learning context with the aim of offering the best possible education for their students. In an era when change has become an integral feature of society, when schools are facing *innovation overload* (Hopkins *et al.* 1994), training teachers in the trappings of a particular innovation will have short-term effects and will only serve to exacerbate teachers' frustration when another innovation comes along. Teachers need to be able to cope with change, need to be open to change and make change an integral feature of their working environment. They need to develop the capacity to critique and question imposed knowledge, to discriminate, judge and select the most appropriate for their learners and for their context teaching techniques and practices (Elliott 1994, Hopkins *et al.* 1994). As Fullan and Steigelbauer (1991: 326) succinctly put it:

> Educational reform will never amount to anything until teachers become simultaneously and seamlessly inquiry oriented, skilled, reflective, and collaborative professionals. This is the core agenda for teacher education, and the key to bringing about meaningful, effective reform.

Meaningful, sustainable and continuous improvement will thus be achieved through a comprehensive and systematic programme of teacher education. For such a programme to be effective, however, support from colleagues, headmasters, school officials and

initiators of change and good communications among all stakeholders are absolutely essential.

Communications and support

Case studies of successful innovations (Fullan and Pomfret 1977,
Fullan and Park 1981, Huberman and Miles 1984, Verspoor 1989,
Brindley and Hood 1990, Hopkins *et al.* 1994, Everard and Morris
1996, Hamilton 1996) have revealed the facilitating effect of two
factors for innovation uptake: (1) good communications and regular flow of feedback during the process of implementation and
(2) school support for the innovation.

It has been shown that teachers have their most specific and
pressing problems and concerns in the initial stages of implementation when attempts are made to translate theoretical proposals
into practice. Communication networks between users of the innovation and between users and managers of the innovation are
therefore essential for teachers to clarify the meanings of the innovation, express their concerns and problems and find solutions
to them. Schools need to establish working groups of teachers
who try to support each other as they move through the stages of
implementation. It has been shown that when teachers regularly
meet to discuss their practices, identify problems of implementation, jointly develop action plans, observe each other's lessons and
provide feedback, they become able to clarify the meanings of
the innovation and identify its workable and unworkable aspects.
Groups of teachers will also need to be in constant two-way communication with initiators of change in order to receive appropriate feedback and support. Open feedback channels between
managers and users of the innovation will not only enable teachers
to overcome the initial (often unexpected) humps of implementation and increase their confidence but will also provide essential
information to managers on the progress of the innovation. Information obtained by teachers acts as a monitoring device whereby
ideas are scrutinised and problems are exposed. Information such
as this can and should be fed into the continuing professional
development of teachers, materials support and modification of the
original innovation plan to make the innovation more compatible
to the needs of the teachers and to the realities of the classroom
context.

In addition, administrative and peer support is believed to have a serious effect on a teacher's decision to use an innovation in the classroom. Teachers' attitudes towards an innovation are influenced by how worthwhile and important others within their working environment perceive the innovation to be (C. Kennedy 1996). A supportive school environment will not only facilitate the acceptance of an innovation but will also help reduce the anxiety and difficulty of learning new skills (Stern and Keislar 1977, Hopkins *et al.* 1994). The creation of such an environment is, however, to a large extent dependent on the school leader. School leaders are in a sense the intermediaries between the innovation and the teacher, and through their actions (or non-actions) they can obstruct or facilitate implementation. By showing their support for the innovation, by working with staff on the problems of implementation, by making sure that problems are communicated to appropriate individuals (school officials, initiators of change), by organising and making resources available and by supporting participation in teacher education programmes, school leaders can significantly affect the extent, impact, quality and the sustainable development of change.

The discussion up to this point has focused on the process of change and what individuals need to effect changes at school level. In spite of effective, systematic and continuing teacher education, teachers may also reject innovations which are found to be incongruent with the constraints of the classroom context. Compatibility of the innovation with the wider educational and classroom context, to which we now turn, is yet another factor which has been found to have a serious effect on implementation.

Compatibility of the innovation with features of the instructional environments in which they are to be implemented

Teachers may accept or reject an innovation in terms of its compatibility with existing classroom contingencies and constraints (see Doyle and Ponder 1977). Failure of procedural recommendations to mesh with the realities of the classroom and to take into account the exigencies (or *macro-aspects of the culture,* see Holliday 1994a) of the wider educational context will lead teachers to judge the innovation as unworkable and impractical. Numerous case studies have highlighted the importance of adapting innovations to the realities of the context in which they are introduced. Morris (1985: 15) provides an account of how secondary school teachers in Hong Kong rejected an innovation emphasising a heuristic style of learning despite expressing favourable attitudes towards it because:

> . . . its operational results were judged to be in contradiction with the realities of the context within which teachers worked . . . teachers perceived the new approach to be wholly dysfunctional because it necessitated them to ignore the expectations of their pupils, principals and colleagues.

The new approach did not enable teachers to cover the exam-oriented syllabus. It also necessitated their departure from their usual transmission model of teaching and gave rise to dissatisfaction and complaints from students and parents alike. Another example comes from Sawwan (1984) who examined the implementation of a communicative language-teaching programme in Kuwait secondary schools. The author found that teachers did not implement the programme as such because many of its features were judged incompatible with the philosophy of the education system, the characteristics and needs of Arab secondary school students and the established roles of teachers and learners in the classroom (for similar examples see Canagarajah 1993, Penner 1995). It has been widely recognised (Brown and McIntyre 1978, Doyle and Ponder 1977, Fullan and Park 1981, Kelly 1980, Waugh and Punch 1987, Kennedy 1988) that if innovations are to be accepted they must be judged by teachers as being feasible in terms of time, resources and organisational constraints, as well as relevant in terms of teachers' perceptions of the needs of their students and acceptable in terms of their own teaching style. If incompatibility in any one of these three spheres exists, then levels of implementation may fall. As Hopkins *et al.* (1994: 20) point out, 'changes which do not address the organisational conditions within the school as well as alterations to the curriculum and teaching are quickly marginalised'.

As regards the introduction of communicative learner-centred approaches, some authors (Breen 1983, Tudor 1993) have stressed that when the philosophy of an educational context is incompatible with the principles of such approaches, any attempt to apply a communicative approach would be unreasonable. I would not go as far as to suggest this, since such an attitude would close the doors to any possibility for change and would result in inertia and maintenance of the status quo and would only serve to justify and strengthen teachers' initial resistance to any innovation. However, I do believe that innovation proposals should attempt to mould projects to the teaching conditions and resource constraints of an institution, as well as to the immediate concerns of the teachers. In addition, the relevance and appropriateness of new ideas should be critically appraised and evaluated through application.

Indeed, incompatibility with the classroom and the wider educational context was one of the factors leading to the non-implementation of a communicative approach by teachers in Greek secondary schools. The following sections provide an account of this innovation and examine the degree of its implementation. The case study serves to empirically validate the importance of the factors affecting implementation which were discussed in the first part of this chapter. The study also exemplifies how lack of attention to the process of implementation can result in the loss of time, energy, money and in great teacher dissatisfaction.

Introducing communicative language teaching in Greek secondary schools

Nature and object of the innovation

In 1983, responding to the goals of the Council of Europe for cross-cultural communication and understanding, and the need to provide textbooks responsive to the needs and interests of Greek secondary school foreign language learners, a process of English language-teaching curriculum reform began in Greek state secondary schools.

The revised curriculum, based upon a functional-communicative approach to language teaching (van Ek 1986), was put into effect in 1985. In addition, a teacher-training handbook (Dendrinos 1985b), to familiarise teachers with the theoretical and practical implications of the new curriculum, was developed and distributed free to all state school teachers of English. Following a trial period from 1984 to 1987, new textbooks for the first three years of secondary education were developed along reconstructionist principles (see Clark 1987, for further discussion) and were distributed for implementation on a national level in 1987.

The overriding goal of these textbooks is the development of students' communicative competence, as well as their intellectual and social development through the process of language learning. Apart from the development of students' linguistic repertoire and sociolinguistic skills, the textbooks (mainly through numerous pair and group work activities) strive to have students discover knowledge about the language, make choices and actively participate in the learning process rather than passively accept and digest new information. In terms of teacher roles, teachers are asked to abandon the roles of authority and transmitter of knowledge and are advised to be facilitators, monitors, co-communicators and guides to the students' learning process.[3]

The only training provided to teachers to support this innovation took the form of one-off workshops and conferences in which participation was optional.

The implementation study

In 1991, the author undertook an evaluation of the implementation of the Greek EFL project. The study had two aims:

1. to investigate the extent to which Greek secondary school English language teachers were using the textbooks and applying the principles of a communicative learner-centred approach (as advocated by the curriculum developers) in their classroom practices;
2. to investigate the factors affecting the project's implementation, i.e. teachers' attitudes towards and response to the innovation as well as their knowledge of its underlying principles.

In order to achieve these aims various research methods were employed. The degree of implementation of the project in classrooms was investigated through a specially constructed observation schedule focusing on the nature and types of activity carried out by teachers. In addition, the observed lessons were tape recorded and analysed in terms of (a) teachers' error-correcting behaviour (i.e. the types of learner error corrected or ignored by teachers and the frequency with which the various types of error were corrected) and (b) teachers' questioning behaviour (i.e. the types of question asked by the teachers in the classrooms).

The investigation of the factors affecting implementation was carried out via (a) a specially constructed Likert-type attitude scale aimed at measuring teachers' attitudes towards the communicative approach and (b) a questionnaire and interview aimed at eliciting teachers' opinions of and reactions to the innovation as well as reports of their classroom practices.[4]

Fourteen Greek secondary school teachers in various schools within and around the Athens area were selected to take part in the study. These teachers were observed, interviewed and given the questionnaire to complete. All teachers but one were female, aged from 28 to 65 years; the majority were in their late thirties to early fifties. Two teachers had completed a one-year teacher-training course at the public teacher-training school (SELME) and one teacher held a postgraduate degree in linguistics from a UK university. The other 11 teachers were occasional attenders of conferences or had observed model lessons performed by other teachers or the foreign language adviser in various schools.

In addition to the 14 teachers, the attitude scale and questionnaire was completed by 87 secondary school English language teachers in various schools within and around the Athens area. The field research took place during the fourth year of the project's implementation and lasted for three months (November 1991–February 1992). The following sections discuss the findings of the implementation study, focusing mainly on the factors discussed in the first part of the chapter, which led to the unsuccessful implementation of this innovation.

The use of the communicative learner-centred approach in the language classrooms

The results of the observation scheme and analysis of teacher error correcting and questioning practices in the classroom revealed that the teachers were not implementing the curriculum as intended. Although they used the textbook activities, the teachers followed an eclectic approach in the classroom, exhibiting features reminiscent of audiolingual approaches and (to a much lesser extent) communicative approaches. Classrooms were generally teacher-centred and form-focused. Lessons primarily consisted of activities which provided practice on discrete language items while activities that encouraged spontaneous genuine communication were almost non-existent. Teachers, for instance, regularly supplemented textbook tasks with activities providing controlled practice of a particular language structure or function.

One of the most interesting findings of the comparison between textbook activities and their realisation in the classroom was the vulnerability of the textbooks and activities in the hands of the teachers. The vast majority of the observed teachers transformed open communication activities into structural, controlled teacher-centred ones. This was achieved by changing the participation organisation required for activities or by changing the objectives, language and skill foci of activities. Listening activities, for example, were treated as reading comprehension tasks where students were asked to read aloud the listening transcript and then answer the teachers' controlled comprehension questions. In addition, pair or group work activities (a regular feature of the textbook units) were seldom implemented as such. Most pair work activities were carried out between the teacher and the students.

As far as the roles of teachers in the classrooms are concerned, the roles of instructor, controller and corrector of students' language were the ones most enacted by the teachers, with very few exceptions. The majority (88 per cent) of student errors were corrected by teachers while the majority of teachers' questions were of the 'display' ('known information') type (for the complete set of results and further details see Karavas 1993, Karavas-Doukas 1995b, 1996a).

In conclusion, the analysis of classroom observation data made clear the disparity between intended and implemented curriculum. I turn next to the causes of the limited implementation of this innovation and focus in particular on the previously discussed factors affecting the implementation process.

Factors affecting the implementation of the Greek EFL innovation

Continuing professional development

Predictably, one of the most significant factors impeding the successful implementation of this innovation was *the lack of systematic and ongoing teacher training*. As mentioned above, teacher training focusing specifically on the theoretical and practical implications of this innovation was minimal and participation was optional. Teacher training took the form of occasional local workshops organised by foreign language advisers and an annual or biannual conference dealing with the theoretical aspects of the communicative approach.

Indeed, as was revealed in the questionnaire, only 21 per cent of the sample had taken part in some kind of teacher training during their teaching career. The vast majority of teachers (88 per cent) believed that Greek EFL teachers had been inadequately trained in the communicative approach; for most teachers (52 per cent) this was due to the fact that existing training opportunities focused too much on theory and failed to build bridges with classroom practice.

What was perhaps surprising, in view of their almost non-existent training, was the fact that the majority of the teachers (82 per cent) believed in the effectiveness of the communicative approach while nearly all (92 per cent) claimed to use this approach in their everyday classroom practices (13 out of the 14 teachers who were observed responded in the same way). Indeed, what became evident through the interviews and questionnaire was that teachers suffered from false clarity, i.e. they believed that they had changed their classroom practices but in reality were implementing the innovation on a very superficial level.

Teacher attitudes

Teachers' attitudes towards the innovation were unfavourable. The vast majority (98 per cent) believed that the textbooks needed changes and improvement. The most serious complaint of teachers was that the textbooks were in need of a workbook, of more grammar exercises and more reading passages. Also, a substantial number of teachers (62 per cent) felt that the textbooks did not fulfil their students' needs. Many of the teachers (68 per cent) were also unhappy with the teachers' guides to the textbooks believing that they lacked information on how to carry out activities and present grammatical points.

Furthermore, *teachers' attitudes and beliefs of the teaching/learning process were to a large extent incompatible with the principles of the innovation.* For instance, in the interviews one of major complaints with the new textbooks was their lack of explicit grammar practice, their abundance of open-ended activities, their lack of explicit grammatical presentations and lack of extensive reading passages that could be exploited for vocabulary work, i.e. features that the new textbooks (based as they were on communicative learner-centred principles) deliberately avoided. When asked about their roles in the classroom, the majority of teachers viewed their role in the classroom as the language expert who had the knowledge and skills to transmit information about the language to the learners. The roles of facilitator, guide, monitor of students' learning, so central to the implementation of this new curriculum, were never mentioned by the teachers in the interviews.[5]

Lack of understanding of the principles of the innovations

The results of the attitude scale and interviews also made clear *teachers' limited and superficial understanding of the approach they were asked to implement.* Inconsistent responses to seemingly contradictory attitude statements revealed a lack of understanding of many of the principles of the communicative approach, subsequently verified through the teacher interviews. As an example, for most teachers 'teaching communicatively' meant focusing on oral skills, excluding grammar instruction and ignoring student errors.

Communication networks and support during implementation

The lack of teacher training can be held accountable for teachers' lack of clarity of the innovation's principles and for their failure to revise and refine their attitudes in line with the underlying philosophy of innovation. What compounded this problem, however, was the almost *non-existent communication with other colleagues and programme developers and lack of support within their schools.* Feedback channels between curriculum developers and teachers were never established, while communication with other teachers was limited (as verified in the interviews with the teachers and curriculum developers). Indeed, half the teachers interviewed had poor relations with their appointed foreign language adviser whose role was to provide support and guidance to teachers on an individual level. In sum, interaction processes were extremely limited (or even non-existent); the Greek English language teachers were left to work out the meanings of the innovation and overcome the difficulties of implementation on their own. Support within the school was not mentioned by teachers in the interviews, although one teacher did point out that her school's headmaster did not allow teachers to participate in training activities, 'with the excuse that it would disrupt the programme of the school'.

Compatibility of the innovation with the wider educational and classroom context

Finally, within the interviews teachers made it clear that their limited implementation of the EFL innovation was also due to *its failure to take into account and cater for the constraints of the classroom and wider educational context.* As most teachers pointed out, the constraints of their classrooms, the characteristics of the learners and the nature of the Greek educational context as a whole, made it very difficult, and sometimes impossible, to apply many features of a communicative learner-centred approach. The Greek teachers faced problems in using a communicative approach with large mixed ability and inadequately resourced classes; they faced problems in applying communicative principles with unmotivated learners; they faced problems in assuming non-authoritative roles within an essentially teacher-centred working environment.

Perhaps the most inhibiting factor cited by most teachers was the ever-growing presence and popularity of private language institutes (*frontistiria*). There are approximately 4000 *frontistiria* throughout Greece attended by 900,000 students of English. By being better resourced, employing native speakers of English, being up to date and focusing mainly on the preparation of students for the Cambridge First Certificate in English Examination (a highly regarded qualification in Greece), *frontistiria* are regarded by students, parents (and teachers) alike as the only effective and guaranteed means of learning English. As a result, English language teachers in public secondary schools in Greece feel that the school, as one teacher put it, is the tail of the *frontistiria*, filling in the gaps in students' knowledge rather than providing substantive instruction in English. Experiencing, thus, these problems and not having the skills or support to overcome them, the teachers reverted to their familiar teacher-centred grammar-based pedagogy performing the roles of authority and transmitter of knowledge with which they and their students felt most comfortable.

Managing the change process: concluding remarks

As I have argued throughout this chapter, the change process is a tricky one fraught with problems, anxiety, conflicts and unanticipated difficulties. It can be an extremely disruptive process whereby people are asked to change their habits and routines for the sake of outcomes which are not guaranteed.

The problem is compounded because no hard and fast rules, and no blueprints for success, exist. It is mainly through accounts of failed or successful innovations that we have come to understand the complexity of the change process and some of the factors that facilitate or inhibit the implementation process.

However, despite our increasing knowledge of the change process and the valuable insights gained through case studies referred to in this chapter, many curriculum developers and project managers still seem unaware of, or insensitive to, the factors that lead to successful curriculum changes at classroom level, as the account of the Greek EFL innovation attests. 'Projectitis' or 'addonitis', to use Fullan's (1993) terms, is a syndrome still plaguing education and the ELT sector in particular. Innovations are being introduced on a fragmented basis without proper diagnosis of the needs of schools, without sensitivity to the culture of institutions, and without adequate preparation of the teaching force. The introduction of communicative language teaching is a case in point. As in the Greek EFL innovation, numerous language education projects (Young and Lee 1987, Lawrence 1990, Holliday 1992b, 1994a) have tried to introduce communicative learner-centred practices within school cultures that promote a different type of social order in the classroom, and the consequence is that they have failed. It would appear that no attempts were made to mould and adapt these innovations to the values of educational systems and to the workings of the classroom culture, and only occasionally were feeble attempts made to adequately prepare teachers to handle classroom change.

The school culture and teacher preparation are crucial themes in the change process. Project managers need to develop a thorough understanding and sensitivity to the culture of schools – how people interact, what are their main concerns and needs – and must try to mould innovatory projects to the school's exigencies and realities. As Verspoor (1989: 42–3) points out, 'the critical challenge in designing a programme is achieving congruence between constraints and opportunities created by the external environment and the institutional and educational demands of the innovation'. In addition, teacher education must occupy the centre stage of any reform effort. However, as mentioned above, the success of any innovation that focuses on training teachers for that particular innovation will be short-lived. By the time teachers feel comfortable in using a particular innovation, and it has become institution-alised, other innovations will have been introduced. The training of teachers for each and every innovation that comes their way will only serve to strengthen the 'oh no, not again' feeling and reinforce and justify their resistance to externally imposed change. Teacher education must ultimately aim to develop teachers' capacities to deal with change, so that they actively seek to experiment and improve their teaching practices and their students' learning. Professional development programmes, both pre-service and in-service, must strive to educate teachers or, as Fullan (1992: 23) argues, to make teachers 'become adept at knowing when to seek change aggress-ively and when to back off'. It is only through ongoing and system-atic teacher development that we can make teachers agents of change rather than victims of it.

Notes

1. See also Markee (1993) for a similar argument.
2. By 'fundamental' I am referring to pedagogical innovations or 'sec-ond-order changes' (see Cuban 1988, cited in Fullan and Steigelbauer 1991) which introduce changes in the structure and goals of schools and the roles of teachers and learners within them and which, by nature, are the most difficult to implement. First-order changes seek to improve what is currently being done without bringing about changes in the behaviour and roles of teachers in the classroom. Examples of first-order changes would include the introduction of a newsletter to improve staff communications or the purchase and use of overhead projectors in the classroom.
3. For further information and discussion on the development, nature and objectives of the Greek EFL project, see Dendrinos (1985a) and Karavas (1993).
4. For more details on the research methods employed in this study, see Karavas (1993) and Karavas-Doukas (1995b, 1996a, 1996b).
5. More details on the interview findings can be found in Karavas-Doukas (1995a).

3

Language and cultural issues in innovation: the European dimension

CELIA ROBERTS

Abstract. Given that foreign language learning is also intercultural learning, there is a strong case for using ethnographic methods in the evaluation of FL learning programmes. This chapter raises some of the issues in using ethnographic approaches in evaluation and illustrates its value in a case study evaluating an innovative project on cultural studies in advanced language learning at university level in the UK.

Introduction

This chapter is a case study of an innovatory project in language and cultural studies in higher education in Britain. The theme of the project is intercultural communication within the new Europe and is based on the idea that cultural and language learning interconnect. It uses the opportunity offered by a period of residence abroad, which is a requirement of all modern languages undergraduate programmes in the UK, and is becoming increasingly popular elsewhere, to develop the notion of language learners as ethnographers. The compulsory year abroad, usually in the third year of a four-year degree, is the 'field' where the language learner, like the anthropologist, can collect and analyse data on a particular group or community. And, like the ethnographer, the language learner becomes immersed in the everyday practices of the group, learning both how to communicate and how to understand the communicative practices in which they are participating.[1]

Innovations, especially externally funded ones, compel evaluation. So, this case study will be used to discuss the potential for a symbiotic relationship between the content and methodology of a language education project and the evaluation of it (see also Kiely this volume). In doing so, I shall focus on issues of method and raise questions about the relationship between aspects of ethnography and qualitative evaluation and the importance of cultural theory and method in linking the two.

Cultural theory and ethnography

All second language learning is intercultural. There are good arguments, therefore, for drawing on cultural theory and the method most closely associated with it, ethnography, in the design, implementation and evaluation of second language learning courses and projects. This is particularly the case where the theme of the project is intercultural learning, as in this example. A cultural and ethnographic perspective problematises more widely accepted approaches to evaluation which focus on measurement-based outcomes and argues for a greater emphasis on illumination and understanding. This perspective, particularly in its current, critical phase, questions our interpretations at several levels, from initial notions of what is meant by 'evaluation' (for cxamplc, Parlett and Hamilton 1977, Macdonald 1987, Adelman and Alexander 1987, Burgess 1993 in the educational literature) to our understanding of the different groups and communities of interest in the project, the relationship between researcher and researched and our decisions about the fine-grained detail of implementation and evaluation.

Language and culture are deeply interlocked but there is not, as more recent studies have shown, any simple one-to-one relationship between one language and one culture (Gumperz and Levinson 1996). It would be naive to perpetuate any notion that, for example, English, French or Bahasa Indonesia can be mapped on to the English, French or Indonesians as a national group. Unfortunately, in language education this often happens. Culture is often taught superficially or is viewed as an abstract system of meanings with little relevance to the business of learning grammatical and communicative competence (see Holliday, this volume, on the reification of culture).

However, in the anthropological and sociolinguistic literature the language/culture relationship is construed very differently (Gumperz and Hymes 1972, Gumperz 1982, Bauman and Sherzer 1989, Gal 1989, Woolard 1989, Scollon and Scollon 1994). Agar

(1994: 60) in an uncomfortable but useful term – languaculture – suggests their interconnectedness. But this is not some abstract relationship. Culture and language are enmeshed in the local practices of everyday life: 'Culture is localised in concrete, publicly accessible signs, the most important of which are actually occurring instances of discourse' (Urban 1991: 1).

So languaculture is developed through the local networks of communities. Individuals are socialised into the ways of doing and seeing things in a particular community which may differ from other communities within the nation state.

But the language/culture relationship is not simply a local matter, the local meanings produced by it connect to wider socio-political systems:

> . . . aspects of meaning and interpretation are determined by culture specific activities and practices. Those activities and practices are interconnected in turn with the larger socio-political systems that govern, and are in part constituted by, them.
>
> (Gumperz and Levinson 1996: 9)

It is the taken-for-granted connection between the local and larger systems which has so often led to the simple one language/one culture idea mentioned above. The anthropological and sociolinguistic literature over the last 30 years has begun to show how complex this relationship is, and to emphasise the importance of the local, the fine-grained detail and the ordinary in our understanding of the dynamic process of language/culture learning and use.

The language/culture theories are touched on here for two main reasons. They form the theoretical backdrop to the design of the project described below and they also inform ethnography generally, even where it has a less explicit linguistic focus.

Ethnography can be loosely defined as the study of 'other' people and the social and cultural patterns that give meaning to their lives. It is both a method for carrying out such an investigation (Spradley 1979, Agar 1980, Hammersley and Atkinson 1983, Ellen 1984, Zaharlick and Green 1991) and a written study (Clifford and Marcus 1986, Atkinson 1992). The social and cultural theories upon which ethnography draws are concerned with how people create and sustain their everyday lives through local and particular practices and the discourses around them. For example, two student projects in this case study have drawn on discourses of 'family' and 'personal independence' to look at two quite different groups. One, by a native English speaker, looked at how blind students at the University of Marburg, Germany, managed the tension between personal freedom and family support. Another, by a native German speaker, studied what it meant to be a student from a Panjabi background at a British university.

Ethnography has, of course, been a widely used method in the educational field (Spindler 1983, Burgess 1993, Ball 1994) but remains relatively little used for evaluation in applied linguistics (but see Smith 1991, Holliday 1994a, 1996a). The idea of using ethnographic approaches, particularly from the educational literature, fits well with 'Building Bridges' into new disciplinary areas which is a major theme of this book. But a few words of caution are in order when we consider how such bridges can be built between applied linguistic work in second language education and ethnographic evaluation in education.

Such bridge building is not only laudable but necessary for innovation at a local level and within applied linguistics generally. But if this is to be a metaphor that we live by (Lakoff and Johnson 1980) then it is worth remembering that, in some western languages, those who build bridges for the army, the engineers, are known as 'sappers' – builders of saps – trenches or ditches. Bridge building can end up as ditch digging if we are not careful. So cross-disciplinary borrowing needs to proceed with some caution. I have three major concerns in this respect relating to the ways in which ideas are borrowed from other disciplines.

(1)   The relationship between applied linguistics and other discipline areas

Leo van Lier discusses the danger of applied linguistics splitting into Second Language Acquisition (SLA) and theory on the one hand, and education and practice on the other, losing the mutually strengthening relationship between theory and practice (van Lier 1994a: 5, quoted in Rampton 1997; and see Holliday in this volume). If language education evaluation looks only to education for its practice, then it could end up in a rather uncomfortable space, an atheoretical ditch. The view from the ditch (unlike the view from the bridge) may be a limited one if we only take practice from education and are only interdisciplinary in as far as we have our knowledge from other disciplines mediated through education.

I not wish to underestimate the very real lessons that applied linguistics can learn from education in qualitative and ethnographic evaluation. But I do want to suggest that we can also get our ethnographic theories direct from anthropology and sociology.

(2)   'Off the peg' ethnography

My concern here is that too enthusiastic bridge building can encourage 'buying' in ethnography in rather superficial ways. There are a number of potential problems. Firstly, ethnography was never developed for evaluative purposes (Macdonald 1971) – indeed, it could be said to be antithetical to evaluation. Ethnography is about theoretically driven description and analysis within a comparative perspective, less about making value judgements of the other. This is not to say that ethnography is value free, and indeed the outcome of many studies has been to redeem groups from negative stereotypes. However, its main goal is to describe and analyse. Ethnography can contribute to the descriptive stage of evaluation and indeed to aspects of explanation but it is difficult to see how it could be used for making absolute judgements.

Secondly, ethnography derives from extended periods in the field and from a long tradition of anthropological and sociological interpretive research. The conditions under which course and project evaluation take place are usually very different from this. For example, time scales, pressure to feed into policy and criteria imposed by the sponsoring authority put demands on the evaluator which are not imposed on the ethnographer.

Thirdly, there is currently some debate about what counts as ethnography and on 'writing ethnography' which cannot be ignored. The idea of ethnographic description as unproblematic representation of 'others' has been the subject of much recent critique (Clifford and Marcus 1986). Writing up an ethnography is a translation from one language/culture system to another (Asad and Dixon 1984), or an evocation rather than a description (Tyler 1986b). Discussions on the poetics of ethnography seem a long way from the familiar priorities of evaluation.

Green and Bloome (1997), drawing on similar arguments from Birdwhistell (1970), Heath (1993), Ellen (1984) and Hammersley (1992), suggest that ethnography is often used to label a set of techniques stripped of their theoretical and methodological roots in the particular disciplines of anthropology and sociology:

Recently, researchers in the field of education have been particularly prone to use the terms ethnography or ethnographic to describe studies using participant observation, naturalistic inquiry and open-ended research designs . . . Thus ethnography in education has become a set of techniques in search of a discipline within the social sciences. A variety of researchers, many nonanthropologists, either 'do ethnography' or critique ethnographic methods without reflecting the historical, methodological, and theoretical links of ethnography to cultural anthropology.

(Heath 1993: 33 in Bloome and Green 1996)

Bloome and Greene (1996) argue that there is a need to make distinctions between three approaches to ethnography:

(a) doing ethnography – all aspects of the research process associated with a 'broad, in-depth, and long-term study of a social and cultural group, meeting the criteria for doing ethnography as framed within a discipline or field';
(b) an ethnographic perspective – using the theories and inquiry practices from anthropology and/or sociology to do a more focused, less comprehensive ethnography;
(c) using ethnographic tools – using fieldwork methods and techniques which may or may not be guided by cultural and social theories.

It would be fair to say that a great deal of ethnographically based evaluation falls into the latter category. This, in turn, raises questions about what theory and disciplinary frameworks structure this type of evaluation.

(3)   Classroom ethnography as limiting

This has already been raised by Holliday (1996). He argues that there are limitations to ethnographic research and evaluation if the unit of analysis is taken to be the classroom rather than the whole context in which the innovation takes place. Again, this may be the result of borrowing ethnographic tools rather than 'meeting the criteria for ethnography' (Bloome and Green 1996).

Given that second language education, its innovation, evaluation and management, are by definition intercultural, and given the necessary link between cultural theory and ethnography, I want to argue that ethnographic evaluation is the most sympathetic mode of evaluation for contexts other than those requiring a strictly measurement-based assessment. However, as the preceding discussion indicates, such an approach needs to be dealt with cautiously. In particular, I want to suggest that 'off-the-peg' ethnographic approaches are inadequate and that we need to be careful about both what and how we borrow. This is relevant when borrowing directly from other disciplines or when using approaches mediated through education.

Issues in ethnographic evaluation

Cultural theory and ethnography in applied linguistics assume relativistic, comparative, holistic and reflexive habits of thinking and doing. An ethnographic evaluation of a Cultural Studies in Language-Learning course would need to ask such questions as: What counts as cultural learning for this group of learners, for this group of teachers? How would cultural learning influence students' notions of themselves as cultural beings? How would it influence notions of themselves as communicatively competent? How would the idea of language learners as intercultural communicators impact on modern languages' faculty boards, exam boards, even employment selection interviews? Some of these questions are raised in the case study below. For the present, I want to discuss further the ethnographic habits of thinking and doing mentioned earlier.

A relativistic and comparative approach

This would be one in which the meanings of particular activities and discourses were understood within their specific contexts of production and compared with other, often taken for granted, meanings. 'Comparative' in this sense does not imply anything judgemental, nor does it suggest any simple general comparisons. It is, rather, about a comparative frame of mind in which a particular practice, a way of behaving and knowing, takes on meaning because it is seen in comparison with another: one child's classroom behaviour is significant because in local and detailed ways it is different from another's. An example from a wider context is the concept of 'innovation' itself, and I will take a short detour to illustrate this. A look at the different discourses of innovation within just one cultural area – Europe – will serve to remind us that 'innovation' is itself a contested term arising out of culturally specific ideologies.

This brief illustrative example is from the European Observatory on Innovation in Education and Training[2] which is currently researching the innovative practices within education of the countries of the European Union. If we compare reports from five of the more northern countries, it is clear that 'innovation' is interpreted somewhat differently within each country but that there tends to be a dominant discourse which characterises individual countries. For example, in Ireland and Finland the emphasis is on process, on new ideas and creative responses (Leader and Murphy 1996, Tirri 1996) whereas the key word in Denmark is 'development' (Heidemann 1996). By contrast, in Belgium and Britain 'innovation' is more likely to be described in terms of 'reform' with the focus on planned or external change to systems and structures (Kelchtermans 1996, Roberts and Teasdale 1996).[3]

While much of Europe is struggling with the tension between centralisation and decentralisation in its educational systems, there are contested views of what counts as innovation, even within countries relatively geographically close. Sensitivity to social, political and cultural differences in studying and evaluating innovation is not new but there is a case for increasing sensitivity to the discourses of innovation and, perhaps, their relative untranslatability even across neighbouring countries. Such sensitivity is even more of an issue when the project, curriculum or course concerns an area such as language teaching, which is inherently politically and culturally charged (see Kennedy 1988, Rea-Dickins 1992, Holliday 1994a, on sociopolitical contexts).

A holistic approach

This approach entails drawing in the wider sociopolitical contexts just mentioned, but it does not necessarily involve trying to understand the 'whole' culture in which courses and projects are run. A focused, or what Hymes (1980) calls topic-orientated, ethnography will be more feasible for ethnographic evaluation where the goal is not to produce a full-scale ethnography but a contexted and culturally sensitive evaluation. It can still be holistic, as Erickson (1977: 59) argues:

not because of the size of the social unit but because the units of analysis are considered analytically as wholes, whether the whole be a community, a school system . . . or the beginning of one lesson in a single classroom.

The analytic unit can, therefore, be of any size but it is a bounded unit in the sense that the analyst, or evaluator, has enough evidence from the data to mark it out, in some way, as separate from other activities and practices. Openings and closings of events, for example, are routinely bounded by certain verbal, non-verbal and prosodic features which act to mark them off from what is generally perceived as the substantive elements of the event (Sacks and Schegloff 1974, Mehan 1979, Gumperz 1982).

The second point that Erickson is making is that the analytic unit is studied as comprehensively as possible. So, for example, if a single classroom is to be studied then all aspects of what goes on in that classroom must be researched. This single unit may then be related to a broader whole such as similar lessons or similar activities taking place outside the classroom, and so on. These are always set within an immediate local setting which in Geertz's term is linked to webs of significance which go to make up the wider cultural context (Geertz 1973: 5).[4] I mentioned above the limitation of using only the classroom as the unit of study but, drawing on Erickson, we can see that the unit for ethnographic research can be of any size provided that it is analysed as far as possible as a whole.

The unit of analysis for project evaluation is, unremarkably, usually the whole project and this was the case for the innovation described here. In this project, some of the wider sociopolitical issues arising from the squeeze on resources, and questions about value for money, have a particular impact on the period abroad. Policy questions about its worth at a time of economic constraint were a factor, as were arguments about resource-based learning and student autonomy. Current education policy in Britain has included suggestions to cut down the length of the undergraduate degree. The year abroad on modern language degree programmes has, therefore, been a target for possible cuts. Questions have been raised about its value for money, tangible student benefits and so on. We were, therefore, concerned to address some of these issues in our project. On a more positive note, the increasing importance of resource-based learning and student autonomy should strengthen the case for a period abroad. If the experience of living abroad is used in a rigorous and systematic way, it provides the resources for a continual process of independent student learning. These two issues – value for money and learner autonomy – were linked together in our attempt to use the year abroad as an opportunity for systematic cultural learning.

We also attempted to treat each aspect of the project as an analytical whole. For example, we set the students' reaction to the course within the wider context of the dominant concerns of the department within which the project was run. In addition, without doing a formal comparative study as this was outside the project objectives, we took account of the student-ethnographers' comparisons of themselves with the 'non-ethnographers' while they were abroad, to try to understand what effect 'doing ethnography' had on them. In each case, we tried to collect as rich data as we could so that we could relate immediate and local experiences to wider relevant contexts.

Reflexivity

Reflexivity is defined by Hammersley and Atkinson (1983) as an awareness that we, as researchers, are 'part of the social world which we are researching'. A reflexive habit of mind involves us in the continual monitoring of our experiences in relation to that of others, so that there is a constant interplay between our values and assumptions and those of the groups we are researching.

Issues of reflexivity are central to an ethnographic evaluation. Just as ethnographic researchers need to be conscious of their role in collecting data and aware of the particular constellation of theories and experiences which inform their analysis, so the ethnographic evaluators have to be explicit about their part in collecting and analysing evaluative evidence. In our case, as we discuss below, reflexivity was structured into the project because of the relationship between researcher and researched.

The remainder of this chapter is a brief case study of the 'Language Learners as Ethnographers' project. I first focus on 'case study' as a method since I am using the project as a 'case' and since it is such a central notion in ethnography. However, as I discuss below, I would not claim that our project is presented here as a full case study as this term is used in the qualitative research literature.

Case study method

Despite the increasing numbers of case studies in both education and language education as well as texts and review articles on case study methodology (Yin 1984, Lincoln and Guba 1985, Wilson and Gudmunsdottir 1987, Birnbaum and Ennig 1991, Stake 1995), much of this work still remains merely a description of an individual case. Alternatively, it is represented implicitly as representative or typical of other cases or of general practice. I find Mitchell's essay on case studies particularly helpful in dealing with the particular/general conundrum of case study method:

> What the anthropologist using a case study to support an argument does is to show how general principles deriving from some theoretical orientation manifest themselves in some given set of particular circumstances. A good case study, therefore, enables the analyst to establish theoretically valid connections between events and phenomena which previously were ineluctable. From this point of view, the search for a 'typical' case for analytic exposition is likely to be less fruitful than the search for a 'telling' case study in which the particular circumstances surrounding a case serve to make previously obscure theoretical relationships suddenly apparent . . . Case studies used in this way are clearly more than 'apt illustrations'. Instead they are means whereby general theory must be developed.   (Mitchell in Ellen 1984: 239)

Mitchell's emphasis on general principles and theoretical relationships that can be drawn out of such 'telling' accounts argues for case study as a serious and rigorous method. I cannot claim to be writing a 'telling' case study in the full sense of the term as used by Mitchell. Indeed, it is not much more than an 'apt illustration' but I hope it helps to illuminate the project/evaluation relationship within an ethnographic perspective.

Language learners as ethnographers: a case study

Project rationale

The project on which this case study is based was influenced by three different but overlapping concerns: the theoretical studies on language and cultural processes (see above); the recent pedagogic studies on cultural studies in language learning (Zarate 1986, Melde

1987, Byram 1989, Buttjes and Byram 1991, Brogger 1992, Kramsch 1993, Byram and Morgan 1994, Jurasek 1995); and the practical concerns of how to make better use of the period of residence abroad for language learners on modern languages undergraduate programmes (Freed 1995, Parker and Rouxville 1995, Coleman 1996b).

It is generally assumed that a period abroad provides the basis for acquiring communicative competence but the opportunity to develop an in-depth understanding of sociocultural practices has been given little prominence. In Britain, students of modern language undergraduate programmes are required to spend a period abroad, usually an academic year, in either one or two different countries. This opportunity, combined with the compelling literature on the inextricable connections between language and culture and the pedagogists' arguments to teach 'intercultural competence', led to the notion of language learners as ethnographers. Just as the first 'ethnographer', the anthropologist Malinowski (1923), studied a small group of people on the Trobriand Islands from an 'insider' perspective, so language learners, in a much more limited way, can use the period abroad as a site for ethnographic research. This entails an explicit methodology so that language learners can use ethnographic tools to develop their cultural learning.

But, as I suggested above, using the tools of ethnographic fieldwork does not produce an ethnographic study nor does it tackle explicitly the cultural learning of one's own socially and culturally constructed world and that of the other. For this reason, students are offered a module *Introduction to Ethnography* in the year before they go abroad, which combines ethnographic methods and anthropological and sociolinguistic concepts. After doing what we call a 'home ethnography' on some aspect of life in the UK, they go abroad to carry out a more extensive ethnographic project, which involves going out into 'the field', selecting informants and deciding on a particular research question, collecting data and starting to analyse them, using the conceptual frameworks and ethnographic methods learnt on the preparatory module. On their return for their final year in the UK institution, they write up their ethnographic project with tutorial support. This project is then assessed, both in its written form and in a viva and the grade counts towards their final degree award.

Student projects vary enormously in terms of topic, scope and degree of focus. For example, Antonia studied the relationships between food and religious practices in Seville, concentrating on the ways in which Quino, the five-year-old she was looking after, was socialised into seeing these relationships. By contrast, Chris chose to examine the social identities of a group of transvestite prostitutes in Seville and how they managed the tension between their own sense of self and the stigma of being sex workers.

The rationale behind the ethnography programme was to establish the extent to which cultural learning – both experientially and intellectually – could be made a central and integrated feature of the languages degree, using the year abroad – 'the meat in the sandwich' (Evans 1988: 42) – as the best possible environment for this to develop. In order to answer this question, it was necessary to decide how such a programme could be staffed and supported professionally. The second part of the exercise was thus to assess how far modern language lecturers could teach and supervise an ethnographic programme and ethnographic projects.

Preparing the ground and preparing the staff

Preparing the ground

In preparing to introduce the innovation and in developing the staff to do this, there were a number of challenges to prevailing orthodoxies. The first of these relates to the learning of language and culture through language socialisation (Ochs and Schieffelin 1983). Children and language learners, by participating in different contexts built up out of everyday interaction, gradually learn how to communicate and also, indirectly, learn the sociocultural knowledge which gives meaning to these interactions and is constructed out of them. The argument was that language learners while abroad could develop their communicative competence and sociocultural knowledge together as they undertook their ethnographic studies. This model of language socialisation challenges the prevailing view that the language classroom is the centre of the language-learning endeavour and the year abroad is an opportunity to extend and use the language learned. Instead, here, the year abroad becomes the key element in the undergraduate programme and the classroom experience is a preparation for it.

An example from one of the student's ethnographic projects will illustrate the process of language socialisation. This student was interested in the *pétanque* (a game of bowls) circles in southern France and as a participant observer she learned how to perform the ritual communicative practices of the game. She also learned what these practices meant to the players and began to situate these meanings within the local politics of the club and its functioning within the community. In doing so, she was involved in the process of language socialisation, learning the specific ways of speaking used by the group to carry out their everyday business and construct their identities.

Such an approach to language learning refocuses the priorities of modern languages degree programmes. 'Language people' according to Evans's ethnographic study of modern languages lecturers (Evans 1988) tend either to be literature students or more technical people concerned with vocational language development and the skills of interpreting and translating, usually in a business context. For such students, language is supported by background and area studies courses based on law, politics, economics and so on. An integrated approach to language and cultural studies in which social knowledge is part of the local politics of everyday life is a relatively new approach.

Similarly, the prevailing orthodoxy about the year abroad has assumed that culture is something to be 'caught' not 'taught'. Thorough preparation for this learning and proper integration of it on their return for their final year are not, therefore, considered priorities. Again, the 'Language Learners as Ethnographers' project took a different view.

Challenges to prevailing views are uncomfortable for institutions, both at the level of practical systems and at the level of the discourses that hold institutions together. In the design and implementation of this innovation, therefore, we were very conscious of the need to introduce it as a pilot which did not, at least in the short term, disrupt existing systems. It was presented as an additional opportunity for a group of volunteers, rather than as an alternative to the existing area studies courses. We were also very conscious of the dominant ideologies about modern languages degrees. Firstly, there is the assumption that anything that takes students away from foreign language classroom practice will have an adverse effect on their FL competence. It was difficult to persuade staff that the ethnography course, although conducted largely

in English, would provide students with conceptual and methodological tools which could turn every encounter while abroad into a
learning experience. Secondly, many lecturers still take knowledge
to be positive knowledge about facts and are critical of a social
constructivist view of reality upon which most modern ethnography
is based. For some of these lecturers, therefore, helping students
to analyse their own socially and culturally constructed selves was
dismissed as 'touchy, feely stuff', in contrast to the hard facts of
political and economic institutions.

Given this context, we relied very heavily on what we hoped
would be students' enthusiasm for the introduction to ethnography
course to diffuse the ideas through the department. In the same
way, once the department had agreed to accept ethnographic projects as well as the traditional area studies projects required of all
students on their return for their final year, we hoped that the
quality of these projects would speak for themselves. The department has a long tradition of being sensitive to students' concerns
and perceptions and we considered that students and their projects
were likely to be better ambassadors than a team that consisted of
outsiders as well as insiders who might find themselves causing
'tissue rejection' (Holliday 1992b).

Preparing the staff

An essential element of the project was the development of
modern language lecturers so that they could teach on the course
and supervise ethnographic projects. The relationship between
curriculum and staff development is well established (Stenhouse
1975). It followed, therefore, that if we wanted to develop language learners as ethnographers, we also needed to develop language lecturers as ethnographers. The rationale behind conceiving
of language lecturers as ethnographers was that they were better
placed than any outside anthropologist from another department
to understand the needs of language learners. In addition, given
the language and culture theories that drove the project, the kind
of interdisciplinarity that we were encouraging in the lecturers
seemed entirely appropriate. The role of the anthropological consultant, Brian Street, was crucial here. He was chosen because of
his particular interest in teaching and using anthropology with
non-anthropologists and his research linking ethnography and
language.

The staff prepared themselves in a number of ways, including undertaking their own small-scale ethnographic projects, participating in regular informal meetings/seminars with the anthropology consultant and the project leaders, working jointly on the development of materials, teaching on the course, devising assessment criteria for and marking of ethnographic projects as well as participating in final year student seminars. Their 'newcomer' status as teachers of ethnography placed them with the students as part of a community of learners. The more egalitarian relationship with students which resulted mirrors the more equal footing between informants – or teachers, as Agar (1987) calls them – and ethnographers.

A short section from the initial ethnographic project by one of the lecturers illustrates the uncertainties around this boundary crossing into a new discipline area. She is discussing some of the difficulties and frustrations of data collection for her project on a group of cleaners within the university:

> Worst of all, the unopened notebook became an object of attention to the cleaners, who would remark, 'She's brought her little notebook again!' But who obviously saw I was doing nothing with it. The notebook seemed to me to symbolise my 'failure' to handle my new situation. E [one of the informants] was puzzled by it. 'You're supposed to be writing about us aren't you, but you haven't taken any notes!' Delighted at the invitation, I proposed to ask some questions and do some note-taking next time. At the next session, however, E had other plans: 'Bugger the questions, bingo comes first' was her response when I reminded her of her comments.   (Jordan 1993)

Ethnographic tools for project evaluation

In evaluating the project we aimed to place the content and methods of the project in symbiotic relationship to the evaluative methods. This meant using ethnographic tools within an 'ethnographic perspective' (Bloome and Green's second position, see p. 56 point (b)).

Data were collected using the following tools: ethnographic interviews (Spradley 1979) with students and lecturers; course diaries, end of course questionnaires and the analysis of ethnographic projects. The key informants were the ten students who formed the first cohort of the project and the project lecturers.

Diaries and questionnaires from the first three years of the ethnography course were analysed. Reflecting Agar's approach (Agar 1987), in which he differentiates between core and background data, the data collected in this way represented the 'core data' to which the researchers were accountable. In addition, considerable background data were used to support the core: field notes (Sanjek 1990) from meetings with students while abroad, field notes of the classroom practices, notes from final year seminars, notes from joint assessment meetings on the ethnographic projects and drafts of the projects, notes from project supervision and 'head notes' (Sanjek 1990) from many staff–student discussions.

The lecturers on the team were both researchers and researched and were, therefore, in a crucial participant observation role in relation to the whole project. They played a significant role in collecting and analysing data from the course, in interviewing students and in assessing the ethnographic projects. They were also interviewed by other members of the project team, observed in classes, and their own ethnographic projects were analysed. This dual role meant that the project leaders could research *with* them rather than *on* them (Cameron *et al.* 1992).

Methods of analysis resembled those used in ethnography (Agar 1980, Ellen 1984, Burgess 1993). We moved from initial recording of data to consolidation and analysis. This process of consolidation facilitates 'a constant cumulative dialogue with your material' (Ellen 1984: 283) in which there is a gradual movement from identification of themes to analysis and drawing out more conceptual categories. During this process it is necessary to be steeped in the data, constantly reading and rereading and at the same time to be reflexive. This involves asking questions about how the data were produced and your initial assumptions of those data.

Writing an ethnographic evaluation is the element of the evaluative process most removed from the ethnographic research literature. In this literature, there has been a major critique of ethnographic writing (Clifford and Marcus 1986) which has forced ethnographers to reconceptualise their responsibilities as writers. The ethnography is no longer seen as a simple account of 'otherness' but an active construction of it. The writing process is what creates 'culture'. By contrast, a written evaluation, although obviously constructed through the authority of the narrator (and any writer needs to be aware of this), by definition, takes an evaluative stance. Description is an element of the evaluation but acts in a servicing capacity. So the writer of an ethnographic evaluation can take an interim position – aware of the tropes and discourses which construct a particular view of reality but also committed to taking up an explicit position.

Evaluation of the staff development component

Modern languages staff were asked to add to their repertoire as language teachers (whether from a literature or social science background) some of the perspectives and skills of anthropology, sociolinguistics and ethnography. Like the students they had to take on new ways of thinking and knowing. These included: questioning taken-for-granted assumptions about what is 'normal' and 'natural' in daily life; seeing that apparently trivial surface concerns are deeply rooted in cultural assumptions about knowledge and experience; moving beyond stereotypical conceptions of 'culture' to the idea of active, dynamic cultural processes (the idea that 'culture is a verb'; Street 1993); and being reflexive about the observer's position as both 'inside' and 'outside' as they move between their own cultural contexts and that of their informants.

This kind of staff development has less to do with content knowledge than with developing new perspectives, and less to do with cultural knowledge than with frameworks for understanding cultural processes. In a number of extended ethnographic interviews with staff – observing them in class and learning from their experiences of supervising students – it was clear that development of this kind is achieved not through training but through a complex interplay of factors. These included the experience of undertaking ethnographic projects themselves, ongoing dialogue with the consultant and the rest of the project team, and the habits of reflection and observation on which the theme of the project inevitably focused and which connected to their existing intellectual interests and individual aptitudes for inquiry. The data from the interviews and the many discussions and meetings were rich data, because the staff's developing ethnographic experience produced discourse which was thoughtful, self-aware and critical. The following is an extract from a modern languages lecturer's interview with the anthropological consultant two years into the project:

I think at the beginning because we were insecure we felt we were not getting enough information from you . . . because at first we felt that there weren't formally demarcated times when we were having a lesson . . . we were just picking up what we could from anywhere. I sometimes felt, 'I don't know anything – we're supposed to be getting trained but it seems very loose' . . . It's a bit like the students – most of it sinks in through reflecting on it afterwards or seeing it in action. So, with 'gift giving', I look at gift giving around me, naturally, and that's where it all comes from . . . All we needed was a direction or key ideas – whereas before I would have wanted specific information on each thing – on power, hierarchies, whereas in fact my ideas on power, on hierarchies, have not been from one session but from all your comments and the classes accumulated over the year . . . I think over the year I have learnt to rely more on my ability to connect . . . It was accelerated learning in a way – we just had to do it – there was no time for messing about and therefore you get good at making connections between things . . . I think I'm quicker at looking at patterns . . . It's so much to do with confidence, but also learning to be tentative – before I would have wanted more clearcut things but now I'm more tentative in analysing something – bit of a paradox.

As this extract shows, not surprisingly, the staff expressed considerable anxiety about their role as teachers of ethnography, to do with their confidence and relative lack of authority. Looking back over the first two years, they felt that the actual experience of teaching the course had been the strongest element in their own development but that their new identity involved a holistic process (congruent with the principles of anthropology itself) including interaction with the consultant and project leaders, their own reading and seminar discussions and their own ethnographic work.

Evaluation of the student experience

We looked at three aspects of the student experience in order to examine the benefits and interconnections between the preparatory and returning experiences in the UK institution and the period abroad. These three aspects were: the introductory course in the UK, the experience abroad and doing the ethnographic project.

The value of the introduction to ethnography course

This aspect of the course was mainly evaluated through student diaries and an end-of-course questionnaire. Such evaluative methods are not necessarily ethnographic and can be criticised, if used superficially, for diminishing the student experience. However, within anthropology, diary writing is a basic ethnographic tool, and as students were inducted into a more reflexive understanding of the constructed nature of accounts of social life and of the issues around representation and writing in anthropology, their diaries became richer and provided us with more useful data to evaluate their learning on the module.

It soon became clear from the diaries that the course was not just preparing them for 'culture shock' (Furnham and Bochner 1986) but was itself something of a culture shock. Students frequently referred to the intellectual and analytical demands of the course, to the weekly field tasks and the participative environment of the classes. They described the course, paradoxically, as both more abstract and more practical than they had anticipated. To this extent the project team was satisfied that they had achieved the objective of making the course both conceptual and experiential – as is any ethnographic project. Similarly, the pedagogy aimed to mirror the ethnographic substance of the course so that students were participant observers of their own classroom.

So both content and pedagogy built a course which was a micro-system for the ethnographic experience abroad. As one student commented, 'It clarifies our self-imposed limitations and intolerances'. This kind of learning is in contrast to the largely bureaucratic preparation offered to most students before their period abroad.

The impact of doing ethnography on their experience abroad

> I've been looking around Cadiz with intent to commit ethnography.

Students felt that doing the course gave them both a purpose for, and a new way of looking at, the experience abroad:

> I think I learnt to look at things differently, more carefully, not just to sit there and let things wash over me because I could have easily done that.

Students were unanimous in perceiving an improvement in their understanding of people and their interactions with them. However, they did not always link this to improved language learning where 'language learning' was still conceived as acquisition of grammar. To this extent, the project did not appear to have given the students an expanded view of language at a cognitive level. In other words, their ideologies of language were still in place. However, the projects themselves, and their other comments, suggested that they were living with this expanded view of language in which linguistic and cultural processes were inseparable.

Their improved understanding through interaction contributed to a more general development of cultural learning. Generalisations about a group's behaviour or characteristics were replaced by a more precise, differentiated and cautious view. Conclusions were anchored in specific local experiences and more general comments were carefully hedged:

> Well, I think the conclusions that you come up with in ethnography, you can't just come up with them if you've just seen it once. So you know you need to be culturally aware, you have to spend a hell of a long time actually looking at it. And every time you look at a certain situation you observe different things . . . I don't take things at first glance at all.

Doing the ethnographic project

Undertaking an ethnographic project represented a daunting task to the students and this was made clear in the students' interviews, discussions and from our field notes. The demands were great: they had to formulate an interesting question, collect data – which had both practical and ethical considerations – use data and concepts to illuminate each other and write up the project reflexively and in the foreign language:

> When you are doing ethnography, it's you and the place, it's you and the people. You can't not write yourself into it. You are part of it.

Overall, the strengths of the ethnographic projects lay in the freshness of perceptions and detailed 'life' that came through, giving an insider feel to the studies. For example, the hot dusty pitch where the *pétanque* game was played or little five-year-old Quino's interrogations about how poor people could afford Christmas nougat, were written about in such a way that the reader could sense the 'here and now' of the student's experience. Most projects included a reflexivity section in which the students grappled with their data and the interpretive processes they brought to it.

Weaknesses lay in the integration of data and conceptual frameworks and in the hybrid nature of the writing. This was because the course and the ethnographic examples were largely from the Anglo-American tradition, whereas the students were required by the university to write in the foreign language.

From an institutional perspective, the fact that the ethnographic projects were accepted as an assessed element of the final degree was an achievement. The more recent adoption of the *Introduction to Ethnography* course as an optional module within the Applied Languages programme is a further marker of the integration of the innovation. Integration into the final year has been relatively less successful at a structural level. However, most students felt the experience of cultural learning that doing ethnography had given them could be diffused throughout their final year modules and well beyond. As one senior academic in modern languages who had not been directly involved in the project remarked: 'This group is world's apart, more open, observant, tolerant and self-confident'.

Conclusions from the evaluation

To sum up, then, to what extent were we able to get answers to the kinds of question posed at the beginning of the chapter: What counts as cultural learning? How would cultural learning influence their notions of themselves as cultural beings and as communicatively competent? Both in the interviews and in the ethnographic projects (our core data) students showed that they saw 'culture' not as some body of knowledge waiting prone to be discovered but as a new way of seeing and knowing. This epistemological shift was like turning a searchlight on the local and everyday world – both their own and that of others – so that, perhaps for the first time, they saw themselves, and others, as cultural beings.

However, as I have suggested, they were not always able to recognise the links between language and cultural learning and still tended to see them as separate rather than interconnected. In addition, their particular experiences and those of the staff involved in the project did not always travel beyond this group to staff and students not immediately involved. Despite these limitations, the palpable changes – epistemological, personal and skills based – evidenced in projects and in interviews, discussions and seminars suggest that we asked appropriate questions in our evaluation and arrived at answers that indicated that the innovation was worthwhile and worth trying out elsewhere.

Questions that could not be answered

The ethnographic approach to evaluation described here leaves many questions only partially answered, or indeed unanswered. These would include:

- What are the necessary characteristics required by modern languages lecturers if they are to become effective in supporting language learners as ethnographers?
- How much cultural knowledge did students acquire?
- Is the period abroad a better opportunity for cultural learning if students are prepared for and write an ethnographic project?
- Where is the statistical evidence that compares ethnographic projects with non-ethnographic projects? (The fact that they are very different types of projects raises issues of standardisation and reliability in their marking.)
- Would the project have been as successful if taught by anthropologists from the anthropology department?

There are two main reasons why these questions remain only partially answered or unanswered. The first concerns the nature of cultural learning and assessment and the second concerns the nature of assessment and evaluation more generally. Despite attempts to assess attitude and empathy in the psychological literature there has, until recently, been very little concerted effort to develop forms of assessment which assess language-in-culture (Byram and Morgan 1994). Until assessors and evaluators develop both the objectives and means of assessment to find out the extent of cultural learning and intercultural competence along the lines proposed by Byram (1997), there can be no objective, markable data comparable with test results. However, this does not mean that we should underestimate the significance of the type of illuminative evaluation suggested above.

The objectives and means of assessment for cultural learning will have to be of a rather different nature from those found in the language education literature. For example, I hope it will be clear from what I have said that it has not been possible to devise a syllabus of cultural knowledge which specifies what cultural information is to be learned. Although students develop conceptual frameworks, each one uses them in different ways. Similarly, it is difficult to compare ethnographic with non-ethnographic projects since they are based on a different set of objectives and only some assessment criteria overlap.

Ethnographic projects did not necessarily attract higher grades than non-ethnographic ones. The latter often score higher on linguistic accuracy and overall structure and balance as they are usually book-based and students can draw on the structure and discourses of their bibliographic sources. By contrast, the student ethnographers are 'writing culture' (Clifford and Marcus 1986) from their own data, producing rich, unique and reflexive accounts while having to grapple with their own linguistic repertoire in writing these up.

The second issue concerns the value and nature of illuminative evaluation. Since there is no objective or standardised means of assessing cultural learning, it could be argued that we resorted to an illuminative approach. But that is to suggest that it is some poor substitute for the 'real thing'. If, however, we reconceptualise all assessment (and, by implication, evaluation) as 'educational' rather than 'accountable' (Gipps 1994) then we have a different set of priorities which chime well with both the theme of the case study and the methods used to evaluate it. These priorities include the complex, multidimensional nature of educational assessment, the inclusion of the learners' self-reflection and self-monitoring in the process, the quality of tasks, the recasting of assessment criteria as holistic and the move towards a 'thick description' (Geertz 1973) of learner achievement (Gipps 1994: 159–61).

We can relate each of these to the case study described. The multidimensional nature of assessment is reflected in the different methods of evaluation and the way in which they are triangulated together along ethnographic lines (Denzin 1988). This links also with Geertz's (1973) notion of thick description, as Gipps suggests. Layers of learner achievement – for example, ability to observe, a critical perception of one's own culturally constructed world, the capacity to 'translate' culture when writing up the ethnographic project (Asad and Dixon 1984) and personal development in terms of self-confidence – are all accounted for.

Such a thick description links to the holistic criteria for assessment and, more generally, a holistic approach to evaluation in which the wider as well as the immediate context is drawn upon in making judgements about the project. Finally, the self-reflective element is part of the wider notion of reflexivity which is both part of the students' developing intercultural competence and an element in our own evaluation of the project as both 'insiders' and 'outsiders'.

Conclusion

Any project on intercultural learning (and I would say, therefore, any second language learning project) is particularly susceptible to ethnographic evaluation. There can be a close fit between the goals of such a project and the means of evaluating it. As well as looking to educational literature, we can proceed, with caution, to learn directly from the studies and methods written within the disciplines of anthropology, sociology and sociolinguistics.

In looking at issues of ethnographic evaluation, it is clear how close ethnographic research and evaluation can be in data collection and analysis. But 'writing culture' and writing an evaluation have different purposes and so different discourses. The distinction between ethnographic research and evaluation is also much more obvious if any claims are made for ethnography in evaluation as opposed to an ethnographic perspective.

This does not mean that we should use ethnographic tools without drawing on cultural and social theory. This may land us in the atheoretical ditch mentioned above, where what we are doing is not qualitative but simply non-quantitative evaluation. In these cases, the typical attacks that are levelled against non-quantitative research more generally could also be levelled at ethnographic evaluation: that it is anecdotal, not generalisable, not reliable and so on. What I have tried to convey in this chapter is that it is both possible, and I would say necessary, to elicit rich data, write a thick description and be reflexive about the process to produce, in Mitchell's (1984) terms, a telling account. Such an account would meet the criteria of both internal and external validity within an 'educational' rather than an 'accountable' framework.

So if we recast evaluation as a context-bound process of under-
· standing, rather than as a set of facts which can straightforwardly

predict and replicate other successful projects, we then need to rethink the writing process. Perhaps our greatest task is to write the kind of evaluation which invokes the response (both from those involved in it and those who read it): 'Yes, I understand the project with all its layers of significance.'

Notes

1. The case study described here is based on a research project funded by the Economic and Social Research Council (R232716) based at Thames Valley University, London. The principal researcher was Celia Roberts, and Michael Byram was the co-researcher. The anthropological consultant was Brian Street and the modern languages lecturers who acted as teacher/researchers were Ana Barro and Hanns Grimm. Towards the end of the project, additional funding from the Enterprise in Higher Education Initiative supported the development of two further team members, Marc Bergman and Shirley Jordan.

2.´ The Observatory on Innovation in Education and Training is funded by the European Union and co-ordinated by the Institute Nationale de Recherche Pédagogique in Paris. Of course, the kind of discourses found in these national reports are also reifications constructed out of the discourses of government official reports and interviews. Further ethnographic studies on 'innovation' among teachers and students within national boundaries might reveal intranational differences.

3. If we take a closer look at Britain and compare it with some of the other countries of northern and western Europe we see both similarities and differences. In Britain, the pace and scale of educational change over the past decade has made it increasingly difficult to define innovation in a way that does not mask its creative and process-orientated aspects. In discussing this 'era of change' Hopkins *et al.* (1994) observe: 'ad hoc, self-determined single innovations which by and large individual teachers decided to work on' have given place to a situation where 'the change agenda has increasingly been set by national politicians'. Both the school sector and Higher Education have been radically affected by the increasing government control over policy and direction, and the challenge – as in most countries in western Europe – is to find a balance between these top-down policy initiatives and quality control, on the one hand, and locally developed initiatives on the other (Hopkins *et al.* 1994).

4. 'The concept of culture I espouse . . . is essentially a semiotic one. Believing with Max Weber, that man (*sic*) is an animal suspended in webs of significance he himself has spun, I take culture to be those

webs, and the analysis of it to be, therefore, not an experimental science in search of law but an interpretive one in search of meaning' (Geertz 1973: 5).

Acknowledgements

I would like to thank Richard Kiely, Ben Rampton and Pauline Rea-Dickins for helpful comments on an earlier draft.

4

Programme evaluation by teachers: issues of policy and practice

RICHARD KIELY

Evaluation has an affective element for teachers: at a personal level, evaluation findings sustain a sense of purpose and contribution and, at a professional level, they provide information on the technologies of teaching – classroom activities, homework, materials, etc. – which help plan for the future. Of course these plans are being made anyway, on an ongoing organic basis and the contribution of a formal evaluation procedure is perhaps a validating one confirming, as appropriate, the various hunches and ideas that have held the curriculum together.

However, evaluation is often seen as threatening (see Weir and Roberts 1994, Rea-Dickins and Lwaitama 1995, and Murphy 1996 for accounts relating to the English language teaching sector). In the literature, we find transgressions of good practice in evaluation (and bad management): invalid instruments; inappropriate timing; unethical use of data. In the community of teachers, they constitute a basis for suspicion and distrust for evaluators, inspectors, managers and others who end up making judgements about teachers.

But the threat is only part of the story: the communal distrust of evaluators and inspectors provides an armour which protects teachers, while at the same time allowing them to consider, and use for improvement, elements of truth they recognise in the findings. There is also awareness of more fundamental issues: the evaluation only picked up half the picture; it did not take all the factors into account; findings are not at the end of the day really relevant to the improvement of the teaching or other aspects of professional practice. A formal evaluation whether carried out by an inspector or by means of a test never represents all that a given teacher knows, but will give perspectives not necessarily available to the teacher. It provides the teacher with a need to make self-preserving argument, and at the same time a context to develop new strategies for old problems. The judgement of others, whether an external evaluator or students, however flawed, can have a validating function: it can confirm in a profession where there is no one right form of practice that the personally developed pedagogy of a teacher is relevant and appropriate.

This chapter looks at the evaluation of an English for Academic Purposes programme which is carried out by teachers in a British university. The purposes of the evaluation are a mix of the issues discussed above: improvement of the programme, and accountability to both managers and students. The first section examines the evolution of this form of evaluation in English language education. It discusses the developments in English language teaching evaluation and pedagogy that have in recent decades promoted investigation and dialogue in the language classroom. The second section presents a case study of such an evaluation. It sets out the structure of the investigation, and discusses the issues which arose in the evaluative dialogue of the teachers and students. Finally the paper considers how this form of evaluation might be further researched and developed to improve programme effectiveness.

Evaluation in English language education: theory, policy and practice

Evaluation theory: issues of purpose and method

Awareness of evaluation as a dimension of the English as a Foreign/Second Language (EFL/ESL) curriculum has increased substantially in recent decades. Factors contributing to the enhanced role of evaluation include a shift from rigidly defined programmes to more process pedagogic approaches, and the related need for teachers to assume an investigative role in their classrooms. Theory has been informed at a general level by the shift in educational evaluation and applied linguistics from experimental studies in the positivistic paradigm, to qualitative and multifaceted designs (Mitchell 1990; Rea-Dickins 1994; Lynch 1996). The development of method and approach in EFL/ESL programme evaluation has been a process of inclusion of developments in general educational research, and their application to a range of geographical and institutional contexts. Evaluation has been increasingly invested with the potential to inform on programme and pedagogic needs at local levels (Beretta 1992; Rea-Dickins and Germaine 1992; Greenwood 1985; Lynch 1996). The evaluation of learner outcomes (testing) is no longer seen as the key indicator of programme quality: a range of process factors are equally valid, and more informative on what improvements are desirable. Process evaluation can illuminate the interplay of different aspects of a programme, and thus enable practitioners to make modifications for improvement. Long (1984), for example, sees such evaluations as key contributions to Second Language Acquisition theory development as well as to classroom practice. This view has promoted professional enquiry by teachers, and led to the inclusion of a range of traditions – action research, ethnographic approaches, reflective practice, teacher appraisal and personnel management – within the evaluation paradigm. Evaluation is now not so much about giving definitive yes/no answers to precise questions with universal applicability, as it is about ongoing, multifaceted improvement of programmes in different contexts.

Evaluation policy: how classroom practice is prescribed

Developments in evaluation theory and method have had a significant impact on policy and practice at both classroom and institutional levels. Policy in EFL/ESL teacher education and teacher development – current orthodoxy and prescribed practice according to bodies such as RSA/UCLES[1] – requires teachers to be able to evaluate lesson plans, teaching materials, and learner progress. Increasingly, competency models of teacher education contain explicit statements about the role of evaluation, but do not specify how evaluations should be carried out. It is unclear, for example, whether the evaluation capacities listed as competencies in the RSA/UCLES Schemes are to be understood as skills recognisable to evaluators in other educational fields, or as the intuitive ability to make sound practical decisions. Institutions where EFL/ESL programmes are taught increasingly have evaluation policies, either to demonstrate to validating bodies such as BASELT and BALEAP[2] that there is a capacity for ongoing curriculum development, or to fulfil commitments to listening to students and basing curriculum developments on their needs (Weir and Roberts 1994; Blue and Grundy 1996).

Institutional practices in curriculum management dovetail with another policy framework: the communicative approach to English language teaching. The communicative approach promotes language learning activities with three main features: (a) they involve exchange of meanings, which the learner can shape and direct, (b) they develop linguistic self-awareness in the learner and (c) they have links, in terms of ongoing learning and language use, with the world outside the classroom. The role of the learner here is active, engaged and evaluative.

Legutke and Thomas (1992) give three reasons for a strong role for evaluation in the EFL curriculum: (a) an educational reason linking capacity to communicate in the target language with growth in self-confidence and self-determination, (b) an experiential learning reason, linking reflection on experience to enhanced learning capacity and (c) a language acquisition reason – developing the classroom as a context for real communication. These three reasons encapsulate the pedagogical orthodoxy in which the majority of EFL, and especially EAP teachers work, with the development in learners of a capacity to deal with the discourse needs of their English language situation (see, for example, Brindley 1989, Simpson 1996).

In this perspective, the evaluation process makes a direct contribution to language learning, as well as promoting changes in the learning activities. When reflecting on and sharing experiences with others, the individual student is developing negotiation skills. In the case study described below, the merging of evaluation with language skills practice is one teacher's strategy to locate it in the curriculum.

Learner-centred philosophy is a key element of evaluation policies within institutions where language programmes are taught. Learners, particularly adult learners who are aware and evaluative in relation to their own progress, are likely to be effective learners. They are also likely to be valuable sources of feedback on the 'products' they consume – language-teaching programmes in this case. This feedback can enhance the quality of programmes, and thus, the success of the institution in two ways: in the marketplace, and in achieving or maintaining recognition by the professional bodies.

Teachers, thus, find themselves operating at a convergence of two very different policy traditions: prescribed (or implied) pedagogic approaches from applied linguistics and education on the one hand,

and institutional quality management requirements on the other. The former represents the professionalism of the teacher – the principles that inform and justify teaching activities – while the latter represents the policy framework in which the teacher operates. Both traditions support the idea of evaluation where the students are key stakeholders and informants, though, beyond a broadly supportive framework, neither may provide much guidance on the practicalities, politics or ethics involved. For example, the teacher is potentially the subject of the evaluation, but is also responsible for all phases in the evaluation cycle – from deciding what is to be evaluated, through issues of data-collection, analysis and interpretation, to taking action and reporting on the evaluation.

Evaluation practice: what happens in the classroom

This theoretical and policy framework has generated a methodological diversity in the practice of evaluation. The traditional view that programme evaluation is characterised by the technical rigour of the selected research methodology is hardly tenable if all teachers are to be involved, and evaluation is to be ongoing. On the one hand, where evaluation is for the improvement of aspects of the pedagogy in one or a small set of classrooms, and reporting is limited to brief discussion at a team meeting, there is little need for relating issues of definition or procedure to the literature, or to a wider community. On the other, there is the question of credibility: teacher development has become linked to doing research, both in education generally (e.g. Stenhouse 1975) and in ELT/Applied Linguistics (e.g. Nunan 1989b; Richards and Lockhart 1994; Nunan and Lamb 1996). Increasingly, English language teacher development and in-service training schemes are part of postgraduate study programmes which serve as an induction to the established research community. Investigations by teachers, whether as classroom evaluation or action research, cannot contribute to the profession and the discipline of applied linguistics while living by another, less rigorous set of principles. The discussion of reliability below illustrates how central this issue is in the evaluation literature.

Evaluation quality: reliability and validity

The theory and policy developments in evaluation prescribe an extensive set of professional tasks. Teachers plan for the classroom and respond to situations as they arise. They evaluate systematically and report to the team and the institution on the experiences their students have had and use the classroom to test and further the explanations from the theory, focusing on one aspect of pedagogy such as materials, learner studies, or grammar learning. When they undertake the evaluations implicit in these tasks, there are a range of procedures to choose from for collecting and analysing data. The theory of evaluation in English language education is described in manuals such as White (1988b), Rea-Dickins and Germaine (1992) and Weir and Roberts (1994), and policy is set out in institutional and programme documentation, and in syllabuses for teacher education and development. There are few accounts of teachers doing evaluation in accordance with professional and institutional requirements, and those that that do, e.g. Alderson and Scott (1992), Britten and O'Dwyer (1995) and Murphy (1996), raise important issues. Firstly, there is the question of feasibility: Is it realistic to expect teachers to be evaluators/researchers as well as teachers? Do teachers expect to learn from the experience of peers, and conversely, expect others to learn from their classroom experiences? Is classroom evaluation by teachers sustainable beyond initial hot-housing in contexts such as MA programmes? Secondly, there is the question of reliability. Self-interest and advocacy are inevitably issues in participant evaluation. Where decisions are to be made about the nature of a programme, possibly involving fundamental change, can the judgements of teachers, or those of students reported by teachers, be considered reliable?

Given the complex policy background and methodological diversity which characterises evaluation in English language teaching, there are no easy answers to these questions. In relation to student evaluation, both Marsh (1987) and Pennington and Young (1989) recommend caution in interpreting student evaluations; Pennington and Young, discussing ESL/EFL contexts, recommend greater attention to evaluation in the curriculum, and systematic involvement of teachers in the evaluation process. Alderson and Scott (1992) provide an account of such an involvement: it describes a participatory evaluation of an ESP project in a group of Brazilian universities. Teachers were involved mainly in the data collection and analysis phases, to a minor degree only in the design phase, and not at all in the reporting.

This issue is discussed elsewhere in the evaluation literature for English language education – see, for example, Beretta (1990b),

Lynch (1992, 1996). It is also part of a wider paradigm debate which contrasts quantitative measuring with interpretive approaches. The concerns relating to *objectivity* and *bias* above are informed by the philosophy of the former. Teacher evaluations, however, tend to be interpretive. As Weir and Roberts (1994), Murphy (1996) and the case study described below illustrate, they are designed and carried out in naturalistic settings, and dovetail extensively with other classroom activities, such as needs analysis and learner strategy development.

One aspect of the reliability issue is the role of internal and external evaluators: internal evaluators enhance validity, but may be a threat to reliability while external evaluators have the opposite effect. Mackay (1994), Mackay *et al.* (1995), (and Mackay *et al.* in this volume) set out a useful framework for the linking of internal and external programme evaluation, and the linking of public accountability with both programme and teacher development. The framework involves a team approach to evaluation and methodological rigour in specifying terms of reference, data gathering, analysis and reporting.

A detailed account of the internal evaluation of English language programmes in a British university context in Weir and Roberts (1994) demonstrates how difficult this can be in practice: developing the programme through evaluation, and external evaluation for approval by a professional body, remain quite separate processes, without the structured articulation proposed by Mackay. This account illustrates the diversity of functions that evaluation activity has in situations such as this: it serves to check the validity of the programme objectives; identify problems in the classroom and bring about improvements; and demonstrate quality control procedures, especially in relation to teacher competence. Within this set of functions, there are thus two roles for teachers: teachers as evaluators, and teachers as subject of the evaluation. Beyond general discussion on the need to keep evaluation activity non-threatening, there is no exploration of how these different roles are in conflict, or how each impacts on the pedagogy.

The role of classroom evaluation in curriculum theory and practice raises a number of questions, central to the development of the ELT curriculum, institutional policy and professional development programmes for teachers:

- To what extent is involving students in evaluation a separate process from teaching them?
- To what extent do evaluations focus on problems and explain them such that improvements are brought about?
- To what extent is the experience of others – relevant literature – used in investigating problems and devising solutions?
- To what extent do evaluations influence the pedagogy in terms of classroom activities, materials, assessment procedures, etc?
- How do teachers manage the different agendas – their own personal and professional interests, students' concerns, institutional requirements – involved in carrying out evaluations?
- How do teachers use the time available to carry out the evaluation and deal with other pedagogic demands?

These questions explore the interface between evaluation and pedagogy in the classroom, examining the roles of teachers and students, the structure of the evaluation and the impact on classroom activities, and they constitute an initial set of concerns for the case study described below. Analysis of the data generates a number of themes which illuminate the evaluation/pedagogy interface which can be represented as tensions between goals and outcomes in the classroom. Firstly, there is tension between the classroom as the centre of learning and the resources available outside. Secondly, there is a role tension for the teachers, as they alternate between investigator and responder roles on the one hand, and advocates of a preferred learning strategy on the other. Thirdly, there is a topic issue in the evolving interaction in the classroom, between learning issues such as ways of improving language skills or grammatical accuracy, and programme management issues such as hand-in dates and assessment procedures. Fourthly, there is the issue of language needs and language awareness, where students' lack of awareness seems to impede the exploration of needs. Related to this is the extent to which the students are prepared to disclose needs even when they are aware of them. Fifthly, there is a central evaluation issue in the tension in classroom discussions, between experiences to date and future experiences. Evaluation processes generally analyse past experiences as a means of identifying future direction and strategy; in the classroom there is a tendency to focus on realizing the pedagogy already set out.

The case study

Research methodology

The concern of this case study was to describe how the evaluation of a programme took place, to go beyond an account of procedures and findings, and to examine the dialogue unfolding and its impact on the classroom and participants. The focus of interest was not so much in the classroom strategy of specific teachers, or in institutional practice in relation to evaluation, but in how these came together to shape and develop a specific programme – 'catch the complexity of a single case' (Stake 1995: xi). To do this the programme was shadowed over 12 weeks; observing in the classroom and talking to the teachers and students. The broadly ethnographic approach seemed appropriate for the multifaceted nature of the issue.

The principal method of data collection was classroom observation – low technology watching, listening, note-taking to capture interactions, reactions, and impressions of the teachers and the students.[3] Interactions are especially important where the teachers seek to dialogue with students to understand their needs, and communicate their analysis of the learning activity required of the students. A focus on reactions would inform on action taken by teachers and students. Impressions were interpretations of what was happening, not just as an observer but as a 'human instrument' (Lincoln and Guba 1985) who had practitioner experience and insights into this kind of classroom, and of the wider policy context within which the teaching was taking place. Notes taken in the classroom were augmented from memory immediately after each lesson, and were typed up and given to the teacher concerned to check within a day or two. The observation was complemented by four other procedures: questionnaire studies of the four teachers involved in this kind of programme; detailed interviews with Millie,[4] the teacher mainly focused upon, ongoing discussion of the observation accounts with this teacher, and examination of all documentation including learning guidelines to students and requirements of students' work.

The programme

The programme is located in a British university, with a strong commitment to the student voice in shaping the curriculum.

The institution has a comprehensive evaluation policy which sets out to feed evaluations of the student experience into the design and delivery of programmes, and to bring together classroom process and learning outcomes data in the periodic review of programmes. Teachers are the sole generators of process data – classroom observation or questionnaire studies by managers are not used. The programme involves 36 hours of classes over 12 weeks. Seventeen students are registered, and attendance fluctuates between 5 and 13, with an average attendance of 10. The learning focus is English for Academic Purposes (EAP), and the students are non-native speakers of English from undergraduate programmes, such as Accountancy Studies and Information Management. Two teachers, Millie and Anna,[4] teach a 90-minute class each week. The broad aims of the programme are to help students make the best use of existing knowledge of English in their studies, extend these skills and explore, individually, effective ways of meeting the linguistic demands of their main programme. The task for both teachers and students is an evaluative one: they have to work out specific needs, match existing capacity to these, and develop additional skills required. The focus of this curriculum is the needs of each individual student, rather than a body of knowledge or skills.

The task of the evaluation within this programme is to fine tune classroom and other learning activities so as to better meet students' needs and concerns. Although structured into two events – formative (Week 5) and summative (Week 12) – the evaluation is ongoing. It is a process of planning, drawing conclusions about the effectiveness of tasks and activities, and subsequently planning for the rest of the programme.

The evaluation of the programme

The approach to the evaluation taken by the teachers was largely within the naturalistic tradition (Lynch 1996). Data were collected through a needs analysis procedure at the outset, a structured discussion known as the Nominal Group Technique (Weir and Roberts 1994) halfway through the programme and open-ended questionnaires at the end. This approach was set out as institutional policy in this area, but was widely supported by the teachers. In the questionnaire study the teachers stated that it was easy to manage in the classroom, enabled students to e•press their ideas, and also provided them with a context for negotiation and communication in English. This section describes the evaluation process using the three-stage structure, and examines some of the issues that arise.

Stage 1: Baseline evaluation – understanding the pedagogy

The opening stage of the programme – negotiation of what the focus of learning activities should be, the identification of student needs by teachers and the self-assessment by students – was structured and supported by comprehensive documentation from the teachers. In the first lesson the students did a writing task for diagnostic purposes, and received two sets of guidelines. The first provided procedural information – contacting teachers, calendar, assessment procedures – and a framework for negotiation of classroom activities. Examples of possible topics were given: language areas (articles, verb forms, etc.), study skills (planning an essay, writing an introduction, etc.), and course content topics (studying abroad, travel and tourism, television and young people, etc.).

The second set, the Study Guide, contained a section detailing rights and responsibilities for students: one on academic writing conventions; and another on independent learning, introducing the self-access facilities available and strategies for using the local community as a learning resource.

During the first session, when both teachers were present, there was a guided reading from the guidelines, and questions invited on specific sections. Students were forthcoming with questions: about a specific textbook for the programme; about a specific writing problem; about understanding the comments of other tutors on marked work. In each case, the teachers had a response, which links to the overall approach – a pedagogy based on students' needs. In spite of the carefully structured consideration of the guidelines, it seemed that the students' concerns were about their particular problems, and the tutors' responses were about how central these problems would be to the teaching rather than to solutions *per se*.

In the second session the reading of the guidelines continued, on Independent Study, with an activity to self-assess on the English language skills required of students. The self-assessment sheet provided a list of 16 skills in relation to listening, speaking, reading and writing in different study and professional contexts. In a class discussion towards the end of this activity, introduced by the teacher as areas in which students can work on their own, a number of students introduced their specific needs – essay-writing, reading fast, etc. In reply to each, self-access materials, or a 'self-help' book from the list on the back of the self-assessment sheet, were referred to. Students were then asked to complete this self-assessment procedure as homework.

At the start of the third session the self-assessment sheet is taken up again:

> . . . Millie starts session. Asks students to look at the study guide – explains how the general guidance there can help them. Then refers to the module guide – more specific information for 1534 [code for this programme]. Then to SA [self-assessment] sheets from the last day. Asks students what they are going to focus on. Nominates: Gi: Speaking skills, she says, laughing, that she says a lot of 'stupid things' in class (other modules); Millie says that oral work is important and part of the assessment for the module. Also reading, she would like to be able to read faster, and identifies books listed on back of sheet which will help her. An: Writing essays and summaries. Millie says that a lot of work on the programme will focus on this.   (Classroom observation notes – Week 3)

Millie's intention was to promote learning outside the classroom by focusing on the resources listed for self-access work, and by demonstrating to students how they could work on individual needs using these resources. The data illustrate a pattern which characterises the place of learning outside the classroom: identification of a real problem at a very general level by a student; identification of self-access materials which might help (again, at a general level), and sooner or later the idea that the input in class will deal with the problem.

The role of the classroom in the pedagogy was throughout an interesting aspect of the teacher–student dialogue: the ideal of learning through independent and follow-up tasks outside the classroom was frequently set out, and was the basis for recommendations to individuals. The reality proved different when, for example, separate activities failed to work as intended due to lack of preparation by students:

> Later Millie expressed dissatisfaction with ss work outside the classroom – 'a dead loss': they do not do it, or if they do, they think it is mechanical exercises; they do not think about it in the way they should. She feels that it is not such a good idea to give them work in advance, as they just do not do it, and then the activity planned cannot go ahead.   (Post-lesson notes – Week 4)

The early stages of the programme were characterised not so much by enquiry into students' needs by the teachers as by a systematic process to persuade learners to engage in a certain kind of learning. This approach was defined by the intention: to individualise learning, through provision of a range of resources from which students would select what they required. Teachers were aware that the persuasion task was a challenging one, and were not deflected from it by evidence of limited uptake, and only minor developments in individuals' analyses of their needs.

Stage 2: Formative evaluation – taking stock and moving on

In the early sessions where there was much discussion of the pedagogic approach and independent learning, the place of the formal evaluation events was referred to briefly, but related to the development of the teaching and learning strategy. The key point about it was that it would involve a writing and speaking activity, so that 'the time spent on it will be useful for what you are learning' (Anna, Classroom notes – Week 1).

The evaluation, using the Nominal Group Technique, was carried out in Week 5 and involved small group and plenary discussion led by Anna. Two reasons for the activity were given: to satisfy a university requirement, i.e. to monitor quality, and to give students an opportunity to bring about adjustments. Students were asked to note aspects of the programme under three headings on a sheet:

> What has worked well for you?
> What has not worked well for you?
> Comments

After agreeing a list of points under each heading in small groups, one student would then report to the whole group. Data 1 below represents one small group discussion, while Data 2 represents a segment of the report-back phase. The formal findings in the teachers' report to the students and the institution, which was produced two weeks later, reflected closely the points noted on the OHP during the report-back session. It is, however, the process of evaluation which is revealing here, particularly in relation to the themes outlined above: learning need and language awareness; the teacher role – investigation versus persuasion; and the focus on the future rather than on experiences to date. As the discussion below demonstrates, these themes are themselves related in various ways, and are issues of pedagogy as well as of evaluation.

Learning need and language awareness

A strong rationale was made for the language-learning task aspect of the event, and this was an observable strength of the activity: the students were engaged in getting from their own notes to an agreed list of points to feed into the plenary discussion, i.e. the report back. The requirement of the university was also met – a report on students' perceptions that emerged from the activity. The question of adjustments is less clear cut: the absence of scrutiny of experiences so far, and the lack of awareness of specific learning needs combine to make adjusting the pedagogy difficult. The group discussion (see Data 1) shows that students perceived their needs at a very general level. Essay writing, for example, arises early in the discussion, but there is no probing of what the problems are. Summary writing is merged with it, as if the goal is to include as much as possible in a short group list. In relation to vocabulary, the search for precision in setting out what is needed – using, choosing or selecting – is largely at the level of articulation of the general category, rather than identifying the particular needs that are important.

Data 1: Classroom notes – Week 5

There are four ss in the group near me: Ca, Ab, Aa, and N (new student). Ca starts off by explaining to N what they have been doing – stage 1. She starts explaining what stage 2 is, and asks him:

Ca: What would you like more of?
N: Grammar, essay-writing . . .
Ca: We cannot have too much. How many weeks are left? Only 5?
Ab: Yes.
Ca: So we have to concentrate on the most important.
N: Writing essays
Aa: Did you mention grammar?
Ca (*looking at Ab*): And you?
Ab: Grammar – using tenses. And vocabulary – using vocabulary.
Ca: Choosing vocabulary? Selecting vocabulary – vocabulary selection.

Ab: Yes.

Ca   (*looking at Aa*):   And you?

Aa: Punctuation and . . .

Ab: . . . prepositions.

Ca: I agree grammar as well. Essay writing, writing summaries, which is like essay writing. Vocabulary . . . (*sounds hesitant*).

Ab: If you don't agree, leave it out.

Ca: No no and punctuation.

Ab: Punctuation and some verbs take prepositions, what are they? Like look at, take for, look for.

Ca: Ah, phrasal verbs.

N: Spelling.

Ab: Teacher can't teach you spelling.

N: Well (can't hear, seems to be giving examples).

Ab: That's quite basic isn't it? Like ei, e before i.

Ca: Other comments?

Aa: Frequency of speaking.

Ab: Note taking.

Aa: Reduce time from three hours to two hours.

Ab: No no (*C nodding agreement*).

Aa: (*says something and laughs*).

Ca: Perhaps break is too long.

Ab: Plus your recommendation

Ca: Me?

(*Ab says something I don't hear, which has the effect of closing the discussion.*)

There are two possible explanations for the students' limited detail and insight into their learning: they are unable to further the analysis, or they do not wish to. The case study provides a good deal of data supporting the former: individuals frequently misunderstood feedback given by the teachers; tasks that tutors expected to go well proved too difficult; there was a lack of uptake of opportunities for learning outside the classroom. There is also some evidence that students may hold back on their learning difficulties to avoid representing themselves as incompetent. Ab's response to N's difficulty with spelling may point to a hierarchy of undesirability when dealing with EAP problems. Students do not take opportunities to ask for clarification when they are unclear about what is required in a given activity. The data suggest that there is a complex interplay between what some students understand about their difficulty, and what they are prepared to explain to others – whether peers or the tutor.

The teacher role – investigation v. persuasion

Data 2 illustrates the probing and the search for shared under-standing in the classroom. The discussion has two main features: the centrality, even dominance of the teacher, and the unease of the teacher with this role. The teacher provides the answers, cued by different points from students. These are then noted on the OHP which represents the goal of the discussion and thus orients the process. There seems to be an expectation that the informa-tion provided to the teacher will enable her to pronounce on what students should do to solve their problems. The teacher in turn puts the ball back in the students' court – relating what they seem to want to what is already happening – and genuinely asks them to make a suggestion for a need that has been identified. There is a reminder about the time constraint, and what can be done in the context of individual tutorials, as if the teacher seeks to lower expectations of benefit from the present activity. The teacher's agenda seems to be to help students understand what needs to be done in terms of the overall pedagogical strategy – to develop individual awareness of individual needs, and appropriate strategies to deal with these – a continuation of the process of persuasion which characterised the preceding sessions.

Data 2: Classroom notes – Week 5 (A, B and C represent the three groups; 1, 2, 3, 4 and 5 represent the points proposed and listed on the OHP)

What did not work well *[Heading on OHP]*

C-1. More essay writing.
    Anna: Do you mean in class?
    Ca   (*who made the point*): Well . . .
    Ab   (*helping out/cutting in*): We mean the structure of essays – how an essay is.
    Anna: OK. Practice in the skills of essay writing. Is that what you mean?
    Ab: Yes definitely.

B-2. More grammar. Like the use of articles.
    Ab: Tenses.
    Anna: More on tenses over there.
    Student in B group: No, all grammar. (*Student in B group seems concerned that Ab should not take over his point.*)

A-3. More skills in writing.
    Anna: How do you mean?

G: Structure with the ideas, We have the ideas. We want to know how to present the ideas.

Anna: We need to be more precise, to understand what we can do in the time constraint we have.

Ab: Using our own words. Not using the words in the text.

Anna: Not reading from the text; you want to be able to talk, not with the exact words you have written?

Ab: Yes, but not using the words in the text. Say a summary of a text of 800 words; writing a summary of 500 words in your own words, not with the words in the text.

Anna: We do that every week.

Ab: We need more vocabulary; more building vocabulary.

G: That's what I am saying.

Anna: How should we do it? (*Silence: all seem to hear this as a question for the teacher to answer, not them, though the teacher may intend it as a genuine question.*) Vocabulary directly from the text? We could give you lists of words not in context. We could give you lists to prepare.

Ca: We need to remember a lot of different words.

Anna: Well, you could keep a notebook where you noted all new words that you think you need to learn. We can advise you individually in tutorials, like we will do next week.

Ab: If we look at any book – say for the Cambridge exams – we have to choose vocabulary for sentences. Sometimes prepositions for verbs. That's what I am saying.

Anna: I'll put down *vocabulary building*. Some work we can do in class, but you have to use the book list references we gave you.

B-4. Prepared for our exams.

Anna: That's what we are doing – we have oral presentations, essay writing, and the teaching is to develop skills in these areas.

A-5. Reading. This is difficult for me. To read a book without dictionary, there is some kind of skill. I need that skill. (Sh).

Anna: Yes. Reading skills. Any other comments in this category?

Ab: Punctuation in written texts. S. Pronunciation.

Anna: We only pick this up where there is a communication problem. Many people have different accents and that is not a problem, as long as people can

> understand. Anything else? Next week we will come
> back with proposals. Next week we will have tutorials
> – 10 minutes each. It is not a long time, so you should
> prepare; decide what you want to talk about, and
> then the tutorial will be more useful.

The students' agenda is more complex: each student has his own
individual preferred outcome of discussions on learning. While
these data cannot piece together how the evaluation exercise as
a whole is shaped by students' concerns, the account of Ab illustrates their complexity. He had a problem with plagiaristic use of
text in his writing and, from the start of the programme, he sought
to find a remedy. His attempts (in Data 2, for example) to communicate this problem fail, most probably through his wish not
to represent himself through such a particular problem. He was
not only concerned with his peers – in his individual tutorial with
Anna in Week 6 he seemed intent on avoiding the issue. When
the problem became apparent to Millie towards the end of the
programme, Ab was prepared to argue the point, possibly out
of frustration that he had not found a solution to the problem,
possibly showing that he had not really understood how fundamental the avoidance of plagiarism was to the learning process in
which he was engaged. Ab's story illustrates how daunting a task it
is for teachers to centre a programme on students' needs, and
how difficult it is despite an investigative and evaluative pedagogy
to identify what specifically is at that centre.

The focus on the future rather than on experiences to date

The initial task had three dimensions: two relating to experiences
to date, and one looking to the future. The report back on the
first (what has worked well for you) involved a listing by students
of a range of activity types engaged in without exploring how they
proved useful. The second dimension (what has not worked well
for you) very quickly merged with the third (students suggestions
for the remainder of the programme). Data 2 represents how the
plenary discussion at this stage becomes a shared exploration of
how the learning needs might be met – similar in many ways to
the needs analysis discussions earlier in the programme. The process is thus oriented towards action for the future almost to the
exclusion of the evaluation of what has already taken place. The

trigger here seems to be the use of 'more . . .' to indicate a lack of learning or success. This may be due to a politeness strategy, a desire not to seem directly critical of the activities in class. However, we can see in Data 2, in the discussion in Group C, that it is not just a student strategy for relaying sensitive feedback to the teacher; it is how the students see the problem. The deficit is their failure to learn, so if an activity has not been successful, more of it is needed. Ca (see Data 2), in seeking to explain to and involve the new student, framed the issue: 'What would you like more of?' From there each student states preferences for the remainder of the programme.

Time is not just past, present and future. It is a limited commodity in the programme, and is frequently referred to by teachers and students as a constraint, a reason for not taking a desired or appropriate course of action, or for deferring it till later. We can see this in Data 1, when Ca says: 'We cannot have too much. How many weeks are left? Only 5?' (Classroom observation notes – Week 5). Anna closed the plenary after discussion at the end of Data 2 – without taking points from the Comments category. The allocated time – one hour – for the evaluation activity had expired, Millie had arrived, and it was time for the break. There was one more question:

Ca:	What are your recommendations?
Anna:	About what?
Ca:	About us. You see our work, what do you think we should do?
Anna:	Our expectations are in the module and study guide.
Millie:	What do you mean by recommendations?
Ca:	What would you suggest from seeing our work?
Ca	*(turning to Ab and Aa)*: Is it that?
Anna:	Different things for different people. You see it in your written work.
Millie:	We will talk about that next week and in the tutorial. Or it may be to do with your self-assessment sheet.
Anna:	If there is something from your programme, bring that in – work back, something like that. We are working in the dark here – we really do not know what your programme is asking you to do. (Classroom notes – Week 5)

Ca is the spokesperson for his group and is setting out here what Ab said in the group discussion phase (see Data 1). In the classroom it was clear that the question struck a chord with all the students – as if it was the question they all wanted the answer to. Anna's final comment illustrates the central problem arising from the lack of specificity in the preceding discussion: the insufficiency of illumination from the formative evaluation event. Time as a constraint, a limited commodity, serves as a mechanism for dealing with this difficult issue. At the end of Data 2, and again in the above extract, we can see how deferral till later renders the most difficult evaluation issues manageable.

Stage 3: Summative evaluation – preparing for next time

The summative evaluation was carried out in the last session of the programme. Students were asked to fill in a questionnaire in class, which asked for three positive aspects of the programme, three negative, three suggestions for change, and a series of Yes/ No questions on the use of the resources available. The report of this evaluation, prepared by Millie, listed all the comments made by students in each category. As the evaluation was done on the last day, the report was not relayed to students: the class had already dispersed when it was prepared. The positive comments related for the most part to classroom processes, including the teachers' contributions, rather than learning outcomes: only 3 out of 21 comments related to progress made, and two of these were modified:

> Techniques about writing paragraphs were very useful. I try to put them into practice but still it is very difficult for me to write an essay in the proper style. It takes a huge amount of time to put my ideas in writing.

> To analyse different kinds of reading was very useful, but I still need more practice.   (Summative evaluation report)

The negative comments and the suggestions for improvements focused for the most part on 'more of . . .' and issues of procedure – timetabling, length of break, etc. Responses to the resources section show that one-third of students made use of the resources available on a self-access basis. Millie, in an interview after the writing of this report, found the comments of the students 'unsurprising', but also bland and uninteresting, in that they concentrated on issues of timetabling and procedure rather than:

> whether the content really suited them; whether it matched up with their needs; problems they were having with their other modules;

the issue of what they did outside class; how much help they need to do things outside class; how clear it was what they were supposed to do outside class; why they didn't do much outside class in this programme.   (Interview M2)

Despite the lack of information on these areas, Millie is positive about the contribution of evaluation to the development of the programme:

> *Interviewer*: And from the evaluation of this module will action be taken in terms of shaping the programme for the next time? Will you do it differently?

> *Millie*: I don't think I'll do it differently. I think over the course of this programme we have developed some good strategies and some quite good materials, that will continue to develop. So it is not a change of direction, it is perhaps going further in the same direction. Things we tried out this time [are] as a result of evaluation, and our own evaluation of the last programme.   (Interview M2)

There is a sense at the end of the programme of its being part of something larger, of a contribution to the development of the pedagogy, of the experience of the teacher which will benefit other programmes and students in ways too imprecise to fit into the action points section of a programme report. The programme over, the students cease to be the centre; they take their place as experiences which tell a story, as frames for devising new solutions for similar programmes in the future.

Discussion

This case study raises a number of issues related to the evaluation of programmes by teachers, and to the research of this aspect of classroom and professional practice: the relationship between evaluation and pedagogy; student perceptions of their role; and teacher investigation as a means of improving institutional policy and language programme theory. The data described in this chapter suggest appropriate directions and emphases for further research.

Researching programme evaluation

The case study shows how interwoven are the threads of evaluation and pedagogy in a programme such as this. The evaluation dialogue in the classroom is a dimension of the pedagogy, and a better understanding of the processes involved is important for programme design and teacher education. Evaluation in this context differs in a number of ways from the traditional evaluation for accountability purposes, carried out by external evaluators. These differences seem to preclude the identification of features of evaluation practice which could be used as variables to explore effectiveness within the experimental, positivistic paradigm. Evaluation in this study is characterised by negotiation and persuasion – a dialogue managed to sustain both the classroom process and faith in that process. The dialogue is shaped by the teachers' own principles and institutional policy, rather than established frameworks of educational evaluation – a point which suggests directions for further research.

The broad range of factors currently influencing English language-teaching practice supports a case study approach, where the relationship between the individual teacher, the institutions, and the resources available can be explored in a specific programme situation. The goal is not to produce, in Stake's terms (1995: 7–8) 'grand generalisations' concerning pedagogy or programme design, but 'petite generalisations' about classrooms which teachers one way or another come to work with, and 'particularisations', how one programme differs from others in the same category.

The qualitative approach adopted for this case study permits the inclusion of all the issues and questions that arise in the teaching of a programme, and is especially important where the programme is negotiated and responsive to emerging needs rather than pre-planned in detail. This leaves the problem of what to include, what to describe, what to follow-up in interviews, etc. Many different factors contribute to decision making in planning *for* the classroom as well as *in* the classroom, and the importance of these often does not become apparent till later. Familiarity as a researcher with the context of professional practice was useful in informing on such issues, though this was also a potential pitfall: familiarity with such classrooms as a general class can be a fragile basis for interpretation of case study data. An enquiry of this kind within the ethnographic tradition recommends that ignorance should be assumed in order to maximise the voice of the informant and the data (Spradley 1979). Other strategies for improving the quality of interpretations include engaging with informants at all stages of the research to test the coherence of a given interpretation.

This is necessary for working through situations where the teacher, student and observer seem to have had significantly different experiences:

> *Millie*: It was interesting that you – obviously not busy teaching the lesson – you were able to spend more time looking at the students, and seeing when they were on task, when they were doing something totally different, when they – some people reacted in a way that I hadn't noticed, for example they didn't seem to understand, maybe you heard a comment I hadn't heard. That was interesting.
>
> (Interview M2)

Evaluation and pedagogy

The case study illustrates how evaluation is embedded in the pedagogy. Anna and Millie were at all times evaluating the approach, the materials, what the students needed to concentrate on, etc. They worked systematically at engaging the students in a process of self-evaluation, a pedagogy similar to that of Legutke and Thomas (1992). That this pedagogy did not work out quite as intended was no surprise: the teachers felt there was no real alternative; they did what they could in accordance with the best models available, and in the end were prepared to 'go further in the same direction' next time. In the domains of both evaluation and pedagogy the big decisions are made for the teachers: the former is shaped by institutional policy, the latter by the dominant communicative approach. Within this framework teachers can make decisions on the format of guidelines, materials and tasks. The issues involved in these decisions did not come up in the formal evaluation events, but are important, as Millie's comment on the classroom observation notes illustrate:

> *Millie*: To some extent they were not a bad picture of students' reactions to things, and the interaction that was going on. But there is still – it misses out the students' interaction with the texts, and the tasks they're actually doing, and what effect that has on them. That's very difficult to measure, but that is a big part of the lesson. They are doing an activity – you can comment on how interested they seem to be in it, how they go about it, but you do not necessarily look at what they were producing, or what the materials themselves were trying to achieve.   (Interview M2)

This observation is valuable: while the approach is flexible and negotiated, an understanding of what is happening is not accessible through a focus on the process alone – the planning, and the outcomes are also part of the picture. It is as if the pedagogy is too complex for the evaluation to engage with, and the evaluation which involves the students is only a small part of the decision-making processes at hand.

A key difference between the evaluation described in this study and more conventional evaluation and research, is the management in real time of data generation and interpretation (see Ellis in this volume). Teachers do not engage serially in focusing on one issue, gathering appropriate data, analysing and interpreting these to facilitate appropriate action. This process would involve dealing with what is past, whereas the pedagogic imperative is to deal with the present and the future. The formative evaluation described above constitutes an investigative process, but there is little data generated to permit further analysis and interpretation. Reflecting on, and reinterpreting what has already happened may be an aspect of a teacher's professional development, but it is not teaching, and so is not easily translated into a classroom evaluation event. While in many ways good teaching incorporates practices typical of evaluation, the strategies for dealing with data in the evaluation of the programme are shaped by teaching processes. This interplay between evaluation and teaching may explain the apparent lack of focusing, and the absence of use of the relevant literature in dealing with classroom issues. Ultimately, this interplay can inform our understanding of how teachers manage, in the time available, to deal with the range of tasks involved in teaching a programme, and thus contribute to strategies for teacher and curriculum development.

Students' perceptions of their role

An innovative feature of this programme was the structured approach to engaging students in the kind of learning planned. The student response to this was positive and co-operative in the classroom, though somewhat weaker outside. Although student perceptions were not explored in this case study beyond observation in the classroom, some features became clear. Firstly, students were listeners, and were especially attentive and engaged in tasks which involved rules, explanations and procedures – pieces of information which seemed maximally transferable. Contributions to discussions often seemed designed to support the teachers in giving rules and explanations, and were oriented towards future lessons rather than reflective of learning experiences to date. This view placed the classroom at the centre of their learning, and the teacher as determiner of what is done. Secondly, the students had an awareness of need and purpose, albeit at a general level; each seemed to have a clear idea of what a successful learning outcome would enable them to do, but a less clear sense of strategy on how to get there. Thirdly, their idea of what knowledge and skills they needed to develop was vague, leaving them, in spite of the self-evaluative approach of the programme, with little option other than to listen to the teachers, and make the most of rules and procedures which seem applicable to their work. They were in many ways learners who had performed the self-assessment and reached the conclusion that what they needed was this programme, and what the teachers had to tell them.

Institutional policy

The institutional policy – a kind of house style for programmes such as this – seems a neutral backdrop to the behaviours and interactions that make up the programme. It generates elements such as the role of self-access learning, and the structure of the evaluation events. However, what breathes life into these elements of the curriculum is the individual teacher's pedagogy, the set of beliefs built up from experience and academic study. Millie engages in the difficult task of persuading students to self-assess and develop independent learning strategies, not because it is what the institution wants, or even what the students want, but because in her experience that is what will be of greatest benefit in the long run. In response to specific requests, more familiar grammar exercises and procedures for writing paragraphs are set, but the fundamental goal remains unchanged. Anna is somewhat sceptical of the institutional agenda in relation to evaluation, and sees the report for the institution's committees as a low-priority task. The event itself, the dialogue with the students, however, is carefully structured and managed to understand student perspectives and to get them to explore their learning needs and strategies.

Many of the problems discussed in this chapter arise from the ambitious goals of the programme; to deal with such a range of learning needs in such a short time is perhaps never feasible, especially when the learning has diverse educational and cultural dimensions. These goals have a sound pedigree: the learner-centred curriculum, self-evaluation by students and independent learning are central to the communicative approach and to the programme quality concerns of institutions. In the classroom there is a tension between the goals of the teachers (a process which teachers try to get students to engage with) and those of students (quite simply, to resolve the language problems that make life so difficult for them).

Language programme theory

Language programme or syllabus design theory currently relies heavily on the evaluative pedagogy approach – individual needs analysis and negotiation to develop appropriate strategies. For both EAP and general English students at the post-intermediate levels, the focus is a form of discourse competence – the knowledge and skills for the kind of language-use situations the learner encounters. The classroom discourse evident in this case study seems in many ways insufficient to achieve this: it deals with notions of skill and strategy which remain abstract, and leave students grasping for the certainties of sentence level grammar and vocabulary lists. Is the problem one of implementation, or is the basic rationale flawed? Swales (1989) comments that, in the majority of accounts of EAP programme design and implementation, 'the most commonly identified problems are structural or managerial' (1989: 86), and proposes that it is the 'issues of how and why aims are determined and how and why strategy is formulated, that are of fundamental importance, and thus provide a *raison d'être* for descriptive case studies' (1989: 87–8). The research task implicit here brings together the individual teacher and institutional perspectives discussed above with the language-learning perspectives on which applied linguistics tends to focus.

Conclusion

A central question for this study has been about how teachers manage the different agendas – personal and professional interests, students' concerns, institutional requirements – involved in carrying out evaluations. This is, perhaps, a combination of two other questions: how teachers teach, and how they develop professionally from experience. The traditional evaluation paradigm developed for specially commissioned specific evaluations may not be appropriate for describing the evaluation process, or for developing teachers' skills for the evaluative elements of the EFL/ESL curriculum. The action research and reflective practice traditions are useful for analysing some aspects of professional practice and for training, though neither represents clearly the investigative, pedagogic process in the classroom. We need a better understanding of how teachers meet the demands of programme design and implementation in specific situations, both to provide a better foundation for classroom innovations and to develop our approach to teacher education and professional development.

Notes

1. The Royal Society of Arts/University of Cambridge Local Examination Syndicate is the body which validates many EFL teacher education courses in the UK sector.
2. The British Association for State English Language Teaching and the British Association for Lecturers in English for Academic Purposes are bodies which inspect and approve institutions for general and specifically EAP programmes respectively.
3. The interactions in the classroom were not tape-recorded. Extensive notes were made in the classroom, and were augmented from memory ('headnotes' in the ethnographic tradition) soon afterwards. The dialogues in the data in this chapter are the product of this process of note taking and reconstruction. Although this form of recording is not ideal, it was facilitated by two features of the classroom discourse: the teachers tended to repeat key points, and student interactions (Data 1) proceeded relatively slowly, with a lot of hesitation and wait time between utterances.
4. Names and, elsewhere, pronouns do not suggest the gender of the teachers: rather they follow the pedagogy research convention of referring to teachers as female. Students are referred to by initials with pronouns reflecting actual gender.

Managing evaluation and innovation

Introduction

The contributions to this part of the volume, 'Managing evaluation and innovation' are also concerned with innovations in language education but they reflect a stronger management focus. In particular, they connect with issues of stakeholder involvement in evaluation and democratisation of the evaluation process (see Rea-Dickins and Germaine, Chapter 1 in this volume). They also exemplify some of the tensions between managing, evaluating and innovating in language education.

Chapter 5, 'Using institutional self-evaluation to promote the quality of language and communication training programmes' by Mackay, Wellesley, Tasman and Bazergan concerns the evaluation of English language education programmes within the context of a large language centre, addressing evaluation issues from an institutional perspective to assure programme and curricular developments. A central focus in this chapter is the principled development of a strategy for managing evaluation (see also Markee 1997). One of the roles clearly defined by the authors is that of evaluation as a management activity which takes up the needs of language centre staff for information and knowledge in order to plan strategically, with data from the evaluation activities feeding into this process. Of importance in this is the way in which clear frameworks have been established for evaluation data to feed into. Methodologically, the approach adopted draws on a view of evaluation as a curriculum-focused enquiry grounded in professional practice of an illuminative and responsive nature (Stenhouse 1975, Parlett and Hamilton 1976, Patton 1980) rather than one that is recommendatory. Another focus of this chapter is on democratising the evaluation process and on managing stakeholder participation in the practice of self-evaluation in Programme-Based Review (PBR). PBR is seen as a means of establishing the internal validity of the language centre's work, through staff collaboration in an intrinsically motivated approach to evaluation, in contrast to VFM externally controlled approaches to project evaluation. The chapter identifies a need for clarity (echoed by Karavas-Doukas in Chapter 2 in this volume) in the innovative practice of evaluation through the use of performance indicators (PIs), which need to be adapted to the context in which they are used. This point is emphasised in connection with the non-transferability of PIs, which confirms a view of evaluation as a context-embedded process which, in this case, is used effectively to identify strategic developments for this specific language centre and its programmes.

The self-evaluative and illuminative elements of Mackay *et al.*'s work is taken up in an in-service training context by Hedge in Chapter 6, 'Managing developmental evaluation activities in teacher education: empowering teachers in a new mode of learning'. She describes the use of a series of self-evaluation activities integrated within a 50-hour postgraduate teacher education course. These activities (for which examples are provided), focus on developmental growth. They aim to assist teachers in developing an awareness of issues in managing team work and small group discussion, in developing their perceptions of their own potential to contribute to small group discussion, and in encouraging responsibility in developing critical approaches to modes of learning. Hedge draws attention to some of the problems inherent in using an interactive methodology, where participants may be unfamiliar with this mode of learning, and examines how a programme of developmental evaluation activities may play a useful role in heightening awareness of collaborative group work and in developing teachers' skills in managing it effectively to ensure positive learning outcomes.

Her primary concern is to create self-management capacity in teachers participating in the course, thus promoting the integration of evaluation as part of, and undistinguished from, professional practice. This is achieved through opportunities for self-evaluation and dialogue which aim to prepare teachers not only to learn more effectively through small group work in this specific in-service programme but also, with the broader aim, to prepare them for coping with innovations in their own professional situations which they may be called upon to implement. Stakeholder participation in this study is thus defined as a means of preparing and empowering teachers for the task of implementing new methodologies. In concert with Mackay *et al.* in this part (and Kiely and Roberts in Part I), Hedge's work is embedded within the concept of naturalistic evaluation (e.g. Macdonald 1971, Stake 1975, Parlett and Hamilton 1976): the methodology is responsive to the concerns of the programme participants with the locus of judgement resting primarily within this stakeholder group.

In Chapter 7, 'Managing and evaluating change: the case of teacher appraisal', Anderson (like Mackay *et al.*) is also concerned with institutional systems, and documents the introduction and implementation of a staff appraisal scheme. Her role is that of expatriate manager responsible for introducing a teacher account-ability and development scheme into a large university language school. She documents the complexities involved at every level and, in particular, in trying to secure the involvement of key stake-holders, i.e. the teachers themselves, in the acceptance, uptake and development of this scheme. She deals with appraisal as innovation. As such, she provides ideas on this innovative form of evaluation embedded in an institutional context totally unfamiliar with this type of professional scheme. This provides implicit acknowledge-ment of how appraisal as evaluation can be integrated into a wider innovation process. An evaluation of the appraisal system itself was undertaken and the involvement of stakeholders and outside experts forced a rethink of the appraisal scheme itself, in the form of greater democracy of appraisal processes, thus providing another example of evaluation and innovation being refined and shaped by experience. Once again, this integrated evaluation of the innovation (appraisal scheme) legitimises dissent and resistance (Fullan, Chapter 10 in this volume) and helps produce a more adapted and effective scheme.

The extent to which evaluation is integrated with development and change processes in language education is a theme running throughout this book. The divide between evaluation as an 'inte-grated' or 'separate' activity is not clear cut, with the chapter in this volume reflecting different points on this cline. In this respect, Mackay *et al.*'s contribution is interesting from the perspective of an external evaluator taking on the role of catalyst for actively reducing the distance between the 'evaluators' and those who have the responsibility for the routine implementation of the lan-guage education programmes (see also Mackay 1993, Wellesley 1993). Hedge, too, writes from the standpoint of evaluation as an integral part of a specific curriculum. Although her work is characterised as minimising the distance between stakeholders – in her case, the tutor and the teacher participants – it recognises the dilemma in work of this kind where the relationships between participants are not symmetrical in which 'the fundamental author-ity of the tutor, as an ultimate assessor, cannot be ignored' (p. 147). This is a point which is brought forcibly home in the Anderson evaluation case study.

5

Using institutional self-evaluation to promote the quality of language and communication training programmes

R. MACKAY, S. WELLESLEY, D. TASMAN
AND E. BAZERGAN

Abstract. Those persons who manage and staff schools, language centres and other units (referred to in this chapter as *language centres*) that deliver second language instruction need reliable feedback on their teaching and management activities. With reliable information, programme personnel are able to assess their progress, and adjust their plans and activities to improve performance. Acting on reliable feedback, a language centre can ensure quality service to its students and also demonstrate its efforts towards mission achievement to those authorities to whom it is accountable.

This chapter briefly discusses the benefits to be gained by language centres through the use of participatory evaluation, referred to here as Programme-Based Review (PBR). It illustrates the use of PBR with reference to a specific British Council-sponsored project in Indonesia. The example illustrates how evaluation criteria were arrived at and how a single language centre, belonging to Lemigas, the Indonesian Government gas research and distribution enterprise, undertook an evaluation with the purpose of improving the quality of specific aspects of its performance, in particular those relating to programme delivery, institutional relations and internal organisation, and internal finance.

Programme-Based Review: what it is and what it does

PBR includes participative monitoring and evaluation activities initiated within the unit (school, language centre or programme)

111

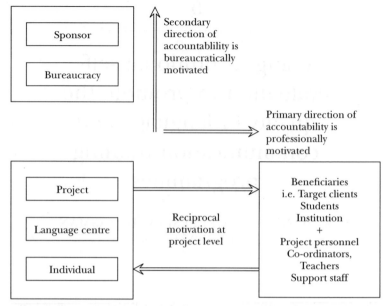

Figure 5.1   A schematic representation of intrinsically motivated evaluation

to facilitate periodic or continuous improvement by programme staff themselves. Programme staff refers to principal, director of studies, head teachers, teachers and other personnel whose direct responsibility it is to run the language centre and deliver the programmes. The intrinsically motivated nature of PBR is shown in Figure 5.1. The participatory character of PBR contrasts with evaluations initiated by persons external to the language centre for the purpose of accountability to higher authorities (Weir and Roberts 1994; Mackay 1994). Unlike PBR, evaluations that are extrinsically motivated seldom permit programme personnel to participate as full and active members, often alienating them from the process thereby denying them a valuable learning experience and putting the utility of the evaluation at risk.

PBR, precisely because of its participative nature, can usually provide information of direct and immediate relevance and use to programme personnel in improving their management and teaching-related activities as well as in demonstrating the programme's achievements to supervisory bodies (founders, government, senior institutional management, boards of governors, etc.)

to whom they are accountable. PBR can be comprehensive in its application. It can be used to diagnose problems in any and all dimensions of the context and work of a language centre. These dimensions include the centre's broader social and institutional context, and the motivation and capacity of the centre to perform in an effective and efficient manner so as to meet the evolving needs of its trainees, ensuring its relevance and thereby its sustainability. PBR at its best becomes a valuable management tool in the hands of the centre's personnel. It permits them, as a co-operative team, to examine all aspects of the centre and to draw up an action plan to address areas where changes and improvements are required. PBR is a form of self-evaluation, the motivation for which comes from within the programme. Within a programme-based review, a centre asks questions about its own activities, e.g.:

- How is the centre doing within the host institution?
- How well is this programme serving the needs of its clients?
- How is the instruction and learning within this course faring?

This may involve a broad look at all aspects of the centre – its environment, stated purpose, curriculum, teaching and learning, etc., or it may require a close look at only one or two specific issues that are causing concern to programme personnel, e.g. the student attrition (dropout) rate, dwindling financial resources, or student placement procedures.

Programme personnel (teachers, managers and other staff) undertake an internal review, with or without the help of an external resource person with relevant evaluation expertise, in order to improve the quality of some or all of their activities. Since PBR is a relatively new activity in second language programme management, the assistance of an experienced evaluator is sometimes sought, as it was in the Indonesian example described here, to introduce and facilitate the initial process. Once programme personnel have been actively involved in one PBR exercise, they should be able to undertake further efforts with the minimum of outside supervision.

A well-conducted PBR will permit programme personnel to address all aspects of their operations, including one or more of the following:

- To determine the nature and strength of the governance and communication links between the centre and the senior administration in the host institution. (It is not uncommon for language centre personnel to be unaware of the opportunities to participate actively in the way in which their centre is governed. Missed opportunities and poor channels of communication with senior administrators can result in less than optimal levels of support.)

- To reassure senior management that the organisation is reflective and self-questioning. (In today's institutions, units that display an awareness of the importance of continuous self-improvement win greater respect – and support – from senior management. They also maintain a relevant function within the institution and are thereby more likely to survive long term.)
- To permit the strength of the centre's motivation to be assessed. A centre with a clear and relevant mission, a collegial and supportive management culture, and purposeful means of valuing and rewarding desired behaviour maximises the motivation of its personnel. (Good teachers are less likely to seek employment elsewhere because they feel that their efforts are in keeping with the goals and objectives of the institution, and are valued and rewarded by management.)
- To answer questions regarding the capacity of the centre to meet its goals and objectives. (Does the centre director demonstrate leadership based on a clear strategic plan in harmony with that of the host institution? Is there a close match between the qualifications and experience of the teachers, the instruction delivered, and the needs of the learners? Are teachers assigned to tasks so that best use is made of their skills and training? Are there continuous close relationships between the centre management and the specialist departments that it serves?)

PBR is capable of generating information for the continuous improvement of the quality of the programme *as well as* information that satisfies the need for programme accountability to funders and sponsors.

While PBR is focused on the individual centre or centre component under review, the exercise must be carried out in a transparent way so that it can be credible to – even audited or examined by – peers and members of the senior administration. The participation of programme personnel ensures that individuals who are intimately familiar with the day-to-day operations of the centre are involved and have a stake in acting on the findings.

Bearing in mind both participation and external credibility, it is necessary at the outset that programme personnel make explicit how they believe the programme works – the logical assumptions upon which their centre and its programmes are built:

- An explicit logical framework provides this conceptual framework.
- A clear conceptual framework is a necessary pre-condition for effective PBR.
- Well-managed PBR offers a learning and development experience for all programme personnel.

Self-evaluation of a language centre can be wide-ranging and complex. Hence this approach lends itself to many of the currently discussed advances in evaluation methodology (Guba and Lincoln 1989, Gosling and Edwards 1995). Traditional approaches involving quasi-experimental designs are usually quite incapable of capturing the complexity required of most PBRs.

Programme logic: inputs, processes and outputs

The concept of the logic of programmes offered by a language centre can help make clear the often implicit assumptions upon which different language programmes are based. By requiring that the assumptions be made explicit, the soundness of the links between instructional materials, activities and learning goals can be examined more carefully. Though this point may be obvious, it is often overlooked in second language programme design. For example, one of the authors, while facilitating a programme-based review of a French second language programme for coastguard officer cadets, helped senior teachers to look at the logic of their most advanced programme. It was based on a line-by-line analysis of the syntax and vocabulary of literary texts. The instruction was enthusiastic and students found the tasks challenging and even interesting – a welcome respite from the mastery of technical features of navigation and maritime law. But logic between the expressed goals of the instruction and the methods used did not stand up to scrutiny.

Any language centre, or language-teaching programme within a centre, can be viewed as a set of resources or *inputs* (e.g. students, teachers, materials, money, space, etc.) which engage in *processes* (syllabus design, materials preparation or selection, classroom teaching and learning, etc.) producing *outputs* (instructional materials, lesson plans, classroom activities, learning assignments, examination results, etc.) with the expressed purpose of producing predetermined *outcomes* (enhanced student language proficiency, professionals capable of performing effectively in a second language, students capable of undertaking higher education in a language other than their mother tongue, etc.).

Ideally, there is a clear chain of anticipated causal relationships between inputs, processes, outputs and outcomes. That chain of anticipated causal relationships represents the theory of action upon which the programme is based. It is also known as the *logic model* of the programme because it represents the logical relationships believed or expected to hold among all of the programme components. According to the theory of action, or programme logic model, changes in outcomes should be predictable by altering the nature and mix of inputs, processes and outputs.

Desired outcomes should determine the nature of the other three components (i.e. the inputs, processes and outputs) in this four-step system. What are of prime importance in second language programmes are the *results* produced by the programmes (i.e. the outcomes). The inputs, processes and outputs are of value to the extent that they produce the desired results. There is no merit in persisting with syllabuses, materials and teachers, or with particular training, instructional strategies and activities – no matter how attached we may be to them, for emotional or theoretical reasons – if they do not produce the planned learner behaviour.

If the system is working as it should (i.e. as we expect it to based on the theory espoused or, more likely, our experience and common sense informed by research results and guess-work), then given types and levels of inputs ought to generate anticipated processes producing predictable outputs resulting in the desired outcomes. That is to say, we do what we do because we believe that by doing so we will achieve our predetermined goals more effectively than by doing something different. The coastguard example cited above reminds us that we sometimes take what we do for granted without subjecting it to the test of logic.

One of the key virtues of constructing a programme logic model for the activities of one's language centre is that it highlights the key characteristics of the centre and its work within a coherent framework that must stand the test of detailed logical questioning. It also ensures that all programme personnel share a common view of the key features of the centre. This common view is a necessary starting point for any serious evaluation exercise.

Key characteristics of language centres

Any given language centre can be characterised with reference to a set of dimensions, including:

- the institutional environment in which it operates (e.g. as a service centre within a focused, public service such as Lemigas, the example illustrated in this chapter, or as a service centre within a university expected to serve a wide variety of different faculties each with its own specific undergraduate and graduate degree courses)
- how the centre is governed and how it receives or generates its financial resources
- the various programmes it offers and how these are managed
- the teaching and support staff it employs to conduct its business and the conditions under which they are employed
- the teaching resources it can count on, and how they are used.

The actual performance of any given language centre will result from the interaction of all of these dimensions. We have intuitive ways of characterising that performance that will vary depending upon the purpose of the characterisation.

If, for example, you were asked to respond to a request for advice from a French-speaking engineer seeking English instruction in order to undertake advanced academic training in an English-medium university, you might describe a suitable place of study in the following way:

> The language centre in X University would serve you well because it is highly thought of by both the faculties of science and engineering and so is given both financial and moral support by the university administration. It has good facilities for both teacher-led instruction and student-directed learning. Students are assigned to classes by an effective screening procedure which includes proficiency tests and individual student learning goals. The classes are small and conducted intensively before the term begins. The teachers are experienced in preparing lessons geared to preparing scientific and technologically oriented students for all aspects of academic study in English.

Table 5.1 The PBR performance indicator framework

Institution	Programmes	Staff	Resources	Finance
Status 1. Access to and support from decision makers 2. Familiarity with parent institution procedures 3. Position in organisation 4. Networking and liaison 5. Reputation *Aims and objectives* 1. SMART plans 2. Monitoring *Internal organisational structure* 1. Positions and delegation *Marketing* 1. Planning 2. Implementation and review	*Course quality* 1. Students' evaluation of courses 2. Appropriate syllabus and materials 3. Assessment methods 4. Documentation and certification 5. Student counselling 6. Self-access learning 7. Attendance *Teaching quality* 1. Feedback from students 2. Systems for monitoring, self assessment and feedback 3. Evidence of adherence to course design documents *Student performance* 1. Client/student satisfaction 2. Test results 3. External criteria 4. Teachers' evaluation *Administration* 1. Procedures and implementation	*Recruitment, retention and utilisation* 1. Recruitment systems 2. Scheduling and deployment 3. Orientation and monitoring 4. Job descriptions *Professional development* 1. Staff development plans *Team spirit* 1. Communication and co-operation with colleagues	*Premises and equipment* 1. Space and furniture 2. Systems for maintenance and updating 3. Availability of office supplies *Teaching and learning materials* 1. A range of suitable materials 2. Systems for selection and ordering 3. Organisation, accessibility and utilisation 4. Development	*Budgeting* 1. Sources of finance 2. Budget planning 3. Book-keeping 4. Cash flow and use of profits *Accountability* 1. Reporting 2. Transparency

Your characterisation of the centre includes those features that you intuitively believe represent important criteria for consideration by an adult engineering student, with limited time and of serious academic intent.

Similarly, for the purposes of conducting PBR, a language centre is characterised by the very programme personnel who will undertake the review on the basis of features that they believe are crucial to the effective performance of their unit according to the logic model or theory of action they adhere to. A formal framework resulting from such a characterisation constitutes a *performance indicator framework*. Table 5.1 contains an example of such a framework.

Performance indicators

Performance indicators (PIs) are contextually relevant quantitative or qualitative descriptions that have the potential to alert programme personnel as to whether the language centre, or any subcomponent of the centre, is performing as it should. The purpose of PIs is to allow programme personnel to make judgements about the performance of the language centre in terms of those components that are perceived to be key to the centre's plans and goals.

Single PIs (e.g. the total number of students scoring above a certain level on a given test) are not sufficient to explain a language centre's performance. Performance is a broader and more complex concept resulting from an interaction between the external environment, the centre's motivation to meet its objectives, and its capacity to do so. Any and all of these three dimensions of performance can be altered and it is the role of a PI framework to identify where change is required so that performance can be enhanced.

PIs are most effectively used in groups or sets representing key areas deemed to be of importance in the logical operation of the centre and the programmes it delivers, e.g. institutional characteristics relating to status within the institution, internal organisational structure; programme characteristics such as course type and quality, teaching quality, student performance, and administrative procedures; dimensions of staffing (recruitment, retention, professional development opportunities, team spirit); resources associated with both premises and equipment, and pedagogical materials; and financial resources and means of income generation.

The framework in Table 5.1 has five components or foci: institution, programmes, staff, resources, and finance. Each focus is broken down into a number of *key areas* (e.g. the focus *programmes* contains the key areas course quality, teaching quality, student performance and administration.

Each key area is characterised by a small set of *performance indicators* (e.g. the key area 'teaching quality' is characterised by the PIs 'feedback from students', 'systems for monitoring', 'self-assessment and feedback', and 'evidence of adherence to course design documents'). Data collection instruments exist for each PI, and the data can be either quantitative or qualitative.

Performance is measured against the language centre's own objectives:

> each level in this model, Focus, Key Areas, and Performance Indicators are identified, agreed upon as important and characterised by the stakeholders involved. Thus the resulting framework is appropriate and sensitive to the context under review.
>
> (Mackay *et al.* 1995)

Criteria for developing performance indicators

The PI framework in Table 5.1 was arrived at in a participatory manner by some 30 language centre personnel representing 16 centres. They chose these specific areas and indicators because they believed that they represent (a) the key features which together determine the ultimate performance of their centres, (b) areas over which they have at least some modicum of control and (c) ideal levels of performance towards which they should strive.

To have maximum value, PIs must be relevant, informative, acceptable, beneficial and cost-effective for those who use them (Fitz-Gibbon 1992, 1996). The PIs in Table 5.1 are deemed *relevant* by those who developed them, in that each relates to policies and/ or goals valued by the language centre personnel and to specific responsibilities of identifiable individuals. They are *informative* in that they address factors believed by programme personnel to influence the outcomes sought by the centre. They are *acceptable* in that each relates to a commonly agreed-upon goal, can be easily

understood, can be explained in terms of the way in which the programmes are believed to work (i.e. the programme logic model),
can be influenced by in-service training, can be defined opera-
tionally, are capable of being confirmed by others, are sensitive to
improvements in the programmes and promote good practice –
which result in benefits if pursued by programme personnel. They
are *cost-effective* in that information on each can be collected and
processed by programme staff without undue investment of time
or money.

Constraints on the transferability of PI frameworks

It must be borne in mind that any given PI framework has been
developed for a particular context and may, therefore, not be
directly transferable to a different set of circumstances. The burden of determining the transferability of any given PI framework
to a new context lies with the adopter, not with the creators. For
example, the framework in Table 5.1 resulted from the combined
efforts of a group of language centre directors and other personnel
during and immediately after a workshop in Bali in 1993 (Wellesley
1993; Mackay 1994). It was created for their own purposes and
uses. It could not be transferred directly and without substantial
modification to a language centre in a Canadian university because
the institutional, political and educational environment would be
substantially different. Moreover, the salience of specific PIs by
which personnel want their centres to be judged may change over
time and according to circumstances. For example, in the case of
Lemigas and most of the other language centres who developed the
PI framework, the areas of resources and finances were considered important. Resources were included because the centres were
expanding and had not yet reached the stage where personnel could
take premises, equipment and teaching resources for granted.

Another easily accessible, well-explained and widely used PI
framework is that produced for secondary school self-evaluation
in Scotland by the Scottish Office Education Department (SOED
1992). This framework provided the foundation for the one that
appears in Table 5.1 and was modified substantially to meet the
particular features of the political, educational and institutional
environments of the Indonesian language centres. The SOED has
also prepared comprehensive PI frameworks for primary school
self-evaluation that include school ethos indicator sets to assess

the more difficult to measure aspects of the school social environment. PI frameworks can be designed to measure and evaluate any and all valued characteristics of education and training. A PI framework such as that illustrated in Table 5.1 represents the logic of the underlying purpose and management of a language centre and its programmes. PBR employs the PI framework of a given language centre in order to examine the validity of the assumptions underlying its management and instructional activities and the extent to which these activities are producing the desired outcomes. The review will allow programme personnel to identify the strengths and weaknesses of the centre and pinpoint areas where improvement is required.

The nature of projects and programmes

It is appropriate at this point to discuss briefly the notions of project and programme as used in this chapter. A project is different from a programme in that, whereas a programme is ongoing, a project is a unique, non-routine activity undertaken to provide a clearly identified service with a fixed goal within an identified time period and a limited budget. Once the terms of reference of the project have been fulfilled, the activity may proceed, even multiply, as a programme or set of programmes become more or less routine.

The metamorphosis from project to programme(s) in the Indonesian context under consideration is characterised not only by the notion of project goal attainment (i.e. the establishment of a set of well-organised language centres inside Indonesian government departments, para-public institutions and university departments, with trained staff and programmes relevant to the needs of their host institutions) but also the notion of sustainability in the sense of centres that are valued, respected and well supported politically and financially by their host institutions because they meet their current needs and are sufficiently adaptable to meet evolving needs. Once the target outcomes – the planned language-training services – of the project have become demonstrably sustainable by the human and financial resources devoted to it, then the activities of the project can become more routine programmes, monitored regularly to ensure that they follow their intended function and are adjusted as necessary.

Background description of Lemigas

The Research and Development Centre for Oil and Gas Technology, more commonly known by its Indonesian abbreviation Lemigas, has been operating since 1972. Many of its activities involve interactions with other oil companies and institutions, both national and international. For this reason managers and technologists are aware that English is one of the keys to increasing the productivity of this institution, especially in the transfer of technology.

Prior to 1987, Lemigas ran English courses on an irregular basis. In 1987 a language centre was set up under the auspices of the British Council through the Projects Unit. The objective was to ensure regular English classes as a way of systematically upgrading the English of key employees to enable them to be more effective in relations with international institutions and to be able to take advantage of overseas training opportunities. Since the Projects Unit's input to Lemigas ended in 1991, the institution has entrusted the language centre with all English language training for the institution's employees.

What started as a project, i.e. an undertaking to create a language centre offering work-related ESL instruction, has metamorphosed into an established programme within the institution.

Now a new undertaking – evaluation for continuous improvement – has begun in the language centre, prompted by the responsibility felt by the programme personnel to develop, expand and improve the centre and its activities, as well as themselves, professionally. This undertaking has been prompted by a number of disparate but important factors, which include:

- the growing respect which the language centre and its courses have attracted within Lemigas
- a demand for a wider variety of courses from a broader section of Lemigas employees than that originally perceived to represent the potential client base
- the opportunity to market courses to learners from outside Lemigas in order to maximise the use of classrooms and to generate revenue from external sources
- the need to keep abreast of professional developments in the management and delivery of second language programmes.

The Lemigas language centre concentrates its efforts on running 3–4 broad-based courses each year, as well as a larger number of more specialised, one-off courses tailored to the individual needs of particular groups of technical clients. The institution provides an adequate but modest budget to cover the costs of these activities. Centre personnel consist of the director, one full-time teacher, three full-time support staff, and a number of part-time teachers from both inside and outside Lemigas. Those part-time teachers from inside the institution tend to be specialists in technology with a high level of proficiency in English and a desire to teach. Those part-time teachers from outside tend to have more traditional TESL qualifications.

The first language-related project at Lemigas was to establish a language centre to ensure effective communication between donor and recipient technologists. This centre has now become a strong, institutionalised unit delivering language programmes not only to Lemigas but also to the Department of Mines and Energy and other government organisations.

A subsequent project was initiated to provide the language centre with self-monitoring and evaluation skills to ensure and improve upon the quality of the courses delivered. The role of these courses in facilitating scientific and technical communication is essential to the success of a very important component of the Indonesian economic development plan. Hence, continuous quality improvement of the centre's activities is regarded within Lemigas and within the language centre as a priority.

There are no obvious institutional constraints to the sustainability of this centre. It has come to be recognised by administrators and technologists alike as a key training department within Lemigas. It has its champions at the senior administration level of the institution; its core budget is secure. Nevertheless, a constant effort on the part of the centre director is necessary to ensure that the appropriateness and quality of the services provided are maintained at a high level. In all language centres, wherever they may be located, training personnel with administrative responsibility are constantly reminded that their organisations are dynamic entities requiring continuous monitoring if standards are to be maintained and improved so that their clients are well served.

The framework within which this sustainability is maintained at Lemigas, and the very instrument of this maintenance itself, is PBR.

The implementation of project improvement at Lemigas

In this evaluation improvement project, one of the main stakeholders – and the principal information user – was the centre director. *Project improvement* was initiated by her from the outset. She is in the enviable position of not having to carry out evaluation for purposes of detailed accountability to the institution's administration. The administration demand only that the Lemigas employees be effective in their professional relationships with international counterparts, and, on this criterion, so far appear to be satisfied that the language centre is making its planned contribution.

The Lemigas language centre has reached the stage of sustainability in that an adequate operating budget is secure and an appropriate number of full-time and part-time teachers, as well as a director, are in place. The programmes are not dependent on but are enhanced by external revenues. However, as a professional ELT practitioner with substantial management training, the director determined to make a systematic investigation of the characteristics of the centre, the programmes, and its clients in order to provide the basis for current improvements and future planning.

To set *project improvement* in motion, Lemigas language centre invited the two evaluation facilitators from the Projects Unit to work with the centre staff in identifying the weaknesses and strengths in the programme, building on the latter and making systematic plans for the improvement of the former.

This improvement exercise, using PBR, employed the PI framework (Table 5.1) as a starting point. Participatory evaluation, i.e. evaluation activity in which key stakeholders contribute to the identification of the instruments by which the programme will be measured and the standards by which it will be judged, places a strong emphasis on utility to all stakeholders, including those at the programme implementation level. In the Lemigas language centre, the evaluation team consisted of the director and the senior teacher – the critical mass in this programme – together with the Projects Unit's evaluation adviser. The director and senior teacher were aware of the potential benefits of empowerment that could come through the evaluation, and all other programme personnel and representatives from the institution's senior administration were encouraged to become involved. However, participation of individuals other than those mentioned above was limited. This raises the question (a question which will not be resolved here): How many key stakeholder groups must be directly involved in order for the evaluation to be truly *participatory*? The Lemigas part-time teachers were unable to devote the time to participate much in the evaluation itself, though some of them subsequently involved themselves in implementing the recommendations. To participate in a substantial way, stakeholders may have to have part of their regular workload recognised as being dedicated to the evaluation. They also have to believe that their participation will make a difference. In many current situations, neither of these conditions holds, and the reasons for this need to be documented, with thought given to how the situation might be changed.

How project improvement was implemented at Lemigas

In keeping with the participatory nature of PBR, all stakeholders' views on priorities for evaluation were invited, and the critical mass of Lemigas language centre staff together with the evaluation adviser agreed on three foci (out of the five possible) for the evaluation. These were programmes, institution and finance. Centre personnel believed that the programme focus was the most in need of attention. In particular, they wanted answers to the questions:

- Is the language centre accepting the most needy clients?
- How do heads of technical departments and potential clients find out about the courses on offer?
- Are the procedures used to place clients in specific levels and programmes effective and efficient?

Institutional and financial foci were, for the most part, operating well but specific questions also needed to be addressed, in particular:

- Does language centre staff have access to specialists in the technical departments of Lemigas who can advise on language use and content?
- Who bears responsibility for the language performance of technical staff once they complete a second language course?

- Are trainees assured the opportunity, after completing a course, to use the language they have learned in work-related situations?
- Does the Lemigas institutional budgeting process permit the language centre to make long-term plans for courses with the assurance that the predetermined funding will be available?

The PIs within these three foci were recognised as being interdependent elements of the organisation and operation of the language centre, and it would not have been easy, or helpful, to draw conclusions based only on an assessment of the single Programmes focus alone. Successful implementation of programmes obviously relies on the appropriate number of part-time (and full-time) teachers being paid on time, cross-institutional support to ensure the release of those scientists and technologists in need of language training to attend the courses, and so on. The language centre staff wanted to confirm that these, and other systems, were in place and operating efficiently and effectively.

The evaluation data were co-ordinated by the evaluation adviser. They were collected by means of a series of semi-structured interviews conducted as discussions between the evaluation adviser and the language centre staff. The focus and questions were jointly agreed upon prior to the discussions. The centre personnel as a group, led by the director, examined the linkages and channels of communication between the language centre and examined the policies and procedures of the senior administration of Lemigas as they related to the centre. Finally, a collaborative examination of programme documentation and materials was undertaken on a file by file basis.

The responsibility for writing up the reports fell to the evaluation adviser. This responsibility was undertaken by the evaluation adviser only after considerable discussion with language centre personnel and on the understanding that final responsibility for the content and conclusions of the report lay with them. It was also agreed that future reports would be written in their entirety by language centre personnel.

The evaluation results confirmed the director's hunch that the language centre was institutionally fairly secure. The director of the language centre enjoys easy and rapid access to the director general of the institution and an adequate level of funding is assured, though it is sometimes subject to delay. The main areas of concern were found, as predicted, to be in the programmes

Table 5.2   Action plan based on findings based on assisted programme-based review

Evaluation recommendation: April (Year 1)	Actions to be completed before 1st follow-up visit: November (Year 1)	Actions to be completed before 2nd follow-up visit: April (Year 2)	Actions to be completed before 3rd follow-up visit: November (Year 2)
Repeat placement test at end of course	Equivalent versions of placement test and procedures for repetition reviewed	Equivalent version of placement test repeated at end of 1 course	Equivalent version of placement test repeated at end of 3 courses
Standardise rating system for oral tests	Rating system for oral tests selected and adapted	Rating system for oral tests adopted	Video used to assess oral/aural performance of students
Develop self-access materials and programme into course	Supervised self-access sessions account for 15 per cent of course hours	Additional self-access listening materials developed	Additional self-access reading and writing materials developed

themselves. Specifically, these lay with the centre's assessment methods, and procedures surrounding the use of self-access facilities. Accordingly, procedures to address these concerns were identified as high priorities in the centre's action plan for the following year. The specific steps to be taken were clearly specified (Table 5.2).

The impact of the evaluation was traced over a series of follow-up visits by one of the evaluation facilitators at approximately six-monthly intervals. One striking effect was that, on their own initiative, the two key staff who had been most closely involved with the evaluation began to pay much closer attention to student test results and student progress over the next few months. As a result of this attention, by the third follow-up visit, they had drawn up a longer term plan designed to further improve programme quality. Each step in the plan was based on the data yielded by the PBR and the follow-up emanating from it listed in Table 5.2. Results from the placement tests given on exit, for example, indicated that minimum scores representing successful completion of course objectives needed to be revised upwards. The results of investigating certain limited aspects of the placement tests in detail, e.g. minimum acceptable achievement scores, led to innovations designed to remedy the problems associated with students graduating from courses but still unable to operate at certain required performance levels in the workplace. This information forced programme personnel to review other components of the tests (e.g. the types of test items employed, and the skills tested) and their relationship to the instructional courses delivered. The innovations adopted by the director and the teachers as a consequence, included the use of video as part of the oral assessment to simulate more closely both instructional and work contexts. Reflection on inadequate student performance also led to discussions with the senior administration of Lemigas and directors of technical departments regarding changes in language course schedules in an attempt to improve attendance. It had been noted that attendance was often disrupted by course participants having to undertake fieldwork outside the institution or having been scheduled to attend simultaneous technical training courses.

Conclusions to be drawn from project improvement

It might be too optimistic to expect that, within the space of two or even three years, a radical change within any system will take place as a result of having practised participatory evaluation. Cumming and Mackay (1994: 8) observe that 'finding out what might happen within one school or one year is vital, but the most important effects . . . may only be apparent over the very long term and in diffuse ways'. To be truly effective in terms of changing practice and thereby performance, PBR must become institutionalised – that is, adopted as a continuous activity directed at improving areas that give rise to concern. However, recording, discussing and reporting what has, and to some extent why things have, been happening in the centre is an appropriate task to encourage and motivate teachers to better understand their situation, to self-evaluate their practice and to seek ways to improve. It is important to equip teachers with the ability to see evaluation in its broad sense, i.e. not only to measure achievements, but to gain insights into how they were achieved (Nunan 1985; Weir and Roberts 1994).

In Lemigas the evaluation leading to quality improvement is still a *project* in that it is a non-routine task with a clearly identifiable goal, limited resources and a specified time frame. However, within a few years, PBR could be a recurring or even continuous part of the language centre's activities. That is to say, continuous quality improvement through PBR is likely become an integral part of the *programme*. The key to institutionalising PBR is found in the attitudes of the programme personnel themselves. If they are convinced that, through evaluation, they will gain insights into the programme they are implementing, and will empower themselves to take more control over its quality and direction, they will be motivated to continue.

This first attempt at PBR in Lemigas has given all stakeholders the opportunity to become familiar with the discourse of self-evaluation and the use and application of a PI framework. The process of becoming familiar with the concepts integral to PBR and mastering the discourse of self-evaluation is a critical step in the successful practice of continuous quality improvement within the management and delivery of second language training.

One important indicator of the utility of the evaluation is that it widens and legitimises the sources of information about the language centre and its performance. It encourages stakeholders – in particular those at the day-to-day management and implementation levels – to see patterns and to take a more informed role in planning, making recommendations and acting. For the Lemigas English language centre, this means that it will not only be able to react to the demands of its parent institution but also to work with them, and with human resource development departments in other institutions which purchase the services of the Lemigas language centre, to recommend strategies for increasingly effective modes of language and communication training.

Those involved in this Lemigas language centre PBR crystallised out of the experience the following principles:

1. Project (and programme) evaluation is most effective, when it is motivated by a desire, in those involved in the programme, to improve practice rather than when it is imposed by a bureaucracy for accountability or compliance purposes.
2. Within an intrinsically motivated evaluation framework, teachers (and other stakeholders) are given the opportunity to engage in self-evaluation and to examine and reflect, communally, upon their practices. They may then embark upon self-initiated change based on information they helped to collect and interpret so

that subsequent action flows from teachers' (and other stake-holders') own enhanced appreciation of how their programmes are functioning.

3. Programme-based review permits (but unfortunately does not always assure) the voluntary and democratic participation of all programme personnel.
4. PBR is capable of providing a framework within which all of the factors that are believed to impinge upon a centre's performance can be examined. Such factors include those related to the governance mechanisms within the host institution, the financial, administrative and management contexts in which the programme exists as well as the more familiar factors relating to curriculum planning, materials development and selection, classroom pedagogy, student assessment, and teacher quality and training.

Possible future directions

The experience of Lemigas personnel with PBR, and their sharing of that experience with teachers and directors from other language centres in the network, has promoted interest in self-evaluation and its credibility as a practicable means of programme improvement. All participants in the process have been encouraged by the opportunity PBR represents for learning about the processes involved in and the uses of the results of evaluation.

Future attempts to engage in PBR will place greater emphasis on the active participation of all programme personnel, even to the extent of providing paid release time from teaching. It will also stress the clear division and assignment of responsibilities for different parts of the review to identified co-ordinators. It will stress the need for the development of an action plan with the names of persons responsible for follow-up and deadlines for implementation. Increased confidence in the process of conducting PBR suggests that the evaluation adviser will be used more as a resource person – to suggest appropriate evaluation tools and techniques and to assure the quality of the operation – rather than as the leader of the review.

6

Managing developmental evaluation activities in teacher education: empowering teachers in a new mode of learning

TRICIA HEDGE

Abstract.   An interactive methodology, using small group work, discussion and design teams has become common practice on English language teacher education courses which aim to encourage reflective practice. However, collaborative work carries with it inherent problems, particularly where participants are from a variety of cultural backgrounds and where many may be unfamiliar with collaborative work in education. This chapter argues that if participants are invited to engage in a particular mode of learning, they need to be able to manage it effectively to ensure positive learning outcomes. The implication of this is that teacher educators should take on responsibility for providing and managing the groundwork necessary for successful collaborative work. It goes on to discuss how a programme of developmental evaluation activities might play a useful role in this task.

The concept of the educated teacher

In recent years a substantial number of teacher educators have contributed to clarifying the difference between training and education or development. Lange (1990: 250), for example, describes teacher development as:

> a process of continual intellectual, experiential and attitudinal growth of teachers, some of which is generated in preprofessional and professional inservice programmes.

The aim of facilitating that continuing process is now firmly established as an ideologically acceptable base of teacher education programmes, at least with regard to in-service programmes and to many contexts in the Western world.

In recent literature on teacher education, it is therefore common to find attempts to formulate principles for education as opposed to training. Richards (1990: xi), for example, characterises teacher education as involving teachers in 'developing theories of teaching, understanding the nature of teacher decision making and strategies for critical self awareness and self evaluation'. Ramani (1990: 204) discusses the need to provide a point of access into theory which derives from practice:

> teachers' theoretical abilities can be engaged and strengthened if their intuitions are afforded value and if the entry point into theory is close to their experience as practising teachers.

Nunan (1989a: 112) proposes a further principle when he says: 'Content should, as far as possible, be derived from the teachers themselves.' The outcomes of applying these principles to the formulation of a programme, it is hoped, will be the educated teacher. Before accepting such principles and attempting to implement them, the teacher educator will then need to explore the concept of the educated teacher and arrive at a professionally and personally relevant definition.

One source of insight on this may be derived from Peters, who, in his book *Ethics and Education* (1966: 30–1), proposed four criteria for a person to be educated. The first was that a person should possess more than 'mere know-how or knack' but a body of knowledge and 'some kind of conceptual scheme to raise this above the level of a collection of disjointed facts'. This implies an understanding of principles and having a critical framework through which to view and appraise practical classroom procedures. Peters called this the 'understanding of principles' criterion. The second he called the transformation criterion. This implies that a person's outlook is transformed by what that person knows. This could be related to educational thinking about encouraging the practitioner to reflect on received professional knowledge, and that gained from experience, in order to achieve development. The third criterion is the caring or commitment criterion, that a person must care about the standards immanent in his or her field of interest. In education this would relate to finding evidence for our assumptions, looking for coherence and consistency in our own professional practice, developing criteria for self-appraisal, and building our own standards for that appraisal (see Anderson, this volume). Fourthly, the educated person must have a cognitive perspective and see the connections between what he or she is doing and other areas of activity. Many would judge that teachers need to see the place of education in the pattern of life and to recognise the issues for particular learners, age groups, conditions and contexts while, at the same time, appreciating wider educational concerns. Adopting Peters' interpretation of the educated person suggests a teacher who is substantially more than an agent in the educational hierarchy and gives a strong sense of the educated teacher as professionally self-aware, with a critical capacity to reflect on experience. In turn, this implies the capacity of a teacher to engage in evaluation in ways appropriate to his or her teaching context.

Encouraging teacher reflection on in-service programmes

Many teacher education programmes are premised on the belief that an educated teacher is a reflective teacher and that reflection is a professional disposition to be encouraged. A major question for the teacher educator, then, becomes how to encourage the development of these attitudes and qualities.

In recent years we have seen moves towards procedures in the training classroom which aim to do this. One example often used at the beginning of a course enables teachers to make explicit their assumptions about teaching (see Appendix 6.1). This 'Teacher's Credo' (based on Ellis 1988) presents a set of principles to which teachers might adhere in their teaching and which reveal their underlying beliefs about what constitutes good practice. The rationale for this activity type is that all teachers have theories which motivate their classroom practice but these are covert and implicit. They need to be brought to the surface and explored through a procedure which allows teachers to engage in self-evaluation at the beginning of a course and to build profiles of themselves. It takes into account the attitudes and personal constructs of teachers and their beliefs about their own professional practice. It begins the process of critical self-evaluation.

An extract from a second example (see Appendix 6.2) demonstrates the growing interest in dialogic pedagogy, in what Kramsch (1993: 29) has called 'an exchange of ideas and emotions . . . which has the potential of putting in question the status quo'. The aim of this task is to encourage teachers to consider their own practice, the institutional ethos within which they work and the ways in which these relate to educational tradition. It hopes to create an exchange of perceptions and experiences among participants; it also tries to give teachers an opportunity (a) to respond to ideas, by dismissing, adopting, or adjusting, and (b) to build a rationale for any of those options. The outcome from the task for each individual may be divergent.

These task types are now firmly established practice. They demonstrate the current preoccupation with enabling teachers to reflect, to challenge the assumptions which underly their own professional practice and to explore new strategies in appropriately critical ways. In this sense they perform an evaluative role as a means to teacher self-development.

The role of task-based collaborative work in teacher education

It is significant that the examples above all require teachers to engage in collaborative work in small groups, in which discussion, decision making and design feature strongly. Such activity has become a feature of in-service teachers' courses. Teacher perspectives on this major mode of learning are instructive:

> I found that this collaborative work really helped me in finding solutions to problems which I couldn't find entirely from my own experience or from the theory I had learned.

> I think in a teachers' workshop such a method is indispensable and I would surely apply it myself to get teachers feeling they are part of the learning, to draw from their experience and knowledge.

> Working in a group, sharing my opinion with others was instructive. I learned a lot from my colleagues.

> Group work I sometimes felt to be irritating and so polarised. So much time is spent before inter-subjectivity is achieved and discussion seems to progress. So often I've been tempted to chip in and

to direct discussions the way I think is right. But group work is a co-operative process that necessarily involves a warming-up period and interpersonal skills. I shan't push the river. It makes me realise what I ask of my students in discussion.

Such comments (extracted from the teachers' diaries in the programme described later) highlight the values felt by course participants to be inherent in group work: the possibilities for sharing problems and solutions; the possibility for peer comment and criticism of beliefs and perceptions which can motivate self-evaluation; the possibility for enhancement of confidence and self-esteem if group work is productive; the need and incentive to develop interpersonal skills; the training it provides for future work in teams; and the insights it provides into group processes to teachers who use group work in their own classrooms. Their perceptions are reminiscent of Handy and Aitken's assertion (1986: 64) that:

> groups allow individuals to reach beyond themselves, to be part of something that none of them could have attained on their own, and to discover ways of working with others to mutual advantage.

Yet collaborative work is a notoriously difficult mode of learning within the context of in-service teacher education, and the difficulties of handling this and of handling one's own effective contribution to collaborative work is exacerbated by the implicit role of group discussion in the process of critical self-evaluation and development. For many teachers it involves new ways of looking at their teaching, a transformation of perspective (in Peters's words) and this will impinge on personal theories underlying their professional practice. These may be strong and resistant and the process for the individual of making them explicit, confronting them in the light of new ideas and information, and adjusting them, can be challenging and uncomfortable. Group participants engaging in a process of critical self-appraisal can be vulnerable. However, understanding one's own personal theories is a necessary basis for change and for developing new ways of interpreting professional work. As Easen (1985: 83) puts it: 'The great value of other people can be the interpretative lenses they give us for looking at familiar phenomena in new ways.' Thus, a methodology of encounter, which encourages dialogue and response to other people's perceptions and values, given the vulnerability of participants, holds substantial potential for difficulty.[1]

Paying attention to these factors and processes is crucial to the successful management of group work on multicultural courses where assumptions, expectations and conventions can differ radically. This is well demonstrated by the comments of an American teacher following an MA programme with Japanese teachers of English in Tokyo:

> In particular our group work has helped me to explore more consciously the substantial cultural differences we have. I come from a society where great value is placed on the performance of the individual: here the ethos is one of achieving consensus. How does that affect our discussions?

Moreover, in multicultural groups of teachers drawn from a wide range of educational and cultural backgrounds, there will be a complexity of personal and interpersonal factors at work in using a methodology which is probably new to many participants. It is not unlikely that some will come from backgrounds where group work is uncommon for a variety of reasons and these reasons will affect their attitudes towards participation in groups. The ethos at home may be competitive rather than collaborative, the tradition of individualism may be strong in the local culture, educational tradition may emphasise convergence with the teacher's view; or the logistics of class size may inhibit explorations with classroom collaborative work. The fact, then, that some course members may be working with a new mode of learning, can exacerbate an already sensitive and demanding situation for both participants and tutor. This, it is suggested, needs careful management.

Managing collaborative work in groups

It is now generally recognised that if we invite our language learners to engage in a particular mode of learning, we should take on the responsibility, as far as possible, for ensuring that it is successful. This recognition has been the basis of recent moves in English language education towards learner training, the ultimate goal of which is the capacity of individual learners to manage their own learning in a responsible and self-directed way (Holec 1982, Dickinson 1987, Wenden 1991).

If teacher educators take on a similar responsibility on in-service courses for ensuring that teachers can learn effective strategies for managing their collaborative work, this may involve providing time for participants to feel comfortable together, to learn about working together, to address and get beyond the problems, and to draw up ground rules for working in teams. It may also mean managing the course in such a way that participants gradually uncover for themselves the principles of effective team work and try to put these into practice. But what is meant by effective group and team work?

Everard and Morris (1990: 172) provide one perspective from the field of educational management:

> A team is a group of people that can effectively tackle any task which it has been set up to do. 'Effectively' means that the quality of the task accomplished is the best achievable within the time available and makes full and economic use of the resources available to the team. The contribution drawn from each member is of the highest possible quality, and is one which could not have been called into play other than in the context of a supportive team.

This is a useful definition as it marks out not only the quality of the product but also implies a quality in the experience which would lead to personal satisfaction and continued motivation. Teamwork has been much discussed in management literature and useful insights are available to inform teacher educators in considering the factors that influence effective group work and in managing the training process.

For example, although each group will develop in its own way it is generally acknowledged that a group may well pass through a number of phases (Bennis and Shepard 1956, Tuckman and Jensen 1977). The first phase is called *forming* and involves each member finding out the personalities of colleagues, sorting out who might assume authority and how the group is going to organise itself. It is characterised by guardedness and anxiety. The next phase, *storming*, is usually characterized by competitiveness and conflict about leadership and working methods. In phase three, *norming*, the group formulates roles and procedures that are acceptable to all members, and settles down into a greater cohesiveness. The final phase, *performing*, involves commitment to the effective functioning of the group and a focus on productive collaborative work, with mutual support among members.

The issue for a course tutor is whether this process can be managed and facilitated through activities which enable participants to break the ice, confront the issues at the 'storming' stage and resolve them as quickly as possible so that effective 'performing' is possible. For instance, it has been suggested that keeping a consistent membership and having longer meetings in the early life of a group will help the group to establish itself.

Another perception of group effectiveness is that it needs at least one member who is interested in keeping the group on task and achieving an outcome, and at least one member who is interested in maintaining good relationships within the group. This will ensure that a variety of essential functions are undertaken within the group: those which help the group to perform the task, such as suggesting new ideas, giving opinions or providing relevant information; and those which build cohesiveness in the group, such as making compromises between different points of view or eliciting contributions from quieter members (Bales 1950, Johnson and Johnson 1987, Jacques 1991, Falchikov 1991). A further issue for the course tutor, then, is how to raise awareness of these functions so that members can diagnose problems arising from non-performance of certain functions or learn to perform a wider range of functions themselves.

It is now standard practice in many professional fields to train for group work and a range of training activities have been developed (e.g. Johnson and Johnson 1987, Jones 1991, Christopher and Smith 1991). The following section discusses an exploratory training programme in English language teacher education aimed at assisting participants in a process of building initial awareness of issues in group work and learning to deal with these through practice, review and evaluation.

Designing and managing a programme of developmental evaluation

Preparing teachers for collaborative work: rationale

A programme of developmental evaluation was introduced to a multicultural group of teachers following a 50-hour core course in Professional Practice[2] on a postgraduate programme. Collaborative work on this course ranged from a 15-minute discussion and decision making session on some aspect of syllabus design to four-hour design sessions on units of learner material, some of this continuing outside the training sessions.

The aims and methodology of the Professional Practice course developed through five stages and collaborative work assumed a different role at each of the first four stages. Stage 1 encouraged teachers to reflect on experience and to gain insights on their own professional practice through reading, observation, input from tutor and peer presentations, and discussion. Stage 2 enabled teachers to evaluate ideas critically and to relate experience and new ideas in professionally meaningful ways, through collaborative evaluation tasks and discussion. Examples of discussion tasks during these two stages appear in Appendix 6.3. Stage 3 aimed to help teachers, working in design teams, to apply insights to the formulation of curricular specifications and design of materials for local teaching contexts. Stage 4 assisted teachers in evaluating their applications through peer critique and stage 5 encouraged teachers to apply ideas individually to the design of specific materials for their own learners. Teamwork took on importance at stages 3 and 4. This was characterised by integrating a number of tasks, similar to those in Appendix 6.3, in order to undertake the decision-making processes involved in designing a sample syllabus and sample materials, by working on design outside class and by presenting materials for peer comment and review.

The programme of developmental evaluation activities was integrated into this Professional Practice component with a number of aims:

- to help teachers develop a growing awareness of the issues involved in managing teamwork and small group discussion
- to help participants develop perceptions of their own potential to contribute to teamwork and discussion
- to encourage responsibility through awareness raising
- to increase the effectiveness of modes of learning used on the course
- to encourage reflection so that participants could build on the experience in their own professional work to develop critical approaches to modes of learning.

Opening workshop

The initial activity in the programme was a five-hour workshop in which participants designed an access course[3] in groups of four or five. This task was in the nature of a simulation with information provided about prospective students, institutional facilities, available staffing, etc. Participants were requested to make a series of strategic decisions, to design the course components and to arrive at the point of preparing the weekly timetable. Three evaluation instruments were used to help teachers reflect on the issues arising from the use of collaborative methodology: a pre-session questionnaire; a post-session questionnaire, and diaries.[4]

Evaluating and building insights into group management processes

Two particular outcomes of this initial workshop are noteworthy. The first was an immediate awareness among the teachers of a need to discuss the issues that had arisen during the group work, particularly any problems encountered. They perceived a need to negotiate procedures for further workshops and to make decisions about whether the composition of groups would vary, whether the tutor should intervene during discussion, whether documentation of the discussion was desirable, and what roles might be allocated within the group – for example, timekeeper, chair, reporter. This had an immediate beneficial effect on the management, by the groups, of their own time, performance and achievement.

The second outcome was an awareness of the factors influencing the success, or otherwise, of group work. For instance, information from the diaries suggested a set of categories which the tutor identified, listed and exemplified with anonymous extracts so that participants could build a growing understanding of these, a sensitivity to their influence and strategies for managing them. A sample set of categories is provided in Appendix 6.5. Many of the issues raised at this early stage (concerning procedures, participation, conflict, roles, etc.) were later taken up for comment by individuals and groups in further evaluation activities: the need to review the task and share perceptions at the outset; the extent to which divergence or consensus were appropriate outcomes to a particular task; the phases through which a group evolves; management of time; the meaning of silence in groups; and management of the task.

The programme of developmental evaluation

Following the preliminary workshop a full programme of developmental evaluation proceeded through four main stages: at the first stage, enabling participants to reflect on intitial experiences and to identify issues of personal relevance; at a second stage, encouraging groups to look at their performance and consider ways of improving their procedures; at a third stage, asking participants to analyse their personal contributions to teamwork and think how they might wish to develop and expand these; and at a final stage, inviting course members to assess the ways in which they might be developing expertise in this type of collaborative work.

Two of the activities used will serve as examples. The first is a group performance checklist, adapted from Everard and Morris (1990). The checklist contains a set of statements (see Appendix 6.6) which describe the ways in which the group may have performed in relation to six factors thought to be important in effective group discussion: participation, system, relationships, decisions, disputes and leadership. Unsurprisingly, some of these categories reflect those arising from the participant diaries (see Appendix 6.5), thus making use of the checklist a natural progression from the evaluation activities in the initial workshop. After scoring their own checklist, group members can then compare scores with other members of their group and the ensuing discussion of both common and differing perceptions of performance can move into suggestions and decision-making for future discussions. This *process review* allows, as an example, comment on behaviour which somehow impeded the functioning of the group or which caused concern in terms of group rapport. It enabled members to begin the process of considering what roles they might play in eliciting contributions from all members and assisting group communication.

A second procedure is a self-perception inventory of functions undertaken in group work (see Appendix 6.7) which moves the participants' attention from the working of the group as a whole to their individual roles, functions and behaviour within the group. The inventory is divided into task functions (i.e. getting the work done and achieving outcomes) and team functions (i.e. building productive relationships). The dichotomy reflects the assertion that an effective team is one which pays attention to both results and relationships. The categories of the inventory were drawn partly from the studies mentioned earlier (Bales 1950, Johnson and Johnson 1987, Jacques 1991, Falchikov 1991) and adjusted, with reformulated descriptors, in line with queries and feedback from participants. This activity was used for consciousness raising, for individuals to develop perceptions of their preferred types of contribution, and of functions in which they felt they could and would like to develop expertise, particularly with regard to any they observed as lacking in the group. One advantage of this activity at this stage is that it not only increased critical self-awareness but also an understanding of group interaction.

Perceptions of group management: participant self-evaluation

Having presented the programme rationale and sample activities, I present here two brief case studies with extracts from the teachers' introspections. They are offered as informative instances which can contribute to a picture of how individuals gained insights into the collaborative mode of learning in which they were engaged and how the experience could inform their future work as teachers or teacher educators. The teachers in question came from markedly different teaching backgrounds, cultural contexts and prior experiences of collaborative work.

Case study 1

T was a teacher trainer of some experience from Eastern Europe. She identified several characteristics of a training session of particular importance to her: that it should enable teachers to develop perceptions of themselves as teachers, trainers or course designers and that it should help participants clarify to themselves their personal value systems. The methodology she preferred as a participant was the lecture with time for questions afterwards as she felt that this was the most efficient way to provide new information, clarify misunderstandings, build links with previous knowledge and raise significant issues. After the first session she wrote that her concept of a training session and her views of learning had changed, and she went on to present her perceptions of the collaborative work she had experienced. Some of these were to do with the product of group work:

> When people are sitting and thinking together . . . it helps us to see different dimensions of the same issue. You can't possibly see all the dimensions of this or that issue by yourself.

and others were to do with the learning process:

> The fact that we were not given ready-made answers but could find them by putting together our knowledge and experience was very important for me. I believe that by actually doing the task first we set a certain framework, got questions on difficult issues ready.

Her initial experiences at the 'forming' stage of the group were positive as she felt a degree of tolerance within the group, but she felt anxiety about having performed the initiating role and perhaps having dominated too much. She wrote in her diary:

> I wanted the task to be done properly but nobody else took much initiative at the beginning.

and developed this later in discussion in the following way:

> I find it sometimes quite difficult, because maybe I am more open, playing the function of a person who brings in ideas . . . and sometimes I am carried away with those ideas. But I am very conscious that that doesn't let other people talk. And I am really worried about that. Recently I started thinking about the group and trying to control myself so that other people could talk.

This concern stayed with her for much of the programme but awareness of the danger of dominating led her to take on other functions within the group. She specified that she had developed expertise, through practice, in information seeking, responsive listening and clarifying, and felt that she was beginning to manage these well. At the end of the programme she reported:

> I have never thought so much about group work as this term. In a way for me it was a very valuable learning experience . . . I have been trying very hard to monitor my own and the group's behaviour. At group sessions I was trying to make a conscious effort to involve other people.

Case study 2

L was an experienced teacher of adult learners who had worked in a variety of contexts and countries. She had been exposed to collaborative learning in small group work quite extensively during undergraduate studies and, as a result, her preference was for training sessions with a mixture of tutor presentation, small group work, summary plenary and discussion. She appreciated the potential for exchanging ideas that this mode of training offers. It fitted with her perception that training should focus on currently significant controversial issues and that participants ideally should be able to share problems and solutions as they are experienced in different training contexts:

> I find sometimes I have tunnel vision and other people pick up things, or sometimes I'm completely out of it, like completely off the idea, so other people can show me different ways of looking at something, or just bring up other issues I would never have thought of.

She was concerned for structure in group work and was aware of her own need for organisation. This came through strongly in her diary, in which she acknowledged a need to organise and delegate, and in discussion where she described herself as 'the kind of person who likes to decide what it is we have to do, or divide things into little tasks to delegate'. It is perhaps not surprising, then, that her contributions to small group work tended to focus on the task. She proved to be a strong initiator and direction giver, and a good clarifier. The degree to which she made a contribution in a range of task functions was consistently high. She was aware of team functions and felt she had built a facility with these through her earlier experiences so she tended to take them for granted in her own behaviour and to let other people in the group focus on them. She explained herself in the following way:

> In areas of management I do not think I improved as I am not conscious of my actions in this matter. I had to do a great deal of group work as an undergrad. Items such as letting a member finish what he has to say or including others just seems courteous and effective. I don't give these matters much thought.

With regard to standard setting, however, she felt she had made progress during the term, and the tutor also noted the way in which her management of this role pushed a group with good relationships, which could otherwise have settled into a satisfied complacency, towards more worthwhile products. She was also concerned about how training could be done for group work as she had learned by trial and error in her undergraduate days:

> I think it would help us to grow as individuals . . . maybe a lot of people have never had to do group work before and . . . it might make them think a little more about their contribution and some of the problems that come up, what they can do to solve those problems. It might get people to think a bit more.

Her recommendation was for some consciousness-raising activity at the very beginning of a long post-experience course, which would start the developmental process.

Criteria for the effective management of the programme

As the programme evolved, a set of criteria emerged for the design, sequencing and management of the developmental evaluation activities. For example, progression is desirable in the focus of activities, moving from preliminary issues in the forming of groups, to activities which would help the group move from storming to norming as quickly as possible, and finally to activities which would help individuals refine their contribution to the performing of the group.

It is also clear that each developmental activity needs to fit the type of curricular task being undertaken. The self-perception inventory of roles in group work can only realistically be used when the task offers opportunities for each individual to play a variety of roles in a sustained period of activity and, ideally, will be used as participants are becoming aware of their strengths and weaknesses with regard to these roles. In this way an optimal match between task and developmental evaluation activity facilitates the participants' growing perceptions of personal and interpersonal issues. Another criterion is that the evaluation activity should not be so time-consuming or demanding as to be intrusive. In creating a regular sequence of activities for the review and reflection on various aspects of group work, this should not dominate the collaborative tasks themselves. A further and sensitive factor in the success of such a programme concerns the role of the tutor and fellow participants when it becomes obvious that a member of the group is experiencing difficulty. Among other criteria to emerge are perceived relevance of the activity, the motivation of teams and individuals to give continued time to the evaluation tasks, the cultural sensitivity of the evaluation activity used, and the accessibility of the tutor for informal discussion as issues arise in out-of-class teamwork. All of these need careful management.

Developmental evaluation for managing learning

It will be recalled that the original aims in setting up a series of developmental evaluation activities were to gain a better understanding of the dynamics of group work in task-based learning and to reflect on the issues arising in order to inform future activity and build on what seemed to work well. The approach taken in this exploratory study can be characterised in a number of ways, much of which falls within the paradigm of action research, as self-reflective enquiry into a form of educational practice in order to assess the assumptions underlying that practice (Carr and Kemmis 1985, McNiff 1988, Elliott 1994, Hopkins 1985). Four of these characteristics are considered below: democracy, collaboration, empowerment and self-evaluation.

Democracy

The characteristic of democracy is one which, in this context, gave pause for thought. Albeit that the ethos of this postgraduate course was one of informal relations, easy access to tutors and open discussion of course affairs, the fundamental authority of the tutor, as an ultimate assessor, cannot be ignored. In these circumstances there can hardly be a symmetrical relationship between participants in the programme, suggested by Holly and Whitehead (1986) to be one of the aspirations of action research. Notions of authority and democracy impinged on programme development in several ways. Firstly, consideration had to be given to the point at which and how the tutor gave feedback on concerns brought out by participants in their diaries. This democratisation of the issues – crucial for awareness raising – needed handling with sensitivity as well as ensuring confidentiality for the individual. It was for participants themselves in ensuing discussion to decide whether they wished to acknowledge publicly their own anxieties, irritations and concerns as expressed in initial writing. Secondly, the tutor had to negotiate her own role with the groups, whether or not to intervene in group interactions, whether and when to act as mediator. This negotiation was set in motion during the intitial workshop activity when the tutor announced her intention not to intervene unless invited and then feedback on this issue was sought in the post-session questionnaire. Thirdly, there was an issue regarding the degree of control exercised by the tutor over the design of the evaluation activities themselves in relation to the freedom of the participants to modify them in useful ways and to supplement them with their own activities. For example, one participant supplemented the evaluation activities by engaging in writing for dialogic reflection, a kind of discourse with herself (Hatton and Smith 1995) which she wished to share. Motivated by the experience of collaborative work and by a debate about its potential in teacher education to continue reflection on the issues by herself, she wrote:

> I am writing in response to the discussion about the role of self-help groups as the follow-up stage of training courses. Two controversial opinions were put forward at the session. The first one suggested that groups have a significant potential for continuing the educational process after a course. The opposite claimed that the work of such groups is repetitive and often ineffective. Furthermore, a certain warning was expressed that occasionally some poor ideas can be reinforced and brought into the classroom. It would seem that the latter view is based on negative experience as well as certain beliefs about teachers. Let me summarise those that were expressed. First it was asserted that the agenda of these group meetings becomes a 'cry on my shoulder' matter when teachers predominantly express concerns and complain about their problems in classroom practice. By limiting their discussions in this way they often leave out the consideration of improvement of the situation.
>
> This is an attempt to justify the necessity and potential productivity of self-help groups. First I look at the nature of educational improvement. Then I consider how educational improvement can be brought about through reflexive communities. Then I look at some factors that enable successful work of such communities . . .

Collaboration

Another characteristic is collaboration (Kemmis and McTaggert 1988). In this programme the collaboration was between tutor and participants and among participants. Both parties were stakeholders in the success of the collaborative work during the course, and the participants were themselves teachers or teacher trainers who had a personal stake in investigating a mode of learning they used or might use in their own classrooms. Reflection on the experiences of group work included the responses, perceptions and opinions of everyone involved, in both formal and informal discussion.

Empowerment

A third characteristic is empowerment. The primary aim of the evaluation activities was to enable teachers to build the competence and confidence to self-manage the collaborative learning mode successfully. A secondary aim was to empower teachers with regard to future responsibilities and roles. In other words, activities were selected and managed so that participants could look critically at the workings of an educational practice in order to make informed and rational decisions about its future use in their own professional work. In this sense the experience would give them the power to be decision-makers rather than consumers of other people's imported practice. It was also the aim of the programme to empower participants for future professional work in teams by building confidence in contributing to the various roles necessary for teamwork to function well.

Self-evaluation

A further characteristic of action research is that it is self-evaluative, involving the regular, iterative evaluation of actions. It is what Jacques (1991) has called 'evaluation as learning', giving individuals a chance to reflect on the behaviour of groups and their personal functioning in groups. This kind of developmental evaluation is thus a source of learning of benefit to both the individual and the group if it enables participants to talk about their experience in the collaborative work and to learn from it. It also integrates evaluation into learning activity so that an integral part of the learning becomes the students' developing understanding of their own preferences and styles, needs and problems in relation to the a major mode of learning on the course.

The concepts of collaboration, democracy, empowerment and self-evaluation have been drawn from the field of action research but can equally well be drawn from the field of developmental evaluation. This type of evaluation activity lies at the interface of action research and evaluation. It is equally appropriate to apply the terms 'illuminative' and 'formative' to the kind of evaluation activity performed by participants in supporting reflection on the process of their learning during the programme.

Conclusion

This chapter set out to describe an exploratory study in the use of developmental evaluation with regard to collaborative small group work on teacher education courses and its demands for sensitive management. The sample case studies – using data from diaries, group discussion, and a self-perception inventory – demonstrate the ways in which the evaluation activities can contribute to making collaborative work a constructive educational experience, to strengthening the confidence of participants to make a range of contributions to teamwork, and to create awareness of how the teachers themselves could incorporate developmental evaluation within their own professional practice.

Part of the exploration considered the relevance of such concepts from the fields of action research and evaluation as collaboration, democracy, empowerment and self-evaluation and their implications for the procedures used to manage the programme. Another part was discovering practical criteria for the design, sequencing and management of the programme.

There will never be easy solutions to the issues of people working together or, indeed, to issues in developing the self-critical but confident teacher. However, there is an argument for giving teachers the opportunity to explore and understand the issues. Reflective investigation and developmental evaluation activity can build strong motivation among participants on teacher education courses. And the fundamental rationale for this kind of activity is to create a quality of learning experience for teachers which might enable them, in turn, to create a quality of learning experience in their own classrooms.

Notes

1. And this is quite apart from all the other issues of group interaction which can create difficulty: for example, our need to judge the extent to which we seem valued or accepted by the group or our need to maintain self-esteem.
2. The Professional Practice course focused on syllabus design and its interface with materials design and methodology for the English language classroom. The aim of the course was to develop participants' practical expertise in these design areas and the assessment for the course was the production of a partial syllabus with the materials to show its classroom interpretation.
3. An access course is designed to prepare overseas students for studying in the UK for a period of time (4–16 weeks) before they begin their undergraduate or postgraduate studies. The content is based on an analysis of student needs for language development, study skills, social English, etc.

4. The aims of these procedures were as follows:

- A pre-session questionnaire was completed individually by the teachers. This asked them to think about the modes of learning they had experienced in their previous education, e.g. lecture, seminar, group work, and to consider whether they had preferred modes and why. It also asked them to reflect on their expectations of a training session and the principles which might underlie its methodology.

- Similarly, post-session questionnaires were completed after the workshop. These asked participants to reflect in more detail on the issues that had arisen in trying to work with colleagues in small groups, on the role of the tutor, on methods of organising feedback and other details of session management.

- Participants elected to complete either a concurrent diary as the sessions proceeded or a retrospective diary reflecting after the event. Guidelines to diarists were formulated in some detail to suggest possible content, not to pre-empt or control it, as diary writing was not a familiar cultural activity for some of the participants (see Appendix 6.4). The tutor acted as observer and also kept a diary, with both concurrent and retrospective comment.

Acknowledgement

The present study was motivated by an earlier small-scale study undertaken in collaboration with Pauline Rea-Dickins in which we had the more general aim of evaluating the methodology of teacher education courses. I am indebted to Pauline for her early input to some of the research instruments and for her encouragement.

Appendix 6.1   Example of a teacher's credo

For each of the following statements, indicate whether you agree, disagree or don't have a clear opinion. If you disagree, rewrite the statement so that it reflects what you think. Add any statements you wish, then compare your opinions with those of your colleagues:

- I never allow learners to use their first language in the classroom.
- I correct every error I hear in my learners' spoken English.
- I only ask learners to use language which I have previously taught and practised with them.
- I make certain that a good proportion of my learners' time is spent in group work and pair work.
- I exercise a strong personality in the classroom.

Appendix 6.2   Roles of teachers and learners

Read through the set of quotations below, then discuss your reactions to each one with a colleague. Choose one which you find most interesting, then join with another pair or colleague to discuss your responses.

- Schools are designed on the assumption that there is a secret to everything in life; that the quality of life depends on knowing that secret; that secrets can be known only in orderly succession; and that only teachers can properly reveal those secrets.   (Ivan Illich 1973)
- Who needs the most talking in the classroom? Who gets the most?
                                                                      (John Holt 1979)
- Only when the teacher's authority recedes can the learner be thrown back on his own resources.   (Alistair Maclean 1979)
- If a teacher is indeed wise, he does not bid you enter the house of his wisdom, but rather leads you to the threshold of your own mind.
                                                                      (Kahlil Gibran 1926)

Appendix 6.3   Small group discussion tasks

Generating ideas – e.g. listing and discussing alternative ways of creating audiences for learners in classroom writing tasks.

Listing items from observation – e.g. discussing the strengths and weaknesses of a teaching style as observed on video.

Arguing points – e.g. arguing the applicability of ideas about learner autonomy and procedures for learner training in varied cultural contexts.

Making categories – e.g. reviewing the goals for a secondary school syllabus and categorising these into 'process goals' and 'product goals' in order to assess the usefulness of these concepts.

Setting up criteria – e.g. formulating criteria for the selection of authentic reading materials in a language programme for intermediate learners.

Analysing data – e.g. formulating objectives for a course based on data about students.

Appendix 6.4   Extract from instructions to diarists

Below I have made a list of some of the things that I would be interested in hearing about. If you would like to comment on any aspects which are not on the list, it is important to add them.

I am not suggesting a rigid format for the recording of the diary. I am simply giving you a notebook but please organise it in any way you wish.

It would be particularly useful if you could generally approach the diary from two perspectives: concurrent and retrospective.

(a) *Concurrent.* How do you react to things during the session? Please take a few minutes every so often during your discussions and make a note of anything you want to comment on.

(b) *Retrospective.* After the session please write down your reflections in summary about the various aspects which interested you.

1. *Relevance to your professional work*
   - Is the topic meaningful to you and does the entry point reflect the perspective of yourself as a teacher?

2. *Opportunity to reflect on the issues raised*
   - Did you have the opportunity to reflect on personal experience and was account taken of your knowledge and skills?

3. *Methodologies used*
   - Do these provide an environment in which you can open up and can argue and agree with your colleagues?
   - Do you feel involved in the collaborative work? Why or why not?
   - To what extent do you find collaborative work useful in reflecting on and articulating your own experiences and insights?
   - In what ways are the plenary sessions useful to you? Do these get in the way of small group work?

4. *Groupings*
   - Were you satisfied with the group?
   - Were you able to work well with other people in the group?
   - Did you experience any problems?
   - What do you think are the causes of these?

5. *Management*
   - What were your reactions to the management of the session by participants or by the tutor?

6. *Self-evaluation*
   - How would you describe your contribution to the discussions?
   - What were your strengths and weaknesses?
   - Could you have contributed more?
   - What held you back?
   - Did you dominate? If so, why?

Appendix 6.5 Issues in group management: teacher perspectives

Interpretation
- Different interpretations of the task led us to difficulty in understanding each other.
- Once the objective of the task was established everyone stuck with the task and would have continued through the lunch break.

Procedures
- I felt the need for some organised constructive approach as it was easy to drift into irrelevancies.
- It took us a long time to form the group, to clear the backgrounds, to find a way of working together.

Participation
- The rules of turn taking were not obeyed and this placed constraints on me.
- As for the non-participants, what means of making them participate?

Relationships
- I felt that my relationship with other members of the group overrode the need for objectivity or efficiency in carrying out the task.
- I was sensitive to the need for no one to dominate and to keep a sense of respect and equality among group members.

Personal contribution
- Did I talk too much, was I too pushy, too scattered, too hyper . . . ?
- I still have a long way to go in practising not only listening but taking a real interest and responding to others.

Conflict
- Disputes were as much about procedure as content.
- 'It is clear that we should do this' and 'Of course we must' were phrases that did not promote a sense of collaboration but caused a degree of conflict.

Roles
- I felt relieved that one of us had assumed the role of chairperson.
- Our chair was able to structure very divergent opinions.

Time
- I think the group work was much more productive when we began to feel the pressure of time.

Achievement
- I have the feeling that the group is limited by its own ideas.
- There must be many ideas in other groups that we have not used.

Appendix 6.6   Group performance checklist

How well do you think your group performed while doing the task today? Look at each category below. They represent important factors in successful group work. For each category, distribute 10 points among the statements to reflect your perception of what happened in the group.

When everyone has finished, compare your distributions and decide what you think were the strengths and weaknesses of the group today.

– How do you think you could improve the group's effectiveness?
– What contribution could you make personally to improve its performance?

A: Participation
   (a) Everyone was active and contributed. All contributions were given thoughtful consideration. There was a positive atmosphere.
   (b) Several people dominated and others were quiet and passive.
   (c) We tended to interrupt each other and several people tried to talk at once.
   (d) There were a lot of silences caused by lack of initiative or failure to respond to other people's contributions.
   (e) We were insufficiently focused on the task and made a lot of jokes/irrelevant comments.

B: System
   (a) We agreed to follow a logical procedure and we kept to it. The group work ran smoothly.
   (b) The meeting was over-organised. Keeping to procedure seemed to be more important than dealing effectively with the issues.
   (c) The meeting was disorganised and random.
   (d) The meeting went round in circles with no clear sense of direction.
   (e) Important ideas and information took a long time to emerge.

C: Relationships
   (a) We clearly showed confidence in and respect for each other.
   (b) Relationships were guarded.
   (c) We were not responsive listeners and not open to each other's contributions.
   (d) Subgroups developed with some tensions between them.
   (e) It seemed to be more important to us to keep good relations than to deal effectively with the task.

D: Decisions
   (a) Decisions were reached by consensus after careful consideration.
   (b) Decisions were forced by certain individuals and not everyone's ideas received the same attention.

  (c) Decisions were reached formally by majority vote.
  (d) Decisions were compromised without full discussion.
  (e) Issues were left hanging without proper decisions being taken.

E: Disagreements
  (a) Points of disagreements were worked out carefully until everyone was satisfied.
  (b) Disagreements were smoothed over: keeping good relations was more important than resolving the issues.
  (c) The group polarised into factions and it was important to each faction to win the argument.
  (d) We compromised to the extent of agreeing solutions which might not have been the best.
  (e) Differences were avoided or ignored.

F: Leadership
  (a) We shared responsibility for the quality of the meeting and different individuals took responsibility as required.
  (b) We agreed a leader at the start and that person directed our work and moved it on.
  (c) Several people seemed to be struggling to lead the group.
  (d) The group's need for leadership was not met.
  (e) The group was overcontrolled by the leader: there was little flexibility or spontaneity.

        (Adapted from Everard and Morris 1990)

Appendix 6.7   A self-perception inventory of functions in group work

Please rate yourself (by circling the appropriate number) on the degree to which you contributed each of these possible functions during your group work this morning.

Group function	*Level of contribution* 1=low level 6=high level
Task Functions	
1. *Initiating:* starting up discussion, proposing objectives or new activities	1 2 3 4 5 6

2. *Information giving:* giving facts, providing expertise, and personal experience

    1 2 3 4 5 6

3. *Opinion giving:* stating opinions and beliefs about the topic or issue in question

    1 2 3 4 5 6

4. *Information seeking:* eliciting information, expertise and experience

    1 2 3 4 5 6

5. *Opinion seeking:* eliciting opinions and beliefs about the topic

    1 2 3 4 5 6

6. *Orienting:* focusing the group's attention on the direction the discussion is taking

    1 2 3 4 5 6

7. *Clarifying and co-ordinating:* restating something the group is thinking about, helping the group to clarify its points and put ideas together

    1 2 3 4 5 6

8. *Elaborating:* building on other contributions, expanding them with examples and further points

    1 2 3 4 5 6

9. *Feasibility testing:* analysing the workability of ideas

    1 2 3 4 5 6

Team functions

10. *Encouraging:* encouraging participation, being responsive and accepting to contributions, bringing in quieter members

    1 2 3 4 5 6

11. *Harmonising:* conciliating differences in points of view

    1 2 3 4 5 6

12. *Tension relieving:* keeping an easy atmosphere by joking, suggesting breaks, etc.

    1 2 3 4 5 6

13. *Standard setting:* keeping the group   1   2   3   4   5   6
    to its agreed standards in objectives
    and procedures

---

14. *Responsive listening:* acting as an   1   2   3   4   5   6
    interested audience and responding
    to ideas

Other functions (*please specify*)

---

15.   1   2   3   4   5   6

    ....

---

16.   1   2   3   4   5   6

    ....

Do you think any important functions were not performed in today's group work?

....

....

....

If so, are they functions which you could take on yourself?

....

....

....

Do you feel that you made progress in any particular functions today?

....

....

....

7

Managing and evaluating change: the case of teacher appraisal

JANE ANDERSON

Abstract. The theory on appraisal claims that it is a useful way of enhancing performance and fostering accountability in an organisation. This paper confronts the theory with practice in the context of a large institution over a five-year period. It explores the tensions between the manager's concern to use appraisal as a tool for ensuring standards and the teacher's concern that appraisal is an instrument for personal development. Actual use and evaluation of our appraisal system suggests modifications to existing theoretical frameworks, and suggests a number of ways in which the management of performance and appraisal can be managed.

1 Introduction

Teacher appraisal in the education sector can be seen as an innovation which applies and modifies theories and models of staff appraisal from the world of business and industry. Innovation needs to be planned and ideally should involve an organisation's stakeholders in the process. Not all the members of an organisation will immediately adopt the innovation and some may never do so. Conflict and resistance will inevitably emerge and must be managed. This chapter examines the introduction of a teacher appraisal scheme in Bilkent University School of English Language (BUSEL) in the Turkish tertiary education sector. As a full-time consultant member of BUSEL's management team, I was centrally involved in the introduction, implementation and evaluation of the teacher appraisal scheme, a process which began in 1992.

159

Firstly, there is a consideration of how appraisal theory needs to be adapted to fit an education context. The issues and concerns surrounding the introduction of a teacher appraisal scheme are discussed, drawing on first-hand experience derived from initiating and managing such a scheme. This is followed by details of the case study which documents the implementation of teacher appraisal in BUSEL. A key element in the process is the evaluation of the scheme and its subsequent re-launching. Four years later, there remain a number of tensions: these are discussed and possible solutions offered. In light of the experience of the case study, the chapter concludes with an assessment of the challenges for appraisal in educational contexts which have to be managed effectively if innovations such as this are to be successful and sustainable.

2   The adaptation of appraisal theory to education

The theory of appraisal is full of terms – e.g. staff appraisal, staff development review, performance review, performance appraisal, staff evaluation, and staff assessment – which all have different nuances of meaning and which, if used inappropriately in a specific organisational context, may contribute to misunderstandings about that organisation's approach to appraisal.

For the purposes of this chapter, the term 'teacher appraisal' is used and is seen as the formal process whereby current performance in a job is observed and discussed for the purpose of adding to that level of performance (Randell 1994: 220). 'Level of performance' here refers to the quality of performance rather than the quantity. Although the quality of teachers' performance (the putting into practice of skills, knowledge, training) is their individual responsibility, it is also partly dependent on the context in which this performance takes place (the classroom, the students, colleagues, teaching resources, the school, educational policies). In addition, teacher appraisal is regarded as a managerial activity in which line managers engage in an appraisal process with teachers, for whom they are, in some sense, accountable (Fidler 1989: 191). Hence, it is part of the line manager's job to ensure that teachers develop and improve their teaching performance in terms of quality.

Although evaluation may carry negative overtones, it is central to teacher appraisal, and is integral to teacher development.

Teachers must engage in the evaluation of their own perform-ance in order to know the direction in which to develop. Teacher development would seem difficult to achieve unless teachers and others (students, peers, line manager) are involved in making judgements about their performance. If appraisal represents evalu-ation which links performance with pay or promotion rather than with the professional development of teachers, then evaluation will be viewed as a potential threat which may undermine, rather than promote, the quality of teaching. This is considered later in the case study.

Another controversial dimension to appraisal is outlined by Randell (1994). The controversy is focused on what aspects of performance are observed and how observations are made; why and how these observations are discussed; and what determines the level of performance in a job. These issues are particularly pertinent to educational contexts in which the observation of teach-ing performance is key to the appraisal process. Teachers and their appraisers have concerns about observation, for example: the nature of the conclusions that may be drawn from an observa-tion; the extent to which an observation is representative of a teacher's skills; awareness of the standards against which observed performance is measured. If these issues are not addressed satis-factorily, then appraisal may become dysfunctional because a prin-cipal data-gathering process is viewed with suspicion.

Appraisal is seen as performing a number of different functions (Fidler 1989, White *et al.* 1991, Randell 1994). These include:

- a tool for managerial control
- a way employees can increase their financial reward for effort
- a process which contributes to an organisation's development, i.e. part of performance management
- a process which enhances an individual's sense of achievement and satisfaction in his or her work
- a process which is development-led, i.e. with a focus on change
- a process which is assessment-led, i.e. quantitatively rated.

Randell's chapter in Sisson (1994) provides a succinct overview of the development of appraisal as applied in business and industry. It suggests that organisational leaders (i.e. managers) are currently judged on how well they make use of, and develop, their staff and that employee appraisal is one of the major processes available to help them achieve this (1994: 245). However, the problem of choosing which particular approach to take to staff development remains. Randell concludes that an appraisal scheme must match the needs of the organisation and the expectations of the employees at its particular stage of development, and that appraisal can only be effective if participants (i.e. managers and employees) possess sufficiently well-developed interpersonal skills with which to conduct the process.

When appraisal is transferred to public sector organisations, there are some important distinctions from appraisal in business settings (Fletcher 1993: 129). The effectiveness of a business is generally measured in terms of profit, and that of its employees according to their contribution to that end, whereas the criteria against which a public sector organisation measures its performance are not defined solely in financial terms. Defining the criteria which may be used to judge the effectiveness of teachers and the education service provided by schools has been the focus of much research (Reynolds and Cuttance 1992). Another distinction is that whereas businesses may choose to establish appraisal systems, the public sector may have appraisal thrust upon it as a consequence of prevailing government policy, often leading to resistance. In addition, there are limited resource budgets with which to run appraisal and thus insufficient time may be given to essential training for staff and to the design process which has a negative effect in the future.

The implementation of appraisal in educational contexts is well documented. Evans and Tomlinson (1989) provide a range of experiences from the introduction of teacher appraisal into the education system in England and Wales as a consequence of government policy (see White Papers and reports from the DES, e.g. 1983, 1985a, 1985b, 1989a, 1989b). Millman and Darling-Hammond (1990) provide insights into the American experience associated with the educational reform movement of the 1980s and 1990s, which relies on evaluation for promoting quality improvements for both individual and school development, and curriculum renewal.

Fidler (1989) identifies a number of problem areas of appraisal in education: the management of professionals who traditionally tend to see themselves as autonomous and not needing to be managed; unclear results in relation to unclear purposes; uncertain rewards; the difficulty of assessing teaching (see also Randell 1994); too many bosses; lack of time; and lack of infrastructure beyond the school to support appraisal – personnel and training. Simmons and Elliott (1989: 11) reaffirm that there are no easy answers to some of the questions raised by appraisal and conclude that if there is a consensus on teacher appraisal 'it surely consists of a fear that pressures for easily manageable indicators of performance put at risk the conditions of better teaching and learning, conditions we are slowly coming to understand.'

3   Issues and concerns surrounding the introduction of an appraisal scheme

Below I discuss the major issues and concerns to be considered and addressed when introducing a teacher appraisal scheme. The case study highlights these: some were anticipated and were explored in detail, referring to already established appraisal schemes in different contexts, but others only became apparent and took on significance in the implementation process.

3.1   Purposes of appraisal

Much has been written about the purposes of appraisal and of the need for appraisers and appraisees (senior management, line managers and teachers) to be clear about their purposes (e.g., Trethowan 1987, Turner and Clift 1988, West and Bollington 1990, Green and Sanders 1990, Poster and Poster 1991). Answering the following questions may help an organisation clarify the purposes of its appraisal scheme:

- Is the appraisal scheme being designed to ensure standards and accountability?
- Is it to make judgements about performance in relation to pay?
- Is it to identify poor performers and determine subsequent courses of action?
- Is it to provide data about the effectiveness of the service being provided by the school as part of the school's management information system?
- Is it to make judgements about a teacher's performance with a view to future development (personal and professional) as a way of improving quality?
- Is it a way of getting to know the skills, strengths, interests and problems of a staff group?

■ Is appraisal designed to meet individual or organisational needs and priorities?

Some of these questions will be taken up later in the case study. It can be argued that several of these purposes overlap and some may be in conflict. Thus, during the initial phase of the design of an appraisal scheme it is important to decide which purposes the scheme aims to fulfil, and to consider the implications of the choice of purposes with reference to implementation.

3.2 Evaluation

The purposes of teacher appraisal and evaluation are closely connected. Weir and Roberts (1994: 4–8) outline the relationship between evaluation, accountability and development at organisational, programme or project level. Caldwell and Spinks (1988: 143) suggest that if evaluation is viewed as an equation of quantitative descriptions (measurement) and/or qualitative descriptions (non-measurement) plus value judgements, then it occurs continuously in the instructional and management process.

Evaluation means different things to different people, with teachers and managers bringing varied experiences of evaluation and being evaluated to their workplace, some of which may be negative. Thus, before introducing a teacher appraisal scheme it would be useful to explore the level of knowledge of techniques and approaches to evaluation, as well as the attitudes towards evaluation that exist among the staff. Such data would inform the ways in which training for appraisal (of both appraisers and appraisees) is planned. In addition, by creating an organisational climate where evaluation is an integral part of whole-school improvement, some of the negative associations of evaluation may be removed, and the evaluation element of appraisal accepted as something positive.

Another type of evaluation which takes place in educational organisations is student evaluation of programmes and teaching. The ways in which such evaluation is conducted (if at all) can have a significant effect on the implementation of a teacher appraisal scheme, depending on the uses to which the data are put by both the teacher and the management, and the degree of maturity with which the students participate in the evaluation. This is of particular relevance to BUSEL.

3.3   Power and authority

Integral to the process of evaluation and appraisal is the issue of power and authority: who is appraising whom, and what power and authority do the participants have? Because teacher appraisal is essentially interactive, consisting of dialogue between two individuals, the way the power and authority relationship between the two is defined and the approach adopted by individuals to stimulate this interaction will impact upon the design of the scheme and the quality of the ultimate experience of appraisal. There are a number of questions to be answered during the design process in relation to this balance of power dimension:

- Should the student appraise the teacher? How?
- Do teachers appraise each other? How?
- Does the line manager (head of department) appraise the teacher? How?
- Does the teacher appraise the line manager (head of department)? How?
- Who else appraises the line manager (head of department)? How?
- Who, and how are senior managers (heads or principals) appraised?
- Does the size of the organisation and its structure lend itself to the establishment of an appraisal scheme?
- How are hierarchies, power and authority perceived in an organisation?

If an organisation's structure defines teachers as being accountable to a line manager, the extent to which this particular role relationship is accepted by teachers may have an impact at several levels: on the quality of interaction; on attitudes towards the scheme; on the outcomes for all involved. Traditionally, teachers tend to see themselves as autonomous professionals and may not be disposed towards being managed by fellow professionals who have been promoted within the system and who now have the responsibility for the management of the teacher appraisal scheme. The case study reveals a tension here, which is discussed in Section 4.4.

Winter (1989: 50) highlights an apparent tension in educational organisations focused on the issue of who has power and authority. This relates to the purposes of a teacher appraisal scheme and to the quality of the interaction between an appraiser and an appraisee. A school management team is described as a bureaucracy presiding over a profession with its ideals of professional practice and development, and teachers as professional educators operating within a bureaucracy with its ideals of regulation and accountability. There is immediately potential for a conflict of ideals, heightened by the fact that managers typically have power and authority. However, Winter's description assumes that the members of a school management team do not see themselves as professional educators sharing the ideals of their teachers. In fact, many school managers have been teachers and would feel uncomfortable with the notion of not retaining the identity and function of a professional educator. What is more problematic for appraisal schemes is that teachers may not fully embrace regulation and accountability as viewed from a manager's perspective. Winter goes on to question whether a single appraisal scheme can combine the ideals of professional practice and development, and the principles of accountability (i.e. whether both purposes can be achieved). The case study takes this up further.

3.4   Motivation and reward

Whatever form an appraisal scheme takes, the issue of motivation and reward needs consideration, especially as the appraisal process requires teachers to take on tasks additional to their normal work, and may be seen as added workload with all its negative consequences. Teachers may well ask: why should I participate in an appraisal scheme? What's in it for me, other than more work to be squeezed into what seems to be an ever-shortening week? There is an assumption that teachers, as professionals, tend to have high self-motivation for their work. However, this can be undermined if the conditions in which teachers work are perceived by them to have a negative impact on their ability to deliver quality teaching. For example, they may have limited access to appropriate teaching materials; class sizes may be large; students may be unwilling learners; salaries may not be perceived as an adequate reflection of the demands of the job. Therefore managers need to consider the levels of teachers' motivation when introducing an appraisal scheme and not assume positive attitudes towards appraisal.

Another assumption is that teachers are eager to expand their knowledge about teaching and learning and to enhance their skills. This finds its manifestation in the notion of the reflective practitioner (Schön 1983, Wallace 1991), teachers as collaborative learners (Smyth 1991) and teachers as life-long learners (Fullan 1991). Managers can promote such approaches by ensuring that a teacher appraisal scheme emphasises target-setting, action-research, self- or peer-observation and evaluation, with line managers adopting a facilitative critical-friend type function.

The extent to which teachers are motivated to participate and find some form of reward through engaging with the appraisal process will differ from individual to individual. Motivation theory, particularly that of Herzberg *et al.* (1959), McGregor (1960), McClelland (1961) and Vroom (1964), provides useful insights into how people are motivated at work. Their work is of relevance when designing an appraisal scheme so that people with different motivations can benefit from participation. Reward may be derived from the experience of the process itself; or may take the form of additional opportunities for self-development (e.g. in-service training); or may be found in opportunities to gain further qualifications, to participate in conferences or network with other professionals. There may also be opportunities to acquire and demonstrate new knowledge and skills in order to move up the promotional ladder within the school or to gain a better job elsewhere. The management of motivation and reward in relation to an appraisal scheme is a key issue for those designing any scheme.

3.5 Criteria for appraisal

A further crucial dimension of the appraisal process is the identification and clear specification of appropriate criteria against which performance is judged. Because appraisal may have different purposes – i.e. ensuring standards and accountability, or teacher development – the process of determining appropriate appraisal criteria is complex. Criteria may be required to embrace not only classroom teaching, but also other areas relating to a teacher's overall effectiveness within the educational institution. Poster and Poster (1991: 152) include communicating (with colleagues and students), record keeping, decision making, planning of student learning, leadership, motivation, educational philosophy and personal qualities as being areas for appraisal. The DES (1985b) provide an example of competencies and criteria for use in teacher appraisal for some of the areas set out above. However, no one set of criteria will serve to evaluate teaching in all contexts. The performance of a teacher who has just completed initial teacher training and one with several years' experience might well be appraised according to different criteria, given that they are at different stages in their careers. Again it is important to have fully articulated the purpose(s) of the teacher appraisal scheme, as these will, in turn, determine the extent to which appraisal criteria and definitions of what constitutes effective teaching will be developed.

There is a connection here with the issue of power and authority. The acceptance by teachers of such criteria and definitions will depend on the extent of their involvement in the defining process, and on their respect for the power and authority of their managers who will be using the criteria. Some form of standard or benchmarking is essential if teaching quality is to be improved, but this may be achieved through initiatives other than the appraisal scheme (see Section 4.5).

3.6   Involvement, ownership and consultation

When an organisation introduces a teacher appraisal scheme, it initiates a change process which, according to the literature, will only be successful if it is owned by those on whom the change most directly impacts (Kanter 1983, Fullan 1991, Bennett *et al.* 1992, Newton and Tarrant 1992, Wilson 1992). Thus, in ideal circumstances, it is desirable to take the time to involve as many people as possible in all stages of the introduction of a teacher appraisal scheme. However, given real-life practical constraints, it is difficult to have the whole staff group involved in full consultation about all the dimensions of a teacher appraisal scheme. It seems more workable then, to secure the involvement of the group who will have responsibility for appraising, together with a sample of those who will be appraised, and keeping all staff informed at the different stages of the design process. While all staff will be affected by an appraisal scheme, not all will actually want to be actively involved in the detail: many are content to comment on the work of others without taking the responsibility of breaking new ground themselves.

Ownership requires shared values which develop over time. This entails a shared belief that the appraisal process will lead to quality improvements of both the staff and the institution. Hence, key players must be involved in the various stages in the development of a teacher appraisal scheme: design, criteria, procedures. At the outset, appraisal awareness-raising and training must be systematic and perceived to be a valuable use of time. In an expanding organisation, or one which has a regular staff turnover, induction into the existing scheme is important to encourage the continuation of shared values; 100 per cent ownership is unlikely to be achieved and a major concern is the maintenance of an appraisal scheme's impetus and vitality. These issues are of particular relevance in the context of BUSEL.

3.7 Culture and diversity

The issue of culture, both national and organisational, and the management of diversity is relevant to the development of an appropriate teacher appraisal scheme. Hofstede's work on national cultures and the transferability of models of management (1980, 1991) offers some interesting insights. Issues to be taken into account include:

- the extent to which appraisal fits with the perceived or expressed values of national culture
- the extent to which subordinates in the society feel free to comment openly on or question their organisation and superiors
- the power–distance relationships
- the extent to which the organisational culture reflects the national culture
- the degree of fit between the appraisal scheme and the organisational culture.

These issues are of particular importance within the BUSEL context: in Turkey, in a university modelled on American lines, with two-thirds of its teachers Turkish, one-third expatriate teachers of different nationalities, and a management team which, in the past, was predominantly from the UK.

The effective management of an organisation's culture has been considered the key to its success (Peters and Waterman 1982) and this view has been transferred to the education sector (Sarason 1971, Handy and Aitken 1986). Following Handy's typology (1993), elements of role, task and person culture are useful in defining BUSEL as an institution. From the management's perspective,

BUSEL may be characterised as participative, dynamic, and having a clear sense of mission. Thus, if the teacher appraisal scheme is to fit with the culture, it should have a target-setting, problem-solving focus geared towards improvement.

With a staff group from different national cultural backgrounds, different ranges of work experience (some have only ever worked in BUSEL), different types of professional training, different expectations about the workplace and different motivations for working, management of diversity is a major issue. Appraisal itself can be seen as being about managing diversity: line managers knowing their staff well and enabling senior management to be constantly up-dated about the strengths, potential and problems of the organisation's human resources.

3.8   Opportunity cost

In addition to the costs of the teacher appraisal scheme design process, considerable resources are needed to set up, administer and evaluate a scheme, with implications for the resourcing of resultant action (e.g. the provision of in-service training opportunities). At some point, some kind of assessment of the opportunity cost of running an appraisal scheme will be necessary to determine the extent to which appraisal makes a significant enough contribution to the improvement of quality, or proving quality to justify the resource use and allocation. The question managers might ask themselves is: What difference(s) does appraisal make? In my view, it is difficult to predict or to measure the value appraisal adds to the quality of what an organization does in advance of the implementation and evaluation of an appraisal scheme.

3.9   Appraisal as part of performance management

The last issue to be considered is the extent to which a teacher appraisal scheme is part of a whole system of performance management. Elements of such a system are the organisation's mission statement and objectives: a development (business) plan; effective communication, so that all staff are aware of the objectives and can contribute to their formulation; clarified responsibilities and accountabilities usually defined through job descriptions; shared understandings of differing roles; defining and measuring individual performance; appropriate reward strategies; and staff development programmes (Fletcher 1993). Appraisal enables an individual member of staff to translate organisational goals and objectives into personal targets. In its appraisal training package, LEAP (1991) stresses the importance of linking appraisal to other school processes and of making its relationship with the main themes of the development plan and the mission statement explicit. For example, in the BUSEL context, a major development plan objective is to strengthen test development expertise. This has been translated into the appraisal process by individual teachers setting targets for themselves whereby they will improve on their ability to write tests, taking up training opportunities provided by the school. In other words, BUSEL has been developing its performance management, and the introduction of a teacher appraisal scheme is an essential part of the system.

4 Appraisal in practice: a case study

This section illustrates how, in a large university school of English language, a group of people introduced a teacher appraisal scheme, drawing on theory and the experience of others; analysed problems encountered during the first year of operation through systematic evaluation of the scheme; revised the design of the teacher appraisal scheme; and is developing further an approach to the management of teachers, addressing issues of quality standards, school improvement and the professional development of teachers.

4.1 The Bilkent context

Bilkent University is a private English-medium university in Ankara, Turkey, which was established in 1986. The objectives of BUSEL are to ensure adequate levels of English language proficiency to enable students to study their chosen discipline through the medium of English. There are approximately 2500 students in BUSEL who follow a curriculum specially designed to meet their academic language and skills needs. There is a system of continuous assessment and level achievement tests with a final proficiency test, all of which are developed and written by the school's team of testers. BUSEL is also responsible for providing English language support courses to students in their Faculties and Schools. In addition, it offers its own Diploma in Translation Studies.

It has a teaching staff of approximately 230, some of whom have posts of responsibility and are therefore on a reduced teaching timetable. The staff are a heterogeneous group comprising one-third expatriate teachers on renewable contracts, and two-thirds Turkish teachers. Across both groups there is a considerable range in the teachers' qualifications and experience.

Since 1986, BUSEL has experienced periods of growth, change, innovation and consolidation with all the attendant features. The management structure has been developed over time and currently comprises a mixed team of Turks and expatriates, two of whom are employed as full-time management consultants. Teachers are organised into teaching units of 12–15 teachers, each managed by a head who has line-management responsibility for the performance of each teacher in the unit. In addition, there are six specialist teams, each managed by a head, who support the teaching and learning: curriculum, testing, teacher training, student services, textbook project, self-access.

BUSEL is engaged in the ongoing process of improving the quality of the education it provides. A major element in the process is the quality of the teachers themselves, and considerable resources are devoted to their selection, the further improvement of their performance and their professional development.

4.2 Design and implementation

The management team faced a number of problems in 1991/92. Questions were being asked about the quality of what was actually happening in classrooms. There were no records of any individual teacher's performance apart from documentation related to observations when teachers first joined the university. No formal mechanism for obtaining feedback from teachers about the problems they faced existed. It was difficult to write references as there was no accurate information on which to base them. Teachers' interests, their special skills, or their potential were not systematically known by those in management. There was no way of knowing what in-service training or staff development provision should be. As teachers form the most important resource in a school, the development of a tool to really get to know them seemed imperative, especially in an organisation as large and as diverse as BUSEL.

Being aware of some of the issues and concerns outlined in the previous section, and with others emerging as we progressed, the design and implementation of the teacher appraisal scheme in BUSEL is really a story of evolution, and a story of a group of people, the membership of which changed over time, working together to introduce and implement a scheme that we believed would be beneficial to individual teachers and to the organisation as a whole.

There were six stages towards the implementation of a fully-fledged teacher appraisal scheme.

Stage one

In semester two of the 1991/92 academic year the ideas, principles, purposes, processes, skills and documentation of appraisal were reviewed and discussed among the senior teachers, through a series of weekly workshops and discussion sessions. (The current teaching unit structure with Heads of Teaching Unit (HTU) is a development of the senior teacher function). Each senior teacher's main activity was the observation of a group of teachers' classroom practice, the provision of constructive feedback, and support for any problems that were diagnosed through the observation, or which came to light elsewhere. Any part of the teaching and learning process could form the focus for each observation and this was agreed between the teacher and the senior teacher. The senior teachers had received training in approaches to classroom observation, active listening and the rudiments of counselling through a series of workshops.

Stage two

In 1992/93, an Appraisal Special Interest Group was set up to discuss the issues and engage in an appraisal cycle. The aim was to involve teachers in awareness raising about appraisal and to run a pilot scheme from which lessons could be learned during the year, before introducing a whole-school appraisal scheme. However, the pilot scheme did not materialise as planned, largely due to a lack of willingness among teachers to participate. This should perhaps have been a signal that the climate was not ready for appraisal, and that further preparatory work was necessary. However, the senior teachers continued with classroom observation and a handful of teachers did follow an appraisal cycle through.

An End of Year Summary form was administered to all teachers, as a way of gathering data about their reflections on the year. These included recognition of successes and problems; discussion about dealing with the latter and building on the former; evaluation of processes and services; and making future plans. Teachers completed it and then discussed it with their senior teacher. In addition, there was a Teacher Profile form which the teacher completed with information about workshops, courses attended, interests and so on. The analysis of the data obtained from the completed End of Year Summaries and the Teacher Profiles indicated strengths, and problem areas within the school, which required management attention.

Stage three

The senior teachers and teacher trainers developed the existing End of Year Summary, by making the connection with observations more explicit, and including the Teacher Profile form. This became the first version of our appraisal scheme and was known as the Teacher Profile. They prepared an explanatory booklet on the purposes of appraisal, the components of the appraisal cycle and the role of observation. They drafted appraisal documentation for inclusion in the Teacher Profile; devised a series of training sessions for appraisers; and prepared a briefing session for teachers about the appraisal scheme. The appraisal scheme was formally introduced in the 1993/94 academic year:

> At BUSEL we are committed to regular appraisal of work in order to develop the institution and the individual within it. As a means of achieving this aim, it is necessary to have regular formal contact with teachers in the form of appraisal meetings to identify interests, skills and needs.

> There are various components of your work in BUSEL which provide opportunities to monitor and reflect on your teaching, e.g. observations, student evaluation of teaching, and participation in workshops and INSET courses. During the course of your work you may also become involved in other teaching related activities, e.g. test-writing, materials production and/or adaptation, exploitation of video resources. The purpose of the appraisal meeting is to focus on all these areas in order to:

- recognise successes and problems;
- discuss how the successes might be built on and the problems overcome;
- evaluate processes and services, e.g. how effective your HTU and others have been in responding to your needs and in assisting you in meeting your objectives;
- make future plans for teaching/career goals.

(BUSEL 1993: 1)

The appraisal cycle consisted of three stages: an initial meeting to open the Teacher Profile, i.e. to open the appraisal documentation, by setting targets; a progress review meeting; and an end of year meeting to reflect on the whole year. Observation was an integral part of the cycle, with teachers being required to engage in four observations focusing on their targets during the year, for which records were kept. Each stage of the cycle was documented. The first appraisal cycle was completed in July 1994.

Stage four

Because the appraisal scheme was an innovation in BUSEL, and was being managed by the HTUs, who were a newly established middle-management structure, it was agreed that it would be useful to evaluate how the scheme was working. This evaluation is looked at more closely in Section 4.3.

Stage five

As a result of the evaluation there was a halt in the operation of the appraisal scheme while the whole process was refined and reworked, and HTUs participated in further training for appraisal during the 1994/95 academic year. This period also saw preliminary work on the introduction of a staff development policy and programme, and time released for staff to participate in a Staff Development Programme (SDP) which would support the appraisal process.

Stage six

In 1995/96 the Teacher Appraisal Scheme (TAS) was re-introduced through *The Teacher Appraisal Scheme Handbook* and teacher appraisal briefing sessions. The first cycle of the revised scheme was concluded in July 1996, and data from the appraisal meetings collated. These are used by the management team for planning the Staff Development Programme, and addressing issues of concern.

4.3   Evaluation of the teacher appraisal scheme

Evaluation is an integral part of good professional and curriculum practice and can be defined as the process of systematically collecting and analysing information in order to form value judgements based on firm evidence. These judgements are concerned with the extent to which particular targets are being achieved either at organisational or individual levels. They should therefore guide decision making for development. The two main purposes for evaluation of performance can be defined as: accountability to prove quality, and development to improve quality (Rogers and Badham 1992).[1]

In order for the evaluation of the teacher appraisal scheme to be designed and carried out appropriately, it was necessary to provide some training for key BUSEL staff. An external consultant was brought in to hold a workshop with the HTUs. The aims of the workshop were defined as follows:

- to reflect critically on the teacher appraisal scheme (strengths, weaknesses, conflicts, etc.) and to summarise implementation to date
- to evaluate the observation component of the teacher appraisal scheme
- to identify other potential inputs to the teacher appraisal scheme (e.g. self-evaluation, teacher self-report, student evaluation)
- to develop a framework for the evaluation of the teacher appraisal scheme, and to identify appropriate procedures
- to analyse the relationship between the teacher appraisal scheme and the staff development processes, and the nature of the staff development process itself and responsibilities within it.

The workshop proved to be a valuable training experience and its aims were achieved, with the HTUs proceeding with the implementation of the evaluation framework. The questions the evaluation sought to answer were as follows:

- To what extent is the rationale for the teacher appraisal scheme understood?
- To what extent are the components well-integrated?

- How effective are those charged with responsibility for managing the scheme?
- To what extent is the information gathered during the process used, and how?
- Overall, is the scheme beneficial to both the individual and the school?

Data were gathered from two sources: existing appraisal documentation and from the products of a half-day workshop for all teachers in their teaching units using a range of techniques (i.e. pyramid discussions, written responses to a series of open-ended questions, and a questionnaire).

The evaluation revealed that the scheme was considered to be beneficial to approximately 50 per cent of teachers who took part in the workshop, but that the following improvements were necessary:

- a clearer statement of the purposes of TAS, as well as the need for a code of practice
- revisions to the method of documenting the appraisal process
- a series of briefing seminars focusing on the changes that would be made
- further training for HTUs as appraisers, and awareness raising about skills for appraisal meetings for teachers
- the addition of appraiser and appraisee evaluation checklists
- the development of a systematic information system, whereby the data from the appraisal meetings would feed into channels for planning staff development and addressing frustrations, constraints and problems
- better integration of the components or elements within the appraisal cycle.

The team of HTUs and the head of teacher training then embarked upon redesigning the scheme, consulting with representative teachers at different stages, participated in further appraisal training, and designed the briefing seminars which included the preparation of a video of an appraisal meeting. All this was completed in the 1994/95 academic year. The evaluation exercise demonstrated that the management team was committed to improving the quality of the appraisal scheme; to a feedback loop improving the quality of communication within the school; and that it was prepared to reassess using appraisal as a tool to ensure that performance standards were being maintained.

4.4   Tensions

With the introduction of any innovation there will inevitably be tensions, seven of which are discussed here in some detail. The main sources of data about tensions are an unpublished MA thesis and the end of year appraisal meetings 1995/96. Akşit (1996: 85) concludes from her study, conducted half-way through the appraisal cycle, that among the sample group there was a fairly even split between those who had positive views about TAS and those who still held negative views.

The first tension relates to three issues: the purposes of appraisal (see Section 3.1), ownership (see Section 3.6) and culture and diversity (see Section 3.7). The purposes of our appraisal scheme were clear for the majority of teachers, who perceived them to be about awareness-raising, self-evaluation, self-improvement and professional development. This can be compared with the introductory statement in *The Teacher Appraisal Scheme Handbook*:

> An appraisal scheme has three purposes: to facilitate the professional development of teachers; to improve the quality of classroom performance, i.e. learning and teaching; and to better inform decision-making in the institution.   (BUSEL 1995: 3)

However, half the sample did not consider that they had improved themselves professionally. The reasons given for this were time constraints, heavy workload and lack of belief in the necessity or the value of the scheme. The other half did feel they had improved through TAS. There may also be cultural causes for the differences in attitude, located in the diversity of the staff group, or in the organisation's culture. Negative attitudes to evaluation, perhaps attributable to the university's system for student evaluation of teaching which BUSEL had to implement for some years in the past, may have been transferred to the role of evaluation within the appraisal scheme. So the tension in the staff group between those who believe in appraisal and those who do not sets a further challenge for the school's management team: how to convince those with negative attitudes that appraisal is worthwhile?

The second tension is associated with concerns about motivation (discussed in Section 3.4) and opportunity cost (see Section 3.8). The perceived lack of time and heavy workload were given as reasons why the stated purposes of appraisal were not met for some teachers. The concern for workload and stress is also prominent in data from the appraisal meetings. It is unclear, at this stage, whether making additional time available for teachers to engage in appraisal would actually change their attitude towards it, or whether other reasons for non-participation would be found. The level of stress experienced by teachers is well documented (Kyriacou 1989). If TAS is seen by some staff members to add to their stress levels, their motivation for participation will be reduced, and appraisal is unlikely to improve the quality of classroom performance for those individuals. Thus the cost–benefit relationship of whether appraisal contributes to improvements in the quality of teaching is brought into question, and whether the cost of building in a time allowance for appraisal would yield sufficient benefits for the institution.

Two further tensions are referred to in Akşit's study: reward for participation, effort and achievement in the appraisal process; and the standards and quality of the line managers themselves. The earlier discussion of motivation and reward (see Section 3.4), and power and authority relationships in appraisal (see Section 3.3), point to possible reasons for the tensions and indicate areas for improvement to be addressed by the management team. In BUSEL, appraisal is currently not linked to pay, and criteria for judging improvements in performance have yet to be defined systematically. The issue of criteria for appraisal (explored earlier in Section 3.5) is extremely complex, and BUSEL is in the process of addressing it (see Section 4.5). Trying to link appraisal of performance with pay would, in my view, undermine the purposes of our appraisal scheme. Research into reward mechanisms other than pay, which are considered by the teachers to be of value, would be worthwhile so that the rewards of engaging in appraisal become more explicit.

That some teachers do not subscribe to the idea of line management, or do not respect some of those who hold line-management posts, may be viewed in two ways. There is either a problem with the selection and training of line managers, which management action would solve, or with those teachers who have not yet adapted to the changes in organisational structure which introduced the concept of line management and associated accountability. Solutions to the latter may be achieved with more time for readjustment, or a decision by the teacher to seek employment elsewhere.

Data from appraisal meetings revealed concern for operational issues, e.g. timetabling and student contact hours which create frustration and dissatisfaction among teachers. This is indicative of a lack of information among teachers about the constraints under which the management team functions and would indicate the need for improved understanding all round.

The tension of maintaining the continuity of ownership of an appraisal scheme is significant, and BUSEL's annual induction programme attempts to address this. Each year, usually, at least 30 new teachers are employed and thus there is a constant need (i) to recreate ownership of TAS with the changing workforce as the original designers and consultation participants have left, and (ii) to ensure that new staff approach TAS with as open a mind as possible as to the benefits to be derived from active participation in it. Of course, stories that exist within BUSEL's culture about TAS are transmitted to new members, and become part of the cultural web of the organisation (Johnson and Scholes 1993). Consequently, new staff may acquire negative impressions about TAS and the positive introduction to BUSEL's appraisal scheme on the induction programme may be undermined, even though negative views are explored.

The final tension is of direct concern for the management team: the issue of monitoring and quality control cannot be addressed by TAS in its present form. The dual purposes of proving quality and improving quality, or teacher development, in our experience are incompatible within a teacher appraisal scheme. The development of a performance management approach designed to ensure quality and consisting of a number of interrelated systems, only one of which is appraisal, is ongoing in BUSEL, and is outlined in Section 4.5.

4.5   Possible solutions to problems in the management of teacher performance and appraisal

Of the problems confronting the management team in 1992, as outlined in Section 4.2, the experience of designing, implementing and evaluating a teacher appraisal scheme enabled us to use appraisal as a tool to tackle the following: planning for staff development; writing references; knowing teachers' special interests, skills and potential; obtaining feedback on problems faced by teachers. The quality of teachers' performance goes through a number of stages (not necessarily linear) and will be affected by such factors as their experience and professional qualifications; the particular students; their familiarity with and understanding of the curriculum to be taught; their colleagues; the teaching resources available to them; their ability to evaluate, reflect and change; and their individual motivation for their work. Thus, an appraisal scheme is an important element in the management of quality education provision, but alone is an insufficient tool. In order to address the issue of defining and monitoring standards, as well as solving identified problems with teachers' performance, a number of other processes have been developing alongside our appraisal scheme.

Processes to ensure minimum performance standards

BUSEL has been improving the quality and design of the selection process through which new teachers are appointed and is better able to predict the quality of subsequent performance and weed out potentially poor performers. Inevitably, there will be the occasional error. A critical look at the selection process was taken, its effectiveness evaluated and steps are being taken to improve it. These centre on staff training for those with responsibility for selection, and the content and format of the interview itself.

Closely connected to the selection process is probation. BUSEL believes that an effective probation process ensures that newly selected teachers can meet the bottom-line performance standard, however that is defined, and has been improving the probation system in operation. The initial six-month probation period should be characterised by the provision of support for the teacher in a new job to enable him or her to perform effectively as quickly as possible and can be used to establish positive attitudes to evaluation. The establishment of criteria of direct relevance to the job description is essential, in order for the line managers to support new teachers and ensure that the performance standards are met. If problems are identified – as well they may, given that the organisational environment is new – there is time to take positive steps to improve performance so that it can be judged to meet the standards within the probation period. A positive experience of probation for teachers could pave the way for a positive attitude towards appraisal.

A process to solve problems with performance

BUSEL's teacher appraisal scheme does not include among its purposes the identification of poor performance and resultant action. This cannot be addressed in the annual appraisal meeting. Additional strategies are being evolved to manage problems with teachers' performance, which may emerge or are identified subsequent to the successful completion of a probation period. It is the responsibility of the line manager to really get to know the teachers they manage by working with them as closely as possible, supporting them in their teaching in whatever way is appropriate, and building a relationship based on trust and professional respect. It is crucial for the line manager to be sensitive to any indication that there is a problem, the precise nature of which is unspecified, and to engage in a problem-identification and problem-solving dialogue with the teacher aimed at improving performance. Such a discussion results in a joint action-plan designed to address the causes of the problem and to change behaviour over time, so that the desired standard is met (Torrington 1991). Such a plan may involve the line manager in providing support or training. In cases where the standard is not met, then some form of disciplinary action is taken as a reminder that failing to meet the expected standard is not acceptable, and ultimately will result in dismissal.

A process to improve individual performance

This is addressed by BUSEL's appraisal scheme which has professional development as a primary purpose, with an emphasis on target-setting, action-research and dialogue with peers and line managers about teaching, as well as the opportunity to engage in an formal appraisal meeting. The meetings provide an opportunity for the teacher to be heard. Data from the meetings improve communication by informing management of: targets being met successfully; problems with the organisation that are experienced by staff; priorities among the staff for training and development; as well as identifying individuals' strengths and potential for specialist roles or promotion.

A process to meet staff development needs

BUSEL's staff development programme must address both organisational needs, and those of individual teachers for training and development, which have been identified from data coming primarily through the appraisal scheme, and through the organisation's development (business) plan objectives. The staff development programme consumes a lot of resources, and there is an ongoing need for BUSEL to evaluate the programme's effectiveness in achieving improvements in teachers' knowledge, skills and performance – especially as it represents a considerable financial investment. Bramley (1996) provides useful guidelines for evaluating training effectiveness. The design, delivery and management of staff development activities as part of a planned programme provides a parallel challenge to the design, implementation and management of an appraisal scheme, both of which are interdependent.

Processes which lead to the definition of standards and criteria to assist in the monitoring of a teacher's performance

As discussed earlier in Section 3.5, establishing criteria for appraisal is a sensitive and complex task, and depends on the purposes of appraisal. BUSEL has begun the process of defining quality standards and criteria to assist in the monitoring of a teacher's performance in consultation with other teachers. Some of these criteria are integral to probation and solving problems with performance after probation has been completed. The process of definition needs the full involvement of the teachers and includes:

- discussion leading to the shared understanding of the rationale for ensuring and maintaining quality standards in the educational service provided, and about ways of achieving these
- observation of a whole range of teaching in different classrooms
- consultation about draft specifications of standards
- recognition that standards may differ depending on the stage in the profession, e.g. a new teacher-graduate may not be evaluated against the same standards as someone who has been teaching for five years with a postgraduate qualification of some kind
- discussions about the way in which the achievement and maintenance of standards might be related with reward mechanisms in whatever form.

Finding a solution to the controversial issue of performance standards takes commitment, time and expertise on the part of management and teachers alike.

5   Conclusion: challenges for appraisal in educational contexts

The experience of the innovation of the teacher appraisal scheme in BUSEL, and the development of complementary processes (outlined in Section 4.5 above) to the management of performance, point to a number of challenges for educational organisations seeking to adopt appraisal as a tool within performance management:

- There must be a drive for reconciliation between teachers' perceptions of themselves as professionals managing education, and school management teams responsible for running educational institutions, who are subject to external scrutiny and held accountable for the way teachers deliver education, i.e. its quality and standards.
- The establishment of a climate in which all members of the school are committed to ongoing evaluation of their activities and work, as a cornerstone of both individual and organisational improvement, is crucial.
- Involving and equipping teachers with the skills/techniques of evaluation as a part of the process of inquiry into their own practice requires management investment in resources/training.
- Managing the working conditions of teachers in such a way that there is time to engage in active reflection, evaluation and appraisal in a systematic, structured way presents a major challenge.
- The outcomes of the appraisal process must be seen to contribute to the overall improvement of the school, to the improvement of teaching quality in the school and learning outcomes, and to the professional development of teachers.
- Tackling performance problems as and when they appear is important as the quality of the services offered to students may be compromised. Problems with poor performance must be separated from the appraisal process if the latter is to be viewed positively. Within a close-knit team of teachers, when an individual's poor performance is being addressed, maintaining the morale and motivation of the rest of the group requires considerable skill and courage on the part of those with line management responsibilities.

- It is important for any school management team to institute appropriate rewards (which may be context specific) for teachers who do commit themselves to appraisal. BUSEL has yet to address this challenge satisfactorily. It may be a false assumption that the intrinsic satisfaction or reward of engaging in the process of an appraisal scheme is always sufficient for the effective maintenance of the scheme. There is an added problem if there are the constraints of national pay awards, trade union action, etc., or if there is a political (and hence ideological) motivation behind the scheme.

- A school management team has responsibility for ensuring that there are staff development opportunities in the form of time release, courses, workshops, etc., to meet the stated needs of teachers engaging in the appraisal process and to ensure the effectiveness of such opportunities in improving the quality of performance.

- A big challenge is how to win over those teachers who remain sceptical and unwilling to engage in appraisal. There is a possibility that if participation in a scheme were voluntary, as opposed to an organisational requirement, the reluctant adopters would be more willing.

- Finally, schools need to engage in an ongoing review of the extent to which a performance management approach is being successful. The review would focus on establishing the extent to which the quality of the delivery of the educational services has improved. This would involve an analysis of whether the culture of the organisation is more clearly defined and more readily identified with by its members. An indicator of quality might be higher levels of job satisfaction, job involvement and organisational commitment. There should be a positive impact on recruitment and retention, and on human resources policies.

An appraisal scheme takes time to take root and grow into an effective tool for improving the quality of an organisation. The success of any appraisal scheme would seem to largely depend on the quality of the interpersonal and professional relationships between appraisees and appraisers, their mutual respect for the others' skills and roles, which together contribute to the success of an organisation.

Note

1. Hopkins (1989), Millman and Darling-Hammond (1990), Rea-Dickins and Germaine (1992), and Weir and Roberts (1994), all offer insights into issues in evaluation and how evaluation can be carried out within school and project contexts.

Views from the bridge

Introduction

This final part, 'Views from the bridge', aims to introduce and explore additional perspectives on evaluation from those raised in the previous chapters.

Chapter 8, by Holliday, 'Evaluating the discourse: the role of applied linguistics in the management of evaluation and innovation', is written from a broad general perspective and overview. It challenges the reader to look at the diversity of cultural contexts in which management of innovation of integrationist English language teaching (ELT) is exercised and implemented. Applied linguistics can help illuminate the discourse involved in ELT, and he illustrates this by comparing different educational cultures, namely, the academic one of collectivism and the skills-oriented culture of integrationist ELT (see also Holliday 1994a). His case study on cross-communication in an MA degree class situates these issues in a particular context. He invites the reader to adopt an evaluative perspective and to examine the discourse of evaluation itself – even to question the orders of discourse (e.g. Fairclough 1989) in which evaluation discourse is situated – so as to understand the power relations involved between various stakeholders. After all, the social formation of the discourse will often reflect the thinking of the institutions involved as well as the context in which it is produced. Such critical analysis may illuminate the taken-for-granted (and hence ideological) assumptions inherent in the discourse which contribute to the ongoing social construction of reality as perceived by evaluators and commissioners.

In Chapter 9, 'Evaluating and researching grammar consciousness-raising tasks', Ellis explores the connections between evaluation and Second Language Acquisition (SLA). His analysis of the similarities and contrasts between evaluation and research is timely in view of the questioning in some quarters of the value of educational research (e.g. Alan Smithers at the 1997 British Association of Science) and the need to review the relationships between research, evaluation findings and policy making (see, for example, Burgess 1993, Roger Murphy in *Guardian Education*, 16 September 1997). Elsewhere a number of other authors have analysed some of the criterial features of these terms (e.g. Norris 1990, Mackay 1992, Rea-Dickins 1994) but Ellis's approach is unique in that he demonstrates the similarities and differences via two studies as the basis for comparing evaluation and research. The first study is the evaluation of a consciousness-raising grammar task planned and investigated by a practising teacher primarily for awareness-raising purposes. This is followed by a second research-based study of another grammar consciousness-raising task, this time designed for purposes of SLA research. Each is investigated in terms of purpose, planning, data collection, analysis and reporting. Ellis concludes that the task evaluation and the task-based research are complementary in that they inform each other and, thus, Ellis reinforces a central point that research should inform evaluation practice and is, indeed, seminal to the interpretation and validity of evaluation findings (see also Rea-Dickins, forthcoming). He also suggests that 'task-evaluation offers a promising approach to teacher development' (p. 250) through which teachers may develop a theory of action which has much in common with the approach discussed by Hedge in Chapter 6 of this volume.

There are two other views in this last part from contributors external to the field of language education. The first is by Fullan, a leading authority in the area of managing educational change. In Chapter 10, 'Linking change and assessment', he confirms the rather chequered history of the evaluation of educational change and improved performance (see Karavas-Doukas, Chapter 2). He argues, as implicit in many of the contributions in this volume, for a much closer relationship between evaluation and change processes and discusses five ideas he considers key to the understanding of change and the change process. Firstly, searching for the silver bullet, as he puts it, implies a need for healthy scepticism about finding a universal model of change. He then reiterates the view that much about change is personal. He goes on to argue that 'resistance and conflict are positively necessary' and encourages the voicing of dissent as a healthy part of the dialectic process. Conflict and differences are inevitable and should be viewed as an essential and valuable part of productive change (evident in Anderson's account of the process of change in Chapter 7). Fullan is of the view that evaluation of the roots and manifestation of dissent can be a contributing factor to the development of the innovation. For him, *relationships* are by far the most important of all the indicators of successful implementation. Any holistic approach to evaluation necessarily takes the relationships variable into account. Following on naturally from this he places emotion and hope to be considered as part of the constructive theory of change.

Fullan then examines in more depth the nature and impact of collaborative work cultures in schools and is of the view that changes in culture towards collaborative work should precede any restructuring of an organisation. Thus, the development of collaborative professional communities is fundamental to innovation, a point of key relevance to many of the articles in this volume. Finally, with specific reference to changes in assessment, a notoriously difficult area in any case, he examines the relationship between schools and their environments and focuses on how schools should deal with state policies related to assessment of student learning. He argues that the boundaries of the school are permeable and, if we take this as a metaphor, then it can be applied to projects as well. In terms of stakeholder participation and involvement, he suggests a reframing of the relationship between the schools, i.e. teachers and principals, and the outside which would include new approaches to, as examples, parents and community, businesses, state policies, and other agencies. To illustrate this, Fullan takes up the point about how schools should deal with state policies on assessment of student learning, recognising that they (i.e. the assessment schemes) have both an external accountability role to the public and political decision makers as well as providing for improvements and impact on the classroom. Like Stern (Chapter 11), Fullan sees evaluation as something integrated within educational systems, a perspective strongly reflected throughout this volume. In this last respect, Kiely (Chapter 4) pushes knowledge further in seeking to understand the interplay between evaluation for professional practice and policy as well as teacher and student subjective representations of the evaluation process itself.

Within the profession of evaluation (as summarised by Rea-Dickins and Germaine in Chapter 1 of this volume), there continues to be tension between rationalist approaches to evaluation and more humanistic ones (for recent perspectives on both sides of 'truth' versus 'advocacy' see, for example, Pawson and Tilley 1997, Scriven 1996, Fetterman 1997, Chelimsky and Shadish 1997). Fullan's chapter seems to fall into the latter category where the emphasis is on how people are involved in the change process, the culture they generate within an organisation and the links they have with assessment.

However, from an economic and social science background, the second outsider perspective offered by Stern adopts a somewhat different stand, itself a reflection of the debate within the profession. In Chapter 11, 'Eavesdropping on debates in language education and learning', Stern confirms the similarities in terms of approaches, dilemmas, methodologies and theories of evaluation, thus reinforcing our rationale for this volume of bridge building across divides of discipline and fields of application. In terms of purposes for evaluation, he cautions against an over-reliance on two purposes for evaluation of 'managing' and 'learning', at the expense of evaluation for accountability. Referring specifically to the contributions by both Holliday (Chapter 8) and Roberts (Chapter 3), he observes that they 'clearly eschew an 'accountability' purpose for evaluation. This is an interesting view as this trend extends well beyond this present volume (see, for example, Alderson and Beretta 1992, Weir and Roberts 1994). It is explained, perhaps, in part as a reaction against evaluation imposed from outside, of the 'autonomous' functioning of the 'external evaluator', and also as a reflection of the profession itself, with strong influences from humanistic approaches to teaching and learning (see also Kiely 1998). In examining the relatedness of evaluation to innovation, Stern detects a tendency (in several chapters in this volume) to separate innovation from evaluation, and he cites examples such as software engineering where evaluation is at the heart of the development process. In this respect, several writers, elsewhere, have advocated the integration of formative and summative evaluation as a key element in the planning of language projects and programmes (e.g. Murphy 1995, Rea-Dickins 1995, Kiely *et al.* 1996, Kenny and Savage 1997). Stern comments further on the tension that may exist between those who manage, those who evaluate and those who innovate. And, this can be seen in some of the contributions to this volume, e.g. Anderson (Chapter 7) who writes from the perspective of insider manager. In relation to innovation, Stern also invites us to consider two fundamental points and to distinguish between the content and the implementation dimensions of an innovation. Recognising the difficulty in defining 'evaluation', he raises the notion of self-defining innovation, with evaluators having a contributory role in this self-definition through problematising innovation. The knowledge base to which Stern refers includes, minimally, three interdependent theories (in a way completing the circle of discussion running through the chapters by Roberts and Holliday) within the domains of language education, innovation and evaluation. He recognises that all these types of theory are present in this volume, and closes his chapter, provocatively, by suggesting that 'integrating theory and method in the evaluation of innovation always seems just beyond the horizon' (p. 268). This call for integration rejoins the emphasis for a better fit between theory and method running through the chapters in *Managing Evaluation and Innovation in Language Teaching: Building Bridges.*

8

Evaluating the discourse: the role of applied linguistics in the management of evaluation and innovation

ADRIAN HOLLIDAY

Abstract. The management of evaluation and innovation in English language programmes needs to address a tension between two professional–academic cultures. The academic culture of collectionism is often invaded by a skills-oriented culture of integrationist ELT. This state of affairs has important links with a similar tension between academic applied linguistics and integrationist ELT – in turn related to wider tensions within late industrial society. The relevance of applied linguistics to the management of English language education can sometimes be questioned. Also, the presentation within applied linguistics of national or global culture difference and conflict can be counterproductive when analysing institutional factors in language programmes. However, applied linguistics can make a valuable contribution to the management of evaluation and innovation through a critical discourse analysis of the collection–integration conflict, both within English language programmes and in its own relationship with those programmes.

1 Background

In considering the role of applied linguistics in the management of English language curricula, this paper focuses on the cultural nature of the relationships within this role. It shows how the relationship between applied linguistics and English language education is marked by a conflict between a young academic tradition in applied linguistics and the dominant non-academic culture of English language teaching, for which the acronym ELT has become

195

popular. I shall argue that this culture conflict is significant in that it is in essence the same as, and partly gives rise to, that underlying many of the language curriculum scenarios in which evaluation and innovation take place. To be able to manage evaluation and innovation elsewhere, we therefore need first to understand conflicts within our own professional–academic orientation.

I also argue that this understanding is not helped by some current perceptions within applied linguistics, about relations between the West and the developing world and about the nature of culture. The contribution and relevance of applied linguistics to the management of evaluation and innovation is therefore questioned, where other social sciences might be more helpful. Nevertheless, I argue that applied linguistics has a special contribution to make through critical discourse analysis, applied to the cultural complexities of both the curriculum scenarios we wish to manage and our own professional–academic orientation. However, an important condition is that the primary object of study should be language as a significant constituent of culture – as in critical discourse analysis. This would be different to the more common trend in applied linguistics which looks at culture as something which is affected by and behaves in a similar way to language.

Throughout, *English language education* will be used to refer to the whole range of activity implicit in and supporting the teaching and learning of English as a second or other language in the world – including teacher education, all forms of training, programme and curriculum planning, design, implementation and evaluation. The use of the common acronyms ELT and TEFL (for teaching English as a foreign language) represent discoursally loaded concepts – parts of the language which I feel need to be evaluated rather than simply used. Where they are used it will therefore be as artefacts within the discourse. Throughout, *language programme* shall be used to refer to all curriculum processes, from courses to projects, in which evaluation and innovation may take place.

2   An area of interest in applied linguistics

Let us look at the role of applied linguistics by delineating two areas of interest, as displayed in Figure 8.1. On the left, applied linguistics is presented as a specialist branch of social science,

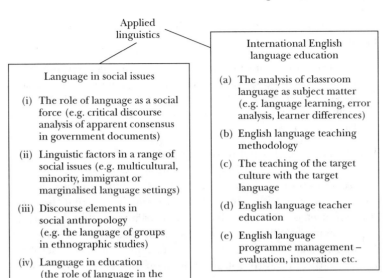

Figure 8.1 Two foci for applied linguistics

bringing knowledge of discourse analysis and socio- and psycho-linguistics to a range of social issues in which language is a key element. Listed there are some examples of this involvement. Because all aspects of social life involve language as a major element, the question may, however, be asked: Where is the boundary between an applied linguistics which can find interest in all aspects of social life and, say, sociology and anthropology which must involve an interest in language in all their fields of study? An interesting case is Baumann's (1996) ethnography of Southall, in which he is very much concerned with language although he is not presenting himself as an applied linguist. Central to his study is the relationship between a 'dominant discourse of culture' and the perceptions of 'culture' among the inhabitants of Southall as exemplified in the way they use the concept. The resulting linguistic analysis of the dominant and local discourses surrounding the use of the term 'culture' nevertheless appears no less accurate or perceptive for Baumann being an anthropologist rather than an applied linguist. Conversely, in ethnographic studies carried out by applied linguists, one might wonder if there is an over-dependence on oral data because of their natural preoccupation with language (Holliday 1996a). On the other hand, there is the argument for a need:

> to convince the increasing number of discourse analysts whose disciplinary base is outside linguistics or language studies that textual analysis should mean analysis of the *texture* of texts, their form and organisation, and not just commentaries on the content of texts. (Fairclough 1995: 4)

I shall return to this point towards the end of the chapter.

The justification of discipline boundaries in these terms is of course a philosophical question which is difficult to resolve. Rather than take a purist line which would presumably say that there is a 'proper' area of interest with a 'proper' balance within disciplines, which themselves have some sort of ontological right to existence, I prefer to take a more relativist stance. The *existence* of disciplines is, in reality, to do with political and economic forces that drive or enable certain groups of academics to institutionalise and territorialise their activities to form or break disciplines (cf. Kuhn 1970). Thus, the boundaries between disciplines are micro-political constructs which become reified into a more general social acceptance. Applied linguistics has in these terms just as much right to be separate from, say, sociology or anthropology as does economics. The areas of interest on the left hand of Figure 8.1 makes applied linguistics behave like economics. However, as an older discipline, economics has achieved a more recognisable image in the public psyche than applied linguistics. One would hope that, eventually, works in applied linguistics will also inhabit well-marked shelves in non-specialist high street bookshops. Even in specialist university bookshops, applied linguistics still hovers between 'linguistics', 'grammar' and, perhaps, 'education'.

On the right of Figure 8.1 are listed examples of the work of applied linguistics which is concerned with English language education. This can be seen as different to the social issues branch presented on the left in that it represents an area of interest which might be compared more to medicine than to economics. Unlike economics, the public view of medicine, despite its academic, theoretical and scientific nature, is of a technical, professional activity. Thus, the relationship between applied linguistics and the English language education profession will be like the relationship of medicine with the professional practice of medicine by doctors and nurses. Another difference is that it can be argued that the

English language education branch has grown more rapidly than the social issues branch on the left, associated with the enormous expansion of teaching English as a second or other language in the 1970s and 1980s (Phillipson 1992). A colleague in education recently asked me why such a fuss was being made about English language education when, in global terms, English plays a relatively small role when compared to the rest of school and university curricula. We were interviewing together a candidate for doctoral research into the effects of sudden English language teaching reform on secondary school education in a small Middle Eastern country. He clearly thought that this was a political issue which had little to do with language *per se*. Why was it under the heading of applied linguistics? From the viewpoint of the social issues branch, the attention to English language education may also appear disproportionate – unless of course the expansion of English language education from the English-speaking West is perceived as one of the major social issues. If this is true, the increased role of applied linguistics in English language education is part of this expansion.

However, looking more closely at the English language education branch on the right of Figure 8.1, there are certain anomalies which lead one to question the involvement of applied linguistics in some areas. While in the analysis of classroom language, language teaching methodology and the teaching of culture with language, (a) – (c), language is certainly central, it seems decreasingly so as one moves down the list to (e). I shall discuss the teaching of the target culture with the target language (c) later. In (e), the management of evaluation, innovation, etc. – the focus of this volume – the difference made by the fact that the programme is about language may not be sufficient to warrant specialist attention from applied linguistics. I am talking here about macro-evaluation of programme processes rather than evaluation as assessment or testing of specifies within the language programme – which would come under language teaching methodology ((b) in Figure 8.1). There is indeed a growing awareness that applied linguistics is less useful in the management of language programmes than other social sciences. This has been due to increased demands within overseas aid projects and the private sector for more sophisticated management approaches, especially within the areas of evaluation and innovation. It is now argued that too much dependence on applied linguistics has created crises in the social domain of

English language education within which the management factor resides (Bowers 1986, Phillipson 1992, Holliday 1994a). The need for better management has also come hand-in-hand with the Thatcherite legacy in Britain, which has refined its demands for accountability and quality into the 1990s, bringing increased governmental instrumentalism and an even greater tendency for aid agencies to exercise 'hyperrational' controls on aid projects (cf. Fullan 1982, Holliday 1994a).

English language teacher education ((d) in Figure 8.1) – now that we are past the lockstep and structuralist regimes of the 60s which bound classroom methodology tightly to a very specific perception of language – also only partly concerns language. In teacher education in Britain, pedagogy (e.g. in the basic teacher qualifying postgraduate certificate of education (PGCE)) can be taught separately to and after the subject matter (e.g. history) is dealt with at degree level. Such a separation in English language teacher education might move the emphasis away from the prescriptions of English language and a language-centred classroom methodology towards a greater sensitivity to the social context of teaching.[1] More time might thus be spent on learning about the whole institutional complexity of teaching and its environment, through mentoring and observation of its culture within the wider institution as well as inside the classroom. This social institutional focus within language teacher education will also better equip the teacher to understand the macro processes underlying the management of evaluation and innovation. Placing the classroom and pedagogy within a wider social environment from the beginning of professional experience will mean that teachers will not suddenly have to master the elements of evaluation and innovation when they become 'curriculum developers' – these sociological skills will be deep rooted within their professionalism.

Therefore, whereas the academic discipline of medicine has a direct one-to-one relationship with the practice of medicine, the relationship between applied linguistics and English language education is ambivalent. On the one hand, applied linguistics has a non-professional social issues heartland which is not necessarily concerned with English language education; on the other, there is mixed relevance where it is concerned with English language education. In some areas of English language education there is a need for linguistic analysis; in other areas, such as classroom methodology and teacher education, and especially in the management of evaluation and innovation in language programmes, applied linguistics may be involved simply because it is there. A good sociology or politics of English language education might well be more useful than applied linguistics for investigating these areas. It has been argued elsewhere that ethnography has an important role to play (Holliday 1996a), though the opportunities made available in many professional contexts demand a distinction between applying methodological principles and doing *an* ethnography (Holliday 1997; Roberts, Chapter 3 in this volume). The same would apply to other social sciences.

3 A dominant discourse

It has been argued above that applied linguistics may have a questionable relevance to some *substantive* areas within English language education (as listed on the right of Figure 8.1). Nevertheless, because of the historical relationship referred to above, it has made significant contribution to the *process* of English language education as a discipline. The resulting *mélange* of relationships governing the formation of this discipline, as depicted in Figure 8.2, has an important bearing on the way in which the management of evaluation and innovation in language programmes is addressed.

Beginning in the centre and lower half of the figure, English language education represents a particular critical reality [A] in that it both influences important activities within its sphere of influence [B] and presents areas of uncertainty [C]. The activities in [B] are not only important in that they govern the whole nature of English language education from the methodology of the classroom to the management of evaluation and innovation connected with these activities; they are also important in that they are the outcomes of clear *choices* about how things should be done. It is becoming established in this postmodern era that there is nothing autonomous about the technologies and principles governing these choices (Pennycook 1989, Coleman 1996a) and that there is little that we definitely know about classrooms (Allwright 1988). Yet, choices are made, which affect not only the treatment of children and adults learning English, but also the careers of English language educators in institutions all over the world. This happens when English is brought in, by whatever government or

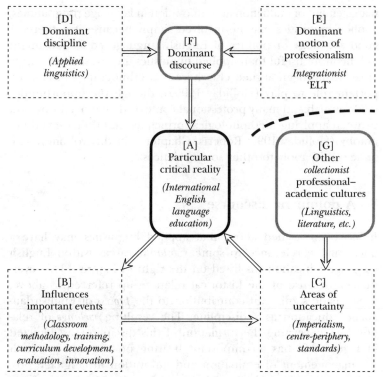

Figure 8.2 *Mélange* of relationships governing the discipline of English language education

international policy, as an innovatory force which might affect wider curricular and administrative practice. In short, English language education, in many institutional contexts, carries with it a technical, educational or political baggage that can affect the lives of a wide range of people. For example, developments in classroom methodology in private language schools in Britain, carried abroad through aid, international publishing and teacher education, may affect what happens in university or state school classrooms in China. It may not only be the teachers and students who are affected, but the work relations of other staff within the institution (Holliday 1992b). Because of the nature of English as a commodity within the international world of work, and as a symbol of educational status in many parts of the world, the aspirations of the wider community will also come into the picture. Hence the uncertainties and issues surrounding English language education ([C] in the figure) may be more internationally, politically and institutionally critical than in some other professional areas. Post-colonial and postmodern discussions of various types of imperialisms that sustain themselves after the decline of empire are often therefore centred around the role of English, not only as national language policy, but in its influence on how education generally should be administered, from classroom to curriculum. The question of managing evaluation and innovation is thus tied up with the whole role and status of English language education and the *mélange* of relationships within which these roles and statuses are derived. Applied linguistics plays an ambivalent yet important part in this.

Looking to the top of Figure 8.2, applied linguistics [D] and a dominant professional culture [E] combine to form the dominant discourse which governs English language education and helps determine the ideological choices inherent in its activities [B]. My understanding of *dominant discourse* is of a set of institutionalised, reified terminologies and ways of expression which influence the thought processes of its participants. It is the linguistic aspect of any professional, academic, technical or other group culture, which articulates the taken-for-granted knowledge and practice of the culture. In Fairclough's (1995) terms, it may be more sinister in that it represents a naturalised, hegemonic, ideological influence on the order of discourse within English language education. Because English language education is a particularly professional–academic formation, the major contributors to its dominant discourse are likely to be a dominant academic discipline and a dominant notion of professionalism. It is important to note, following my discussion above, that the dominant discipline [D] does not have to be applied linguistics. It could be education or another social science. It has become applied linguistics via a particular historical process, in which interest groups within the expansion of the teaching of English as a second or other language funded the setting up of departments of applied linguistics in British and American universities in the 1970s, thus beginning a special professional–academic relationship which has sustained itself to the present day (Phillipson 1992).

The dominant notion of professionalism [E] is essentially *integrationist ELT* originating in the commercial language schools of the English-speaking West and referred to elsewhere as BANA – British, Australasian, North American (Holliday 1994a). The

Table 8.1   Two educational cultures

Integrationist	Collectionist
■ Originating in non-academic commercial sector, adult education, and primary education; adopted by BANA 'ELT' (which has spread to commercial 'ELT' throughout the world)	Mainstream primary, and secondary education in many parts of the world, and tertiary education in most parts of the world (TESEP)
■ Instrumental, accountable, measurable, professionalistic, expertise	Of intrinsic value, professorial
■ Tailor-made, functional small classes, materials, activities	Curricula and facilities defined by generalised educational principles
■ Preoccupation with pedagogy, conformity to methodological principles	Preoccupation with discipline, conformity to academic discourse conventions
■ Skills-based defined competences	Subject knowledge-based
■ 'Learner-centred', teacher as facilitator, 'learner' as client, customer	Education-centred, teacher, lecturer and student roles defined by intrinsic social values
■ Organised classroom activities and arrangement (groups, pairs, etc.)	Centred on teacher and subject discourse
■ Dissolving subject boundaries, low hierarchy	Strong subject boundaries, high hierarchy

characteristics of integrationist ELT are described in the left-hand column of Table 8.1. It has cultural residues in non-academic education such as that found in primary (Bernstein 1991) and adult (Edwards 1991, Edwards and Usher 1994) education. It has been spread to institutions in other countries initially (in the case of Britain) through the establishment of, for example, the British Council direct teaching operation, and has also influenced the various language-teaching institutes within British universities.

The broken line in Figure 8.2 between the dominant and 'other' professional–academic cultures ([G] in the figure) represents a break between two worlds. The second, or 'other' world is that of a *collectionist* professional–academic culture (right-hand column in Table 8.1) which is subject- and knowledge-based and inhabits state education in most parts of the world.[2] This is referred to elsewhere as 'TESEP' – TErtiary, SEcondary and Primary education (Holliday 1994a). A major conflict between the two worlds is that the skills-orientation of integrationism has no respect for the knowledge-based subject boundaries of the collectionist academic world (Table 8.1).[3]

The notion of a dominant discourse is meaningful only in opposition to an alternative discourse. It is important to tread carefully here, because *dominant* is itself politically and culturally divisive. The integration–collection conflict within English language education as described in Holliday (1994a) is similar in many ways, but also significantly different to the centre-periphery argument in Phillipson (1992) and Pennycook (1994a). The Phillipson and Pennycook position suggests a macro global-political, Western imperialism, in which the West is in the centre as a matter of fact with regard to an overall economic and political supremacy of which English language education is a part. The developing world is similarly in a periphery position from which it needs to recover; and a changed relationship with English language education would be an important part of this recovery. The integration–collection conflict is concerned more with the micro-politics of the formation of and conflict within institutions. Integrationist ELT is part of an educational movement operating within specific sectors of the West rather than from the West. The instrumental side of integrationist ELT (Table 8.1) can in turn be associated with the commodification of social processes and the subsequent technologisation and marketisation of institutional, professional and academic discourses which Fairclough (1995) connects with Thatcherism in Britain.[4] The *perception* that integrationist ELT occupies a centre position in international English language education is indeed an ethnocentric characteristic of this instrumentalism based on a conviction that its techniques are autonomous and therefore universally applicable and exportable (see Pennycook 1989). Fairclough (1995: 104) sees the 'tendency . . . for techniques to be increasingly designed and projected as "context-free", as usable in any relevant context' as a logical progression in technologisation of discourse. Unlike the internationalist Phillipson and Pennycook position, the notion of imperialism presented by the integration–collection conflict corresponds very closely with that described by Fairclough (1995: 104) at an institutional level in which 'the projection of such context-free techniques into a variety of institutional contexts contributes to a widespread effect of "colonisation" of local institutional orders of discourse by a few culturally-salient discourse types'. There is a definite infiltration of integrationist ELT technologised discourse into collectionist institutions throughout the world, through English language curriculum projects, teacher education, publications, and the employment of 'native-speaker' teachers (Holliday 1994a). However, this infiltration is more of an outreach action of a confrontation which is still largely located within the West than part of an all-out imperialist confrontation between the West and the developing world.

Unlike the internationalist Phillipson and Pennycook centre–periphery conflict, the integration–collection conflict does not therefore inhabit geographical worlds. Although integrationist ELT originates in the English-speaking West, it represents a techno-logical, instrumentalist ethos that extends beyond ELT and exists everywhere within certain institutional types. Indeed, the teachers and students may move frequently between integrationist and collectionist institutional cultures and the same personnel may work within both. For example, Indonesian ESP teachers may suffer low status within collectionist university departments where subject lecturers and students find it hard to take 'non-academic' ESP seriously. At the same time, the same teachers enjoy high status when teaching the same students in private language schools where integrationist ELT is considered normal (Coleman 1997). The collectionist culture is also common in state education in all parts of the world, including the English-speaking West, and may indeed have its origins in European colonialist education.

The next section illustrates how one well-known scenario, that of the masters course in English language education or applied linguistics in a British university, represents these conflicts and anomalies particularly clearly, and also provides some indication as to how they configure a scenario in which evaluation and innovation need to be managed.

3.1   The masters classroom

The following representation of a masters classroom in a British university does not claim to be scientific, simply a construction distilled from experience. For the sake of this discussion the student body is divided into three types of participant: university lecturers from countries A, B and C, who have been connected with a British Council managed curriculum project; secondary school teachers from countries X, Y and Z; and British TEFL teachers who have been working in private language schools in Britain and for the British Council or International House overseas.[5]

The university lecturers from countries A, B and C all have degrees in literature or linguistics and also teach these as academic subjects. They are therefore collectionist in orientation, seeing the teaching of English essentially as an academic activity. Their work within a British Council managed curriculum project has, however, brought them into contact with integrationist ELT personnel and a technology with a strong discourse of 'skills', 'competences', 'learners', 'communicative', 'activities', etc. (Table 8.1). Their collectionist academic background has made it easy for them to learn this discourse at an academic, theoretical level, but more as a ritual liturgy than as something to put into practice. They may not really understand the integrationist ELT principles behind the discourse, or the aims and behaviour of the curriculum project, its technology and its personnel because it represents a very different arrangement of very different concepts to those behind the collectionist discourse. The integrationist ELT discourse suggests teacher and student roles and realisations of knowledge which may work against the socially intrinsic principles inherent in collectionism. They will take from this alien discourse what they can.[6] They also have little difficulty with the new discourse of academic writing in applied linguistics; and they do well. This is helped by a recognition of collectionist characteristics of applied linguistics as an academic subject.

The secondary school teachers from countries X, Y and Z have also degrees in literature and linguistics and see the teaching of English as very much an academic affair with a collectionist orientation. They have had little contact with the integrationist ELT world, and although they manage to learn its discourse at an academic level, they rely mainly on its extensive literature. They nevertheless continue to be puzzled by the meaning of integrationist ELT. They also find the new discourse of collectionist academic writing in applied linguistics more familiar. Both these groups have to move from a collectionist orientation and learn something of the dominant integrationist ELT discourse in order to get their degrees and get on. They can possibly get by through simply paying lip-service; but they cannot get on with only a collectionist discourse. Their one advantage, however, over the British students, is that there are enough recognisable collectionist characteristics in the applied linguistics content of the course for them to do fairly well.

The British TEFL teachers who have been working in private language schools in Britain and for the British Council or International House overseas may also have degrees in literature or linguistics. However, their careers in a largely commercial integrationist ELT world has taken them well away from academic life. This means that the collectionist academic elements of the course in applied linguistics are very alien. Although they are very articulate in the practical aspects of integrationist ELT discourse, they have to learn from scratch how to re-express this in academic form. They often find academic writing very difficult.

This picture is extremely simplistic. There will be students from other, more varied, backgrounds; and in a modern, shrinking, mobile world, the collectionist and integrationist ELT influences will appear in different balances and combinations with students from both Britain and countries A–Z. Overlaid will be the complexity of the presentation of the course itself. There will be an unavoidable schizophrenia with a integrationist ELT discourse content presented with residues of collectionist academia. The lecturers themselves will have varied combinations of collectionist and integrationist ELT orientations depending on their individual professional–academic biographies. An interesting piece of British university masters classroom archaeology shows the signs of both educational cultures. The furnishing and layout, with a rectangle of tables, belongs to the formal collectionist seminar. On the other hand, the 'tutor' often moves away the front table turning the rest into a traditional integrationist ELT 'U' shape. This is an attempt to remove collectionist notions of the authoritative 'lecture' and also enables the lecturer to walk about close to the students, who have become 'learners', and the students to more easily move around the tables to do 'group-work'. The seminar is thus turned into something very much like an 'active' integrationist ELT language classroom (Table 8.1 and Holliday 1997a). One may therefore move that the part of applied linguistics that has become involved in English language education (on the right-hand part of Figure 8.1) has been ELT-ised through this involvement.

Unravelling the relationships between applied linguistics and English language education, and collectionism and integrationism in the masters classroom is important because the various participants in the masters course represent several of the interests found in English language programmes throughout the world where the management of evaluation and innovation is at issue. The managers of evaluation and innovation need to understand the interests of the programme participants and their own interests. They also need to appreciate how they themselves are participants in the *mélange* of relationships and conflicts that surround the actions within the programme. As in the reflexive ethnographic process, learning about one's own involvement and effect is a large part of the learning about the host environment which is necessary for knowing how and what to evaluate and how and what to innovate (Holliday 1995b). Effective management of evaluation and innovation will require a negotiation and therefore an understanding of these (including one's own) different professional–academic cultures and interests (Holliday 1995a).

3.2   The constituents of dominance

It is therefore necessary to look even further into these relationships. The relationships portrayed in Figure 8.2 and exemplified in the masters classrooms scenario indicate that applied linguistics is somehow involved in a marginalisation of alternative collectionist academic cultures in English language education. This is not to suggest that there is a purposed collusion of academics and integrationist ELT-oriented professionals against the rest of the collectionist world in English language education. Indeed, the masters classroom scenario illustrates that applied linguistics itself has collectionist orientations. That applied linguistics has been building itself as a strong collectionist discipline over the past 20 years can be seen by the rigour which has been invested in the construction of technical standards in academic presentation at postgraduate and doctoral degree level and in academic publishing. This is found particularly daunting by British masters and diploma students who have been used, perhaps, to a more polemic style of academic writing in undergraduate literature. Also, the recent growing concern within applied linguistics, described above, regarding the possibility of imperialism and centre–periphery

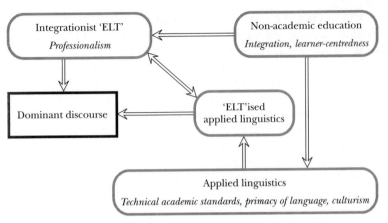

Figure 8.3   Constituents of the dominant discourse in English language education

relations ([C] in Figure 8.2) indicates that the dominant discourse is at least in part addressing the needs of the other side. Applied linguistics is therefore itself collectionist in essence, but, at the same time, those elements of it which are interested in English language education are ELT-ised by the professionalism of dominant integrationist ELT.

What, then, is the basis for the dominant 'other' discourse distinction, and what does it have to do with notions of imperialism and the centre–periphery argument? The basic elements of the dominant discourse are depicted in Figure 8.3. The main constituents are integrationist ELT and the ELT-ised applied linguistics described above. The former brings notions of autonomous professionalism (Table 8.1) suggested in Phillipson (1992) and Pennycook (1989). This professionalism incorporates prescriptive views on teaching and training methodology and the excessive need for accountability and controlled quality characteristic of Thatcherite principles referred to above, which are channelled through a private sector, fine tuned to commercial survival. Behind it are principles of learner-centredness, characterised by a control of the student through manipulative activities and a redefinition of the individual into objective competences (Table 8.1 and Edwards and Usher 1994), in turn derived from skills-based non-academic education growing from the primary (Bernstein 1991) and adult (Edwards and Usher 1994) education sectors.

The influence of non-academic ELT professionalism on the collectionist establishment may have parallels in other professional–academic areas within a dual relationship of discipline-building and profession-building, at least in Britain. Fairclough (1995: 140–1) describes 'the marketisation of discursive practices in contemporary British universities' and the 'pressure for academics to see students as "customers"' bringing a 'transformation in their sense of professional identity' and the incursion of a '"promotional" culture'. Fairclough's conceptualisation of a *technologisation of discourse* – 'calculated intervention to shift discursive practices as part of engineering social change' within institutions (*ibid.*: 3) – fits the invasion of integrationism very well and places such changes within education into a wider change within institutions in 'late capitalist society'.

The integrationist, non-academic movement in education has, however, failed to take over the central formation of disciplines in the university and secondary sectors in Britain, where we see in the 1990s an academic university-isation of institutions which were designed along non-academic lines. However, technologisation of discourse has become an extremely powerful force in the administration of academic subjects, where quality assurance activity has made all academics focus on the definition of the skills, competences and learning objectives (Table 8.1) implicit in the delivery of their subjects, thus creating an integrationist management overlay to the collectionist subject-discipline. There is thus something *like* ELT-isation happening to the whole university establishment. One example of this is the drift towards skills-based coursework in research methodology in doctoral 'programmes' (Rampton 1994).

It is thus the case that the integrationist invasion is not as simple as Western ELT gaining imperialist dominance over English language education in the rest of the world. Neither is it simply a matter of integrationist ELT dominance being part of a more generalised integration–collection conflict within first the industrialised English-speaking West and then carried to English language education in the rest of the world by the expansion of English teaching. The integration–collection conflict can also be seen as part of a wider process of commodification and technologisation of institutions within some industrialised societies.

The other major player in the dominant discourse of English language education, in the more collectionist heartland of applied linguistics, is growing technical academic standards and a primacy given to language and culturism (bottom part of Figure 8.3). By *culturism* I mean a view of culture as a prescriptive, homogeneous set of behaviours and values attached to a particular nation, language group or geographical region. If the language programme scenario in which it takes place is seen as a *mélange* of cultures and interests connected with the collection–integration conflict, the issue of culture becomes central to the management of this scenario. Therefore, culturism coming into English language education through applied linguistics will affect this, and will, I wish to argue, be counterproductive.

3.3   Language and culturism

A particular view of culture has become influential within applied linguistics in its interest in the teaching of culture along with the teaching of language ((c) in Figure 8.1). Here, perceptions of culture are paralleled with perceptions of language; and the concept of target language teaching (L2) is transferred to target culture teaching (C2). The notion of culture is thus modelled on the notion of language and tries to fix culture into families and regional or ethnic identities, in the way that language has been fixed. Thus, *a* culture has an objective identity, based on the physical and conceptual nature of its artefacts, in the same way as *a* language has an objective identity based upon the physical and conceptual nature of its grammar, vocabulary and sound system. It is thus possible to talk of, say, the Japanese culture in the same way as one talks of the Japanese language. Culturism is also predominant in integrationist ELT where there has been a tendency to 'otherise' the cultures of foreign students which do not conform to received notions of participatory communicative language teaching methodology (Holliday 1994b). *Otherisation* is the process whereby the 'foreign' is reduced to a simplistic, easily digestible, exotic or degrading stereotype. The 'foreign' thus becomes a degraded or exotic 'them' or safely categorised 'other'. This way of thinking may have come partly from applied linguistics, but also from tendencies with management studies to address cross-cultural problems within the workplace by looking at national cultural attitudes to work.

Baumann characterises this process as the 'reification of culture' into something which:

> ... seems to connote a certain coherence, uniformity and timeless-
> ness in the meaning systems of a given group, and to operate rather
> like the earlier concept of 'race' in identifying fundamentally dif-
> ferent, essentialised, and homogeneous social units (as when we
> speak about 'a culture'). Because of these associations, ... (it) falsely
> fixes the boundaries between groups in an absolute way.
>   (Baumann 1996: 10–11, citing Lutz and Abou-Lughod)

Of course, this process of reification is not restricted to applied
linguistics. Baumann (1996: 1) is speaking here about British anthropology, in which:

> ethnic reductionism seemed to reign supreme ... (and) whatever
> any 'Asian' informant was reported to have said or done was inter-
> preted with stunning regularity as a consequence of their 'Asianness',
> their 'ethnic identity', or the 'culture' of their 'community'.

This culturism is nevertheless gaining high profile in applied
linguistics, especially in the postmodern vanguard which addresses
the uncertain issues of imperialism fed by the knowledge of 'other'
collectionist professional–academic scenarios ([C] in Figure 8.2).
In the centre–periphery paradigm, 'Western' language (in the
form of English) and culture is seen to be overcoming other world
languages and cultures by means of a hegemonic post-colonialist
imperialism (Pennycook 1994a). Thus, as one language might
be overcome and killed by another through a process of political oppression, so may one culture be overcome and killed by
another through the same process. Pennycook sees the details of
this process through a 'scientific' linguistics which originates in
European rationalisation and standardisation of language (*ibid.*:
121) which, through a 'phonocentric' prioritisation of speech and
phonology, imposes oracy in communicative language teaching
(*ibid.*: 109ff). Thus, Chinese culture, which has had a long tradition of the valuing of written language, is being forced into the
adoption of language teaching in which good lessons have to have
a lot of student-initiated oral activity. Although it is clearly right
to problematise hitherto taken-for-granted aspects of European
and Anglocentric attitudes to language and language teaching,
doing this via a centre–periphery paradigm seems to exacerbate
rather than overcome the rift between a dominant discourse in
integrationist ELT and the other collectionist world. There are
several problems with the culturist point of view implicit in this
paradigm.

(A) It is based upon the cultural reductionism which Baumann (1996) criticises. The notion of 'Western' versus, say, 'Chinese culture' is grossly over-generalised and succeeds not so much in an exposé of an imperialist 'linguicism' as in an other-isation or tribalisation of the victim 'cultures' by reducing them to peripheral, non-thinking automata (Holliday 1994b). Even in the business of cultural generalisation there are studies which reveal the inadequacy of concepts like 'European culture'. Sharpe's work on French primary education (1993, 1995) shows quite clearly that the British and French educational and indeed ideological systems are too different to be easily lumped under one 'Western' cultural heading. The culturist argument which presents an *a priori* notion that centre–periphery differences are set in regional cultures perpetuates an 'us–them' culturist discourse which may be just as powerfully divisive as the phonocentrism it criticises.

(B) Despite its claimed postmodernism, culturism is ironically based upon the same ethnocentric forms in Western nineteenth-century rationalism as the linguicism which it claims to expose (Holliday 1997). Attaching 'culture' to nation, and construing centre–periphery relations in these terms, may itself, like the phonocentrism which Pennycook critiques, be a modernist figment that came with nationalism and a 'methodological nationalist' sociology (Schudson 1994). The fact that such authors as Pennycook and Phillipson are looking to compare the 'West' and the rest of the world – whereas others, outside applied linguistics authors such as Sharpe, are looking to compare education systems closer at hand – reflects the current interests in the respective disciplines of applied linguistics and British education. The former seems preoccupied with the place of English in the world; and the latter is preoccupied with comparisons made between British educational failures and successes elsewhere.

(C) In effect, the world is becoming an increasingly cosmopolitan, multicultural place where cultures are less likely to appear as large coherent geographical entities (Crane 1994). This can be seen particularly with what might have been called 'Muslim culture' which is no longer placeable only within an Asian geographical context. The large-scale settling of Muslim groups within European countries means that 'it is important now to look at these societies as local, as indigenous, not as the other' (Ahmed and Donnan 1994: 5). Hence, the 'Orientalism' upon which Pennycook (1994a) bases much of his argument is 'dated' and 'has itself become a cliché' (Ahmed and Donnan 1994: 5). Baumann's ethnographic study of Southall exemplifies just this state of affairs.

Local people, within a cosmopolitan *mélange*, used the terms 'culture' and 'community' to refer to completely different entities at different times and, dependent on topic, to the extent that a fixed definition of anyone's notion of 'my culture' was very difficult to track down (Baumann 1996: 4–5). It became very apparent that 'stereotyping informants as "belonging to" or even "speaking for" a predefined "community"' could easily result in 'the risk of tribalising people, instead of listening to them, and might end up studying communities of the researcher's own making' (*ibid.*: 8).

(D) A globalist centre–periphery paradigm is itself problematic. Ahmed and Donnan (1994: 3) criticise the 'notion of a hegemonic global culture centre dispensing its products to the world's peripheries' as 'more often assumed than described'. They argue that:

> Even though the same cultural 'message' may be received in different places, it is domesticated by being interpreted and incorporated according to local values . . . Cultural flows do not necessarily map directly on to economic and political relationships, which means that the flow of cultural traffic can often be in many directions simultaneously.'   (*Ibid.*, citing Parkin and Featherstone)

Centres and peripheries do exist everywhere; but it might be more realistic to consider them at an institutional or community level. Wherever there is a dominant discourse, those who do not participate in it will be on the periphery of the centre which the discourse itself has created. At the same time, they may be at the centre of another alternative discourse. The two discourses may then be in centre–periphery junction with each other – and so on. Within curriculum projects in Egypt and India known to this author, it seems clear that although protagonists of integrationist ELT think they are occupying a centre position within their own perception of English language education, local lecturers, who are periphery to the ELT discourse, see *it* as periphery to their centre discourse of collectionist literature and linguistics (Holliday 1994a, 1996b). This means that the alternative 'other' professional–academic cultures ([G] in Figure 8.2) may only be 'other' within the perception of integrationist ELT. Although integrationist ELT has a virtual monopoly of the literature and textbooks in international English language education, collectionism has a strong traditional foothold in English language education outside the English-speaking West where it may perceive itself as 'dominant'.

I wish to contend that the scenarios within English language programmes in which evaluation and innovation are at issue, have therefore become cosmopolitan *mélanges*, similar to Baumann's concept of Southall, in which there are a range of shifting discourses, cultures or interest groups, with complex and differing perceptions of each other (Holliday 1995a). In such an innovative English language programme there is likely to be a similar mix of, and interaction between, integrationist ELT and collectionism as there is in the masters classroom described above. It is therefore likely that an ELT influence, working through materials, syllabi and foreign expertise, will co-exist with collectionist local personnel, students and overall institutional culture. Indeed, that there is a desire to manage evaluation and innovation is itself indicative of an integrationist incursion; and the process of this management will become one of the interactants within the mêlée of cultures within the programme (*ibid.*).

4   Conclusion: coming to terms with discourse

This chapter has painted a complex picture of applied linguistics in interaction with international English language education. Not all the strands are easy to follow, which itself is indicative of the ambivalent position of applied linguistics. On the one hand, it is a traditional academic subject, with high technical standards, fully within a collectionist mould. It is becoming more established as a social science, addressing important issues of language in the full range of social life. At the same time, applied linguistics is deeply involved with English language education, which generates the majority of its work and funding, but which also brings it under the influence of an integrationist, non-academic, instrumental ELT regime. Through this, applied linguistics becomes concerned with areas of professionalism such as methodology, training and the management of evaluation and innovation. In some of these areas, the role of applied linguistics is less clear, where sociologies, anthropologies or politics of English language education may be more appropriate in dealing with macro social issues. Nevertheless, in its ELT-ised form, applied linguistics has become central to a dominant ELT discourse which influences the professional lives of English language educators on a global scale, the majority of whom are in collectionist state education and find the integrationist ELT world difficult to understand or digest. Postmodern sensitivities lead applied linguistics to problematise this state of affairs, but through a centre–periphery paradigm which succeeds only in further tribalising this other collectionist world through an outdated culturism.

4.1 Discourse, evaluation and innovation

A key concept throughout this chapter has been *discourse*. For the successful management of evaluation and innovation it is essential to understand the needs of the collectionist world, whether it be in the English-speaking West or abroad, as well as the effect which integrationist ELT has upon it. A central part of this understanding is through appreciating the nature of the dominant integrationist ELT discourse and how it creates hegemony. This is also one area, from the mainstream social issue branch ((i) in Figure 8.1) where applied linguistics has a great deal to offer. Considerable work has been done by Fairclough (1989, 1995) and others, in critical analysis of technologising discourses in other areas. Similar work is essential in the management of evaluation and innovation, and would be an important contribution to ethnographic approaches.

To escape from the global over-generalisation of a culturist approach, the focus of investigation needs to be 'the institution as a "pivot" between the highest level of social structuring, that of the "social formation", and the most concrete level, that of the particular social event or action' (Fairclough 1995: 37). In other words, an investigation of discoursal and micro-cultural relationships within institutions is a more tangible place to begin than a discussion of global cultural conflict. This focus, in English language programmes, will be cross-cultural, but between professional–academic rather than national cultures, and on the communication conflict between these discourses, evident in the documents (project, curriculum framework, planning, reporting and timetabling) as well as the talk of the day-to-day work of English language education. As Fairclough looks at the apparent consensus of institutional documentation in Britain, we need to look urgently at the apparent consensus of documentation in English language programmes.

At the macro level, applied linguistics and English language education also both need to monitor their own dominant discourse, to enable them to see the same ethnocentricity in their own culturism, just as they have exposed their own linguicism. Only through this self-knowledge and monitoring will the dominant ELT discourse be able to accommodate the discourses of others. To do this, the postmodern vanguard of applied linguistics needs to look deeper than language as a *product* of its activity. It needs also to look at the language *of* its activity, and of its postmodern activity. It might be necessary to go beyond Fairclough's critical discourse approach. Pennycook (1994b) notes that while Fairclough addresses the issue of power in discourse, this is within a Marxist paradigm which focuses mainly on the top-down power of the state, at 'relationships between discourse and society/politics' (*ibid.*: 14). He suggests that a Foucauldian analysis, 'rather theorises discourse as always/already political' (*ibid.*). In other words, the discourse of which we must be aware and evaluate is indeed 'always/already political' and also everywhere in every aspect of our work. This is very clear in the work of Usher and Edwards (1994) in their critique of 'learner-centredness' as a technical discourse of power which pervades every corner of Western education. It is the *internal* imperialisms of our taken-for-granted professional–academic life that we need to watch, just as much as imperialisms that cross oceans. We also need to learn from other professional–academic discourses within the 'other' collectionist world. There is a very developed literature in Indian English studies (e.g. Joshi 1994) which has come of age in a lengthy struggle with concepts of post-colonialism – perhaps an Eastern version of our postmodernism.

Notes

1. It is significant here that some interpretations of 'communicative' in communicative language teaching are independent of language considerations and relate more to a context-sensitive approach to education which might apply also to other subjects (e.g. Allwright 1982, Hutchinson and Waters 1984, Grotjahn 1987).
2. 'Collectionism' here refers to the way in which separate academic subjects are collected together, as opposed to the way in which subjects are integrated in deference to skills in the instrumental culture. *Collectionism* has nothing at all to do with *collectivism*. Some people, on

encountering collectionism, because it represents the 'other', make the Freudian slip of thinking it collectivist – a common folk notion of non-'Western' cultures. The *integrationist–collectionist* distinction is originally used by Bernstein (1991) to refer to different codes in state education. I apply this terminology to a wider variety of circumstances described in a range of literature. There will, of course, be other educational cultures, such as that of *apprenticeship* and perhaps that embodied in traditional Koranic education.

3. The distinction in Table 8.1, of course, represents an ideal typology. Thus, the apparent polarity between, for example, 'skills' and 'knowledge' would therefore in reality be a continuum. Nevertheless, that this is increasingly seen as a polarity is evident in recent discussions about the future of British education. See, for example, the *Times Higher Education Supplement* leader (Opinion 1997), which cites Barnett's distinction between 'operationalism' and 'academicism', which seems to correspond closely to that between integration and collection.

4. This connection between integrationist 'ELT', instrumentalism in education and Fairclough's thesis is entirely my own.

5. International House is an organisation in the British private sector which has franchised schools all over the world. It is a major 'provider' of classes in English as a foreign language to adults, and of English language teacher training.

6. See my discussion of communicative language teaching being taught as a piece of theory within collectionist courses in theoretical methodology, and also of participants in a curriculum project taking the theory of materials design as an important step in keeping 'up to date' but not involving themselves in practice (Holliday 1994a).

9

Evaluating and researching grammar consciousness-raising tasks

ROD ELLIS

Abstract. The purpose of this chapter is to examine the similarities and differences between evaluation and research (specifically, second language acquisition (SLA) research). This is achieved by focusing on a particular type of task for teaching grammar – a consciousness-raising task. A framework for describing and evaluating tasks is provided and illustrated by an evaluation of a consciousness-raising task reported by Hoogwerf (1995). The use of tasks in SLA research is then discussed and illustrated with an account of a study based on a consciousness-raising task (Fotos and Ellis 1991). The similarities and differences between evaluation and research are considered in terms of purpose, planning, data collection, analysis and reporting. Finally, it is argued that task evaluations constitute a kind of action research and can inform task-based research in SLA.

Introduction: evaluation and second language acquisition research

On the face of it, programme evaluation and second language acquisition (SLA) research are very different. This is most evident in the purpose of these two enterprises. Weir and Roberts (1994: 4) characterise the purpose of programme evaluation as follows:

> The purpose of evaluation is to collect information systematically in order to indicate the worth or merit of a programme or project.

In other words, because evaluation feeds directly into policy making or action directed at course improvement, it is an inherently *practical* affair. Stakeholders (i.e. teachers, administrators, aid donors) want to know whether the programme has 'worked' and

220

whether it is worth continuing.[1] Furthermore, each evaluation is focused on a *particular* language-learning situation (i.e. that in which the programme was executed) and is not, except as a matter of interested speculation, concerned with generalisation. There is, perhaps, less agreement regarding the overall purpose of SLA research (see Ellis 1994, ch. 15, for an account of its multifaceted nature) but, following Long (1990: 651), it might be broadly characterised as an activity that involves 'description' and 'explanation': 'The description specifies what is acquired; the theory explains how.' Of course, as Long, goes on to make clear 'description' is not theory-free, while 'explanation' can take many forms, depending on the type of enquiry that is undertaken. Nevertheless, as this definition makes clear, SLA research is ultimately concerned with theory building. As such, it need not be, and indeed often is not, of any immediate practical use. SLA research seeks to develop generalisations about how learners acquire and use L2 knowledge and is only interested in studying particular learning situations insofar as these contribute to such generalisations.[2]

This essential difference in purpose is reflected in further differences. As practical enterprises, evaluations are constrained by contingencies that lie outside the control of the evaluators. Ideally, an evaluation should be planned at the same time as the programme to be evaluated. However, frequently this is not the case. At other times, even when prior planning has occurred, logistical problems or resource limitations make it impossible to obtain the data that are ideally required. As Alderson (1992) points out, evaluations are conducted in 'the real, imperfect and under-resourced world'. As a result 'evaluations are rarely perfect' (Weir and Roberts 1994: 132). Nor, of course, are most research studies. But, in contrast to evaluation, research is typically planned long before it is executed, often in meticulous detail. Researchers, especially educational researchers, may need to adapt the design of a study to take account of local conditions, but they are required to do so in ways that do not seriously imperil the reliability and validity of their research. If the legitimacy of the research is threatened, it can be (indeed, should be) aborted. This option is not usually open to the evaluator.

It is for this reason, among others, that the products of programme evaluations and SLA research need to be judged differently. As Glass and Worthen (1971, cited in Norris 1990) have pointed out, the main criteria for judging the effectiveness of an evaluation are utility and credibility. An evaluation is perceived as being useful if the stakeholders find it helps them to do their job. In the case of teachers, this might mean whether it helps them to improve their instruction; and in the case of aid donors, this might mean whether it helps them to make decisions regarding future financing of a project. To be credible, the evaluation must be seen to have examined those aspects of a programme which are deemed important by the stakeholders, which, as Alderson (1992) and others have been at pains to point out, often varies from one stakeholder to another. SLA research, like all academic research, is judged in terms of reliability and validity. To what extent are the research results replicable? Are the stated conclusions properly supported by the data that have been collected and can they be meaningfully applied to other contexts? There are agreed procedures for determining reliability and validity in SLA research (see, for example, Hatch and Lazaraton 1991). In contrast, the procedures for ensuring the utility and credibility of an evaluation are somewhat less certain, a reflection, no doubt, of its particularistic nature.

Yet, it is easy to overstate the differences between evaluation and SLA for, as Rea-Dickins (1994: 71) notes: 'Distinct boundaries do not operate between educational evaluation on the one hand and educational research on the other.'

The similarities are perhaps most evident where data-collection is involved. The methods by which evaluators collect the data they need to carry out an evaluation are the same as those used by SLA researchers to describe and explain how L2 acquisition takes place. There are four principal methods for collecting data: (1) tests, (2) self-report (e.g. interviews, questionnaires and journals), (3) documentary information (e.g. samples of students' written work) and (4) observation of teaching/learning behaviours. All four methods figure commonly in both evaluations and research.

In this chapter I want to explore more closely the connections between evaluation and SLA. One way in which this can be undertaken is by focusing on language-learning tasks. Task evaluation constitutes a form of micro-evaluation. I shall begin, then, by considering the distinction between macro- and micro-evaluation. This will be followed by an extended discussion of how to carry out a task evaluation, supported by an example of an evaluation of one particular kind of task – a grammar consciousness-raising (CR) task (Ellis 1991). Next, research on language-learning tasks is, more briefly, considered and an example of a research study based on a grammar consciousness-raising task is provided. This affords a basis for comparing evaluation and SLA research. I shall conclude by arguing that task evaluation and task-based research should be seen as complementary activities, each informing the other. I shall also argue that task evaluation offers a promising approach to teacher development as it provides a means by which teachers can investigate L2 learning in their own classrooms and, thereby, develop a 'theory of action' (Schön 1983).

Macro- and micro-evaluation

The bulk of the published work on evaluation in second language education has been macro in nature; that is, it has focused on the evaluation of complete programmes, projects or courses (see, for example, the examples of evaluations published in Alderson and Beretta 1992 and Lynch 1996). As Alderson (1992) notes in his 'Guidelines for the evaluation of language education', there is a wide range of content on which such macro-evaluations can focus, including the outcomes of the programme, the attitudes and opinions of the participants, the impact of the programme within its own context, the process of implementing the programme, the resourcing of the programme and its cost-effectiveness. Alderson expects the evaluator to 'exercise judgement' in determining exactly what is to be evaluated and acknowledges that this will require considerable expertise. More often than not it will be necessary to attend to numerous resource, administration and curricular issues in order to carry out an effective evaluation. Furthermore, a macro-evaluation of the kind Alderson talks about clearly requires a great amount of time. In short, a macro-evaluation is a daunting undertaking, which many (probably most) teachers will not feel able to accomplish on their own account.

   In a micro-evaluation the content and time-scale of the evaluation are narrowed by giving the evaluation a specific focus. The focus may concern an issue related to resourcing (e.g. the efficiency and reliability of publishers in delivering materials that have been ordered for a course), administration (e.g. the organisation of the timetable in a particular school) or curricular (e.g. a teacher's use of correction techniques in a single lesson). Such micro-evaluations lie within the capacity of individual advisers, administrators or teachers to accomplish. They provide a means of addressing specific issues which are important to the stakeholders in a programme, because they are innovatory, because they are perceived as problematic in some way or simply because there is a felt need to obtain information about them. Whereas macro-evaluations are frequently carried out by outsiders (perhaps in conjunction with insiders), micro-evaluations are likely to be instigated and conducted by insiders (sometimes in conjunction with outsiders). As such, it is possible that they will prove more 'significant' to stakeholders, in the sense that they are more likely to be attended to and acted on.

A macro-evaluation can be conceived as being a series of inter-related micro-evaluations. Conversely, through conducting a series of micro-evaluations, stakeholders may be able to put together a macro-evaluation of a complete programme. However, micro-evaluations can also exist independently of a macro-evaluation – that is, a teacher may decide to conduct a single micro-evaluation of his/her teaching with no intention of developing this into a full-scale evaluation of the course. Single micro-evaluations are, perhaps, the more likely given the conditions in which most teachers work.

Task-based evaluation

In this section I want to examine and illustrate one kind of micro-evaluation – task evaluation.

The term 'task' is now widely used in discussions of communicative language teaching (see Long 1985, Candlin and Murphy 1987, and Nunan 1989c). In fact, the term 'task' seems to have become synonymous with 'communicative task' in much of the pedagogic literature. Richards *et al.* (1985: 289), for example, provide this definition of a 'task':

> an activity or action which is carried out as a result of processing or understanding language (i.e. as a response). For example, drawing a map while listening to a tape, listening to an instruction and performing a command, may be referred to as tasks. Tasks may or may not involve the production of language. A task usually requires the teacher to specify what will be regarded as successful completion of the task.

Although, Richards *et al.* do not specifically say so, their examples of tasks imply that the learners' attention will be focused primarily on message conveyance rather than on linguistic form and that, for them, a task is necessarily communicative. It may be better, however, to use 'task' as a generic term for any self-contained pedagogic activity. A task might be described with reference to:

- Objective(s)
- Data
- Procedures
- Intended outcome(s)

On the basis of such descriptions, tasks may then be divided into those that are 'fluency-oriented' and 'accuracy-oriented' (or, of course, those that are both) depending on the kind of objectives, data, procedures and intended outcomes that are involved.

The grammar consciousness-raising task, which is the focus of this chapter, is a special type of task in that it seeks to combine a focus on grammatical form with provision for message conveyance. It attempts this by making grammar (or rather some specific grammatical feature) the content of a task. The students are invited to talk about grammar. A grammar consciousness-raising task, therefore, is directed at (1) developing learners' *explicit* knowledge of grammar (i.e. knowledge *about* a specific grammatical rule rather than ability to use the grammatical rule in production) and (2) developing learners' fluency and catering for incidental acquisition of the L2 by providing opportunities for learners to engage in communication.

In Ellis (1997), I suggest a procedure for evaluating tasks. This involves the following steps:

- Description of the task
- Planning the task evaluation
- Collecting information for the task evaluation
- Analysis of the information collected
- Conclusions and recommendations

To these I would like to add one further step:

- Writing the report

The procedure is potentially cyclical, as the evaluator may decide to act on the recommendations provided by an initial evaluation and, subsequently, carry out a further evaluation.

I shall now discuss this procedure in some detail and illustrate it with reference to an evaluation of a grammar consciousness-raising task carried out by Hoogwerf (1995).

Hoogwerf's students were second-year Japanese college students enrolled in an eight-month College Study Abroad Programme. They were taking a Literature and Writing Class, which met four times a week for 75 minutes. One of the goals of this class was to help the students produce comprehensible prose which was relatively free of typical learner errors. Hoogwerf notes that she habitually carried out evaluations of her teaching in an informal way (e.g. by asking the students to keep class journals) and that what differed in this case was the attempt to formalise the planning and implementation of the evaluation and, of course, to prepare a written report of it.

Description of the task

The description of a task can be carried out in terms of the framework outlined above. 'Objectives' refers to what the teacher hopes to achieve by using the task with a particular group of students. The objectives may be stated very specifically, as in tasks which have a clear linguistic focus (e.g. 'to practise the use of the present perfect continuous tense'), or they may need to be stated more broadly, as is the case of communicative tasks (e.g. 'to give the students opportunities to communicate fluently with each other'). The objectives may also refer to the affective and attitudinal responses of the students (e.g. 'to motivate the students to attend closely to the use of the present perfect continuous tense'). One of the decisions a teacher will have to make is whether to frame the objectives in terms of the task-behaviours the task is intended to elicit (e.g. 'to practise . . .' and 'to give the students opportunities . . .') or in terms of learning outcomes (e.g. 'to develop the students' ability to . . .'). This is an important distinction for, as we shall see below, it is reflected in the kind of task-evaluation that is required.

'Data' refers to the nature of the input made available to the students as part of the task. Various types of input can be distinguished. For example, in some tasks the input is verbal (e.g. a story-completion task) while in others it is non-verbal (e.g. a picture- or symbol-drawing task). Verbal input can be either spoken or written (or, of course, both). Another distinction, of which much is made in the pedagogic literature on tasks, is that between authentic and non-authentic input.

'Procedures' refers to the operations which the students are expected to perform on or with the data. These will vary in the extent to which they call for 'text-manipulation' (i.e. the students operate on the input in very limited ways, as when they are asked to fill in blanks in a sentence) or 'text-creation' (i.e. the students are expected to provide text from their own resources, as in communicative tasks).

'Intended outcomes' refers to what it is that the students are expected to produce as a result of completing a task. For example, students may be expected to write out a list of words or sentences, to produce a ranking according to their personal opinions, to draw a picture, to write a story or to give an oral description of a diagram. There may also be intended 'process features' (i.e. behaviours that the students will manifest in the process of accomplishing a task). For example, students may be expected to negotiate meaning by means of comprehension checks, requests for confirmation and requests for clarification in order to complete a task. As we shall see later, such process features have attracted considerable attention from SLA researchers.

Hoogwerf designed the grammar consciousness-raising task she used herself, and the materials for the task are shown in Figure 9.1. She identified two main **objectives** for the task: (1) to raise the students' awareness of the correct use of subject–verb agreement and (2) to enhance the students' motivation to attend to what was a common, perhaps fossilised, error. The *data* for the task consist of (1) a statement of the subject–verb agreement rule, (2) sentences serving as examples of the rule and (3) sentences to be completed by the students using choices provided. The data are described as 'authentic' by Hoogwerf on the grounds that all the sentences were taken from the students' own free writing. The task *procedures* required the students to (1) read the explanation of the rule and the examples provided and (2) underline the subjects of the sentences and supply the correct verb form from the choices provided. These procedures can be characterised as text manipulation rather than text creation, in agreement with the general requirements of a consciousness-raising task (see Ellis 1991). The *intended outcomes* were (1) the students correctly underline the subjects and (2) they choose the correct verb form to complete each sentence. An intended process feature was that the students would work diligently and with enthusiasm on the task.

SUBJECT–VERB AGREEMENT (using 3rd person subjects)

Rule: With regular verbs (the base form does not change: one need only add -s/-ed/-ing, *et cetera*; no other changes necessary), add -s to singular verbs to match (agree with) 3rd person singular subjects (nouns to which the verbs refer); do not add -s to plural verbs which will agree with 3rd person plural subjects.

Examples:

- The dog (3rd person singular subject) likes (singular verb) running in the park.
- The cats (3rd person plural subject) enjoy (plural verb) lying in the sun.

Practice exercise

I. Underline the subjects of the following sentences and fill in the blanks of each sentence with the correct from of the verb, following the rule above.

   1. As these symptoms _____ (show/shows), victims of childhood sexual abuse frequently suffer from emotional problems for their entire lives.
   2. Children indirectly _____ (explain/explains) what they have experienced.
   3. Officers will often _____ (deal/deals) with this kind of serious incident.
   4. Mothers and daughters both _____ (suffer/suffers) from their lack of communication.
   5. The daughter's fear _____ (force/forces) her to 'tell easy lies' to her mother.
   6. The mother's attempt to 'form' her daughter, _____ (illustrate/illustrates) her desire to control her child.

II. Select one or more of your journal entries or literary paragraphs, and find five examples of subject–verb agreement errors. Correct the errors, using the above rule as a guide. Highlight the corrections and show me.

Figure 9.1   Consciousness-raising task used in Hoogwerf (1995)

Planning the task evaluation

Alderson (1992) suggests that planning a programme evaluation involves working out answers to a number of questions concerning (1) the purpose of the evaluation ('Why?'), (2) the audience ('Who is the evaluation for?'), (3) the evaluator ('Who will do the evaluation?'), (4) content ('What is to be evaluated?'), (5) method ('How?') and (6) timing ('When will the evaluation take place?'). The same set of questions can be used to plan a task evaluation, although, as we have already noted, the process of answering them and thereby planning the evaluation is a lot less complicated.

It is customary to identify two broad purposes for an evaluation (see Norris 1990). In an 'objectives model' evaluation an attempt is made to determine whether the programme has achieved its objectives.. In a 'development model' evaluation the goal is to develop the stakeholders' understanding of the programme, how it has been implemented and what it has achieved, with a view to identifying ways in which it can be improved. A similar distinction, somewhat rephrased, is applicable to task evaluation. In this case, we can ask 'Has the task succeeded in meeting its objectives?' and/or 'In what ways can the task be improved for future use?'. Hoogwerf set about to undertake both an objectives model evaluation and a developmental evaluation. She wanted to know whether her task had 'worked' and how she might improve it.

In a programme evaluation there are likely to be many stakeholders (i.e. aid donors, administrators, teachers, students) with the result that conflicts can arise with regard to whom the evaluation is intended for. However, in a task evaluation the choice of audience is usually much simpler. Hoogwerf conducted her evaluation for two audiences: (1) herself and (2) an academic (the author), for whom she presented a report of the evaluation.

In a task evaluation the *evaluator* is likely to be the teacher who is teaching the task; that is, a task evaluation will be conducted by an *insider* rather than an *outsider*. However, it may sometimes prove possible (and useful) for the teacher-evaluator to invite a fellow teacher to observe the teaching of the task and to participate in the subsequent analysis. In Hoogwerf's case she was the main evaluator. However, she did consult another teacher about the content of the task before she taught it.

One of the most difficult aspects of planning a task evaluation (as in planning a programme evaluation) is choosing what to evaluate. In Ellis (1995) I have suggested that there are three basic choices. In a *student-based* task evaluation, information is collected concerning the students' opinions and feelings about the task they have completed. In a *response-based* evaluation, an attempt is made to determine whether the actual outcomes of the task are the same as the intended outcomes. In a *learning-based* evaluation, it is necessary to determine whether completion of the task has resulted in learning, either in the form of new linguistic knowledge or in terms of enhanced ability to employ specific skills or strategies. These three types of evaluation provide different ways of answering the question: 'Did the task work?' It is, of course, usually much easier to carry out a student-based or a response-based evaluation than a learning-based evaluation, as it is often not feasible and is almost invariably very difficult to demonstrate that learning has taken place. Hoogwerf was relatively ambitious in the choice of content for her evaluation. She decided to try to carry out all three types of evaluation.

The choice of content determines *how* the evaluation is to be carried out. To perform a student-based evaluation it is necessary to obtain information regarding the students' opinions about, and attitudes towards, a task. This can be done most easily by asking them to complete a questionnaire (as in Murphy 1993) or by asking them to comment on the task in their journals. A response-based evaluation requires the evaluator to obtain samples of the 'products' that result from task performance. A learning-based evaluation generally requires the evaluator to obtain information about what a learner knows or can do prior to completing the task and what they know or can do after completing it (i.e. some kind of pre- and post-test). Alternatively, the evaluator might rely on self-report information (e.g. by asking learners to complete uptake charts, recording the new language they think they have learned – see Slimani 1989) or by carrying out detailed analyses of learners' on-task performance to discover whether there is any evidence of learning taking place (see Markee 1994 for an example of this approach). Hoogwerf planned to conduct a student-based evaluation by examining the students' comments about the task in their journals. She planned a response-based evaluation by collecting in the students' written responses to the consciousness-raising task and also through her own observations of the students while they were performing the task. She planned to investigate whether any learning had taken place by examining the students' free writing before and after the task to see if there was any evidence of increased accuracy in subject–verb agreement.

In his discussion of 'timing' (i.e. when to evaluate), Alderson (1992) discusses a number of possibilities; beginning the evaluation before the programme commences, evaluating during the course of the programme and undertaking an evaluation upon completion of the project. These possibilities also arise in task evaluation. Hoogwerf had access to baseline data in the form of the students' free writing before the task. She observed the students carefully while they were doing the consciousness-raising task. She evaluated after the students had completed the task by analysing

LESSON PLANNING	EVALUATION PLANNING
	A. Teacher obtains samples of students' free writing containing obligatory occasions for subject–verb agreement.
1. Teacher introduces the rule and examples to the students, making sure they understand any unfamiliar vocabulary.	
2. The students complete the task. The teacher assists when the students request it.	B. Teacher observes the students' performing the task, paying attention to the time it took them to complete it and the extent to which they concentrated on the task.
3. The teacher goes over the sentences with the whole class, explaining the correct/incorrect choices where necessary.	
	C. Teacher collects in the students' written responses to the task.
	D. The teacher collects in the students' journals one week later.
	E. The teacher collects in samples of the students' free writing completed after the lesson.

– – – – – – designates beginning and ending of the lesson based on the task.

Figure 9.2   An example of lesson/evaluation record (based on Hoogwerf 1995)

their responses to it, their comments in their journals and their free writing subsequent to the task.

Collecting information for the task evaluation

As we have just noted, the information needed to carry out a task evaluation can be collected before, during and after the implementation of the task. It may be useful for the evaluator to draw up a record sheet showing (1) the various stages in the conduct of the lesson, (2) what types of data were collected and (3) when they were collected in relation to the teaching of the task. Figure 9.2 is an example of such a record sheet. The left-hand column shows the various stages of the lesson. The right-hand column indicates those points before, during and after the lesson where the data needed for the evaluation will be collected. Figure 9.2 serves as a record of the lesson that Hoogwerf taught and the various types of information she collected.[3]

Analysis of the information collected

As in research, two ways of analysing data are possible in a task evaluation: one involves a quantification of the information collected while the other involves a more discursive, qualitative presentation. In part, the method of analysis chosen depends on the nature of the data that have been collected. Thus, obviously enough, test scores lend themselves to a quantitative analysis while journal data lend themselves to a qualitative analysis. However, as Brown (1994) has pointed out, it is possible to derive quantitative measures from qualitative data (e.g. to count the number of times students refer to feeling competitive in their journal entries). Teachers with a liberal arts education, which is perhaps the norm for many ESL/EFL teachers, may feel more comfortable with a qualitative analysis. This proved to be so in Hoogwerf's case. Her analysis, presented below, is entirely qualitative in nature.

The student-based evaluation

Evidence of the students' positive response to the task was provided by the students' journals. Many of the students wrote entries asking for similar exercises on other grammatical problems, a response that Hoogwerf says 'totally astounded' her. Hoogwerf discusses the response of one student in some detail:

> One student (not at all given to flattery) commented in her journal entry (about the task) that she had read about subject–verb agreement in her grammar text, but this was the first time she had really paid attention to the difference between plural nouns (add -s) and plural verbs (no -s).

Hoogwerf also notes that the students commented favourably on the helpfulness of working with their own sentences in the task as this made it easier for them to understand the sentences.

Response-based evaluation

Hoogwerf observes that the students 'eagerly attacked the exercise', completing it in less than 10 minutes. She notes that generally her students took a long time to complete exercises they considered difficult or tedious and that the fact they completed this one so quickly, 'in total concentration', was indicative that the task had 'worked'.

Further evidence that the task 'worked' was provided by the students' written answers to the task. These matched the intended outcome in that they were nearly all correct (i.e. the students had underlined the subjects and chosen the correct form of the verbs).

Learning-based evaluation

Hoogwerf reports that 'there was not much difference in the numbers of the students' errors in the students' pre- and post-CR task writing'. However, the top three writers in the class did show substantial gains in accuracy. Hoogwerf reports that these students asked more questions about subject–verb agreement during writing conferences and their first drafts showed more crossing-outs and changes in -s endings.

Conclusions and recommendations

The penultimate stage of a task evaluation is to arrive at a set of conclusions supported by the analysis of the information that has been collected and, on the basis of these, to propose a number of recommendations. Alderson (1992) points out that reaching conclusions can be problematic in a macro-evaluation as different stakeholders may hold very different perspectives on what the data reveal. He also suggests that one of the reasons why evaluation studies are sometimes not utilised is because one or more of the parties involved does not agree with the interpretation of the data. Again, such problems, while not entirely avoided, are less evident in a micro-evaluation, if only because there are fewer parties involved. Hoogwerf, for example, was answerable only to herself and, to some extent, me as the reader and assessor of the report of the evaluation she prepared.

The conclusions and recommendations need to reflect the purposes of the task evaluation. Earlier we noted that there can be two broad purposes, depending on whether the evaluation is based on an 'objectives model' or a 'development model' or both. In the case of an objectives model evaluation, the conclusions need to address the extent to which the task met its objectives. In the case of a development model evaluation, the conclusions need to identify strengths and weaknesses in the design and methodological procedures used to teach the task.

Hoogwerf's task evaluation was concerned with both determining whether the task met its objectives and with identifying ways in which it could be improved. Hoogwerf concluded that she had met both her major objectives; that is, she felt she had succeeded in raising her students' awareness of subject–verb agreement and that she had increased their motivation to attend to fossilised errors in their own writing. She also concluded that, for most students, the task did not result in learning that was immediately manifest in improved production in the students' free writing. She felt, however, that this was to be expected given what is known about interlanguage development (see Ellis 1993 for a rationale of the role of consciousness-raising in language learning). Hoogwerf felt, not surprisingly given her conclusions concerning her objectives, that the task had 'worked'. She points to a number of reasons for its success – the simplified nature of the rule she provided, the provision of clear examples of the rule and, above all, the fact that the sentences in the task were drawn from the students' own writing.

Hoogwerf advances a number of recommendations:

1. Consciousness-raising tasks should be used regularly.
2. If possible, such tasks should incorporate examples from the students' own production.
3. The students should also be asked to undertake a number of follow-up practice activities 'to reinforce the newly-raised consciousness'.
4. Further samples of the students' writing should be studied to determine whether more students were ultimately able to act on their awareness of subject–verb agreement and avoid errors.

Hoogwerf also comments on what she had learned as a teacher from carrying out the task evaluation (see the 'Conclusion' section, on p. 250).

Writing the report

Alderson (1992) views the report of a programme evaluation as 'a critical document'. He points out that it is frequently the only document that stakeholders see. He suggests that sometimes it may be necessary to write different reports for different audiences. In the case of a task evaluation, the report is also an important document, but for a rather different reason. The writing of the report serves as the final step in the process of conducting a *formal* task evaluation. By writing the report, the teacher–evaluator is obliged to make explicit the procedures that have been followed in the evaluation. Also, it helps the teacher–researcher to discover what has been learned from undertaking the evaluation.

Reports of programme evaluations are not typically published; however, there is arguably a case for publishing them. Alderson and Beretta (1992) brought reports of a number of programme evaluations together in a single publication. The case for publishing task evaluations is just as strong (see Rea-Dickins and Lwaitama 1995). It is possible that a journal like the *English Language Teaching Journal* may be interested in articles based on task evaluations, but more likely forms of dissemination are presentations at professional conferences or chapter meetings of organisations such as the Japan Association of Language Teachers (JALT). Crookes (1993) makes a number of suggestions for non-academic publishing of the products of 'action research', of which a task-based evaluation is an example.

Hoogwerf prepared a short paper reporting her evaluation. She submitted this to her course tutor (the author) and received a grade (an 'A') and comments on it. To the best of my knowledge the paper has not been 'published' in any other form.[4]

Researching language-learning tasks

I would like to turn now to how SLA researchers have set about researching tasks, focusing on one study that has investigated a CR task.

Tasks have been widely used by SLA researchers both as a means of eliciting data for descriptive studies and as a means of testing specific hypotheses drawn from theories of L2 acquisition. An example of the former is Long's (1980) study of 'foreigner talk'.

Long asked pairs of native and non-native speakers to perform different tasks, prepared transcriptions of their interactions and then analysed the input and interactional features of the native speakers' talk. An example of a theory-driven study is Pica and Doughty (1985). This study was motivated by theoretical claims that interaction that affords learners opportunities to negotiate meaning will be beneficial to language acquisition (Long 1983). Pica investigated the quantity of interactional modifications (e.g. requests for clarification and comprehension checks) produced when learners were interacting in a whole class environment and in small groups on a task that required a two-way exchange of information.

Tasks have been used to investigate input to the learner, learner comprehension, output produced by the learner and the nature of discourse involving L2 learners. Long's study referred to above is an example of an input-oriented study. Ellis (1987) is an example of a study of learner output. In this study, I asked L2 learners to produce a story, varying the extent to which they had the opportunity to plan their output in order to investigate the effects of planning time on the accuracy with which they used the past tense. Pica *et al.* (1987) used a task that required learners to listen to and demonstrate their understanding of directives in order to investigate the effects of different kinds of input on learner comprehension. Ehrlich *et al.* (1989) analysed the discourse elicited by a task. This study recorded NS–NNS and NS–NS pairs interacting on a picture-drawing task. The interactions were then described in terms of 'a tightly structured discourse' pattern.

It is probably true to say that the research on or with tasks in SLA is still at a programmatic stage. This is evident in two major respects. First, there is no well-established framework of task variables that can be used to inform research systematically – although there have been at least two notable attempts to develop such a framework by Pica *et al.* (1993) and Skehan (1996). As a result, research has tended to select task features for study arbitrarily. Second, despite the fact that the goal of much task-based SLA research is to cast light on how learners learn an L2 (as opposed to the use they make of their L2 knowledge), there have been very few studies that have examined how task-related factors actually influence L2 acquisition. Only recently have a number of studies (e.g. Gass and Varonis 1994, Loschky 1994 and Ellis *et al.* 1994) actually tried to establish cause and effect links between task performance and acquisition.

How is task-based SLA research conducted? The answer to this question will depend in part on the overall purpose of the research (i.e. whether the research seeks to be confirmatory or interpretative) but it is possible to identify a number of general stages involved in planning and carrying out, a task-based study. According to Ary *et al.* (1990) there are five principal stages involved in any research study:[5]

- Selecting a problem
- Formulating a hypothesis
- Selecting a research strategy and developing instruments
- Collecting and interpreting the data
- Reporting the results

These stages will be described briefly. The stages will be illustrated by a study based on a grammar consciousness-raising task carried out by Fotos and reported initially in a paper written for a doctoral course and subsequently published in Fotos and Ellis (1991).

Selecting a problem

Ary *et al.* (1990: 22) comment:

> Researchers begin with a question that they believe deals with an issue of sufficient consequence to warrant investigation. It must be a question for which the answer is not already available, but which the means for finding answers through observation and experimentation are available.

The pedagogic problem that motivated Fotos's study was: 'How could grammar be taught in a manner that was compatible with the principles of communicative language teaching?' This question derived from discussion in language pedagogy and was informed by proposals that I was formulating regarding the role of explicit knowledge in language learning. I argued that one answer to this question might be a task that required learners to talk about grammar (i.e. a grammar consciousness-raising task). Fotos wanted to explore: (1) whether learners could develop explicit knowledge of a grammatical structure efficiently from a consciousness-raising task and (2) whether the talk that centred around the task really was 'communicative' in nature. Fotos felt that these issues could be addressed effectively through an experimental study combined with a descriptive study of learners' performance on a consciousness-raising task.

Formulating a hypothesis

Hypotheses are formulated after reading relevant research and reflecting on it. Formulating a hypothesis requires the researcher to arrive at clear and operationalisable definitions of key constructs.[6]

The relevant literature for the Fotos study consisted of two bodies of research; studies of the effects of formal instruction on L2 acquisition and studies of the kinds of tasks that were most likely to result in the negotiation of meaning believed to be important to L2 acquisition (see Long 1989 for a review of these studies). Fotos (and subsequently Fotos and Ellis in their 1991 paper) did not formulate hypotheses (although, perhaps, they should have done so). Instead, two specific research questions were posed:

1. Is the study of a specific linguistic feature (dative alternation) through performance of a grammar task as effective as study of the same feature through traditional, teacher-fronted grammar instruction, as measured by test scores on a grammaticality judgement test?
2. Is the grammar consciousness-task used (in the study) interactive in the sense that its performance results in the same kind and quantity of interactional adjustments which have been re-pported in other studies based on two-way information-gap tasks performed in pairs/groups?

As can be seen, these questions were constructed in such a way that they provided operationalisations of the key constructs (e.g. 'linguistic feature', 'effective', 'interactive').

Selecting a research strategy and developing instruments

Ary *et al.* (1990: 24) comment:

> Through the process of deductive reasoning, the implications of the suggested hypothesis – that is, what should be observed if the hypothesis is true – are determined.

Fotos deduced that learners would be able to develop an explicit understanding of a grammatical rule as effectively from a grammar consciousness-raising task, where they communicated about the rule in small groups, as they would from a traditional, teacher-centred explanation of the rule. Further, she deduced that if the grammar consciousness-raising task was effective in promoting *communication* about grammar, this would be evident in the kinds of interactional modification which other task-based studies had shown to occur when problems were encountered and negotiated.

These deductions led her to conclude that she required an experimental design in which she compared the explicit knowledge that learners gained from a grammar consciousness-raising task with the knowledge they gained from a traditional grammar lesson. They also indicated that she needed to record the students while they were interacting on the task in order, subsequently, to investigate the extent to which negotiation of meaning had taken place. The study that Fotos finally designed was experimental in nature. It incorporated two experimental groups (a task group and a traditional grammar lesson group) and a control group (who worked on a reading assignment). The subjects were randomly distributed in the three groups. Two sites were used, both involving Japanese college students.

The design of the consciousness-raising task, the traditional, teacher-centred grammar lesson, and of a test for measuring explicit knowledge followed. The task focused on dative alternation (i.e. the use of verbs like 'show' and 'explain', which vary according to whether they allow an indirect object with or without 'to'). The task was constructed as an information-gap task by dividing the 'data' (i.e. the sentences containing grammatical and ungrammatical sentences) into sets and writing them on separate 'task cards'. By pooling their data in groups or pairs the students could complete a 'task sheet' and thereby arrive at an understanding of the grammatical rule. The task materials, which are shown below, were piloted and changes made for the study.[7] The traditional grammar lesson was designed to cover the same 'data' as that included in the task and to last the same length of time it took the students to complete the task. To measure the students' explicit knowledge, Fotos used a grammaticality judgement test (also shown below), which was to be administered before and after the treatment – once immediately after and, again, two weeks later.

CONSCIOUSNESS-RAISING TASK

Task cards: *Students in groups of* four – **one** different card to each member; *students in pairs* – **two** different cards to each member.

1. *Correct*:   I asked my friend a question.
1. *Incorrect*:   She asked a question to her mother.

2. *Correct*:   Kimiko reviewed the lesson for John.
2. *Incorrect*:   Kimiko reviewed John the lesson.

3. *Correct*: The teacher calculated the answers for the students.
3. *Incorrect*: The teacher calculated the students the answers.

4. *Correct*: The secretary reported the problem to her boss.
4. *Incorrect*: The students reported the teacher the matter.

5. *Correct*: I offered her a cup of tea.
5. *Correct*: I offered a cup of tea to the president.

6. *Correct*: The teacher pronounced the difficult word for the class.
6. *Incorrect*: The teacher pronounced the class the difficult word.

7. *Correct*: I bought many presents for my family.
7. *Correct*: I bought my family several presents.

8. *Correct*: She cooked us a wonderful meal.
8. *Correct*: She cooked a delicious dinner for us.

9. *Correct*: She suggested a plan to me.
9. *Incorrect*: She suggested me a good restaurant.

10. *Correct*: The teacher repeated the question for the student.
10. *Incorrect*: The teacher repeated the student the question.

Task sheets: There are some verbs in English which can have two objects. One of the objects is called the **direct object**. The other is called the **indirect object**. An indirect object names the person for whom the action of the verb is performed:

	indirect object		*direct object*
She wrote	**Susan**	a	**letter.**

Different verbs may have the objects in different order, and this is often a problem for students of English. The following exercise will help you understand some confusing verbs.

Directions: In groups, you are to study correct and incorrect sentences using different verbs. You all have different sentences. You must read your sentences to the rest of the group. **Do not show your sentences to the other members! Only read the sentences as many times as necessary!** Work together as a group and decide on the basis of the correct and incorrect sentences where the direct and indirect objects should be located. Complete the following and, choose one student to report your result to the rest of the class. **Please speak only in English during this exercise!**

Verbs: Possible correct order of direct and indirect object.

1. asked: _____

2. reviewed:_____

3. calculated: _____

4. reported: _____

5. offered: _____

6. pronounced: _____

7. bought: _____

8. cooked: _____

9. suggested: _____

10. repeated: _____

Conclusion: Write 3 rules concerning the possible order of objects.

Rule 1: _____

      Verbs which follow this rule: _____

Rule 2: _____

      Verbs which follow this rule: _____

Rule 3: _____

      Verbs which follow this rule: _____

GRAMMATICALITY JUDGEMENT TEST ON DATIVE ALTERNATION

Directions: Read the sentences. Decide if they are correct or incorrect. Write (0) if correct, or (X) if incorrect.

1. _____ She asked the class a question.

2. _____ She asked a question to the class.

3. _____ She reviewed the sentences for Mary.

4. _____ She reviewed Mary the sentences.

5. _____ She calculated John the math problem.

6. _____ She calculated the math problem for John.

7. _____ She reported the police the problem.

8. _____ She reported the problem to the police.

9. _____ She offered her friend a chocolate.

10. _____ She offered a chocolate to her friend.

11. _____ She pronounced the difficult word for me.

12. _____ She pronounced me the difficult word.

13. _____ She bought her friend a dress.

14. _____ She bought a dress for her friend.

15. _____ They cooked a meal for their friends.

16. _____ They cooked their friends a meal.

17. _____ They suggested the children an idea.

18. _____ They suggested an idea to the children.

19. _____ She repeated the word for me.

20. _____ She repeated me the word.

Collecting and interpreting the data

As is usually the case in classroom research, a number of problems arose in collecting the data. Fotos took the role of teacher in one of the sites. However, another teacher provided the experimental treatments in the other site. In this site, the students were not accustomed to group work and may not have been adequately briefed on how to do the consciousness-raising task. The students were not encouraged to use English during group work, with the result that they frequently resorted to Japanese. There were a number of absences in this site when the subjects took the final test. These problems act as potential threats to the validity of the results obtained, at least in one of the two sites. They demonstrate the usefulness of undertaking the same study in two different sites, so that if problems arise in one, the whole study does not have to be abandoned.

Two analyses were undertaken in order to answer the two research questions.

1. Scores obtained by the two experimental groups and the control group on the grammaticality judgement test were compared to determine whether they were meaningfully different. To this end a series of *t*-tests were used, a procedure that might be criticised in that the multiple use of such tests can result in a Type One error (see Brown 1990).

2. A quantitative and qualitative analysis of transcripts of the subjects' interactions was undertaken to investigate the extent and nature of the meaning negotiation that took place during task performance.

A detailed account of the results obtained is not appropriate here (see Fotos and Ellis 1991). The general conclusion, at least for the site where Fotos functioned as the teacher, was that the grammar consciousness-raising task did result in significant and meaningful gains in understanding of the target grammatical point and that these gains were very similar to those resulting from the traditional grammar lesson. Furthermore, the grammar consciousness-raising task was found to promote a similar amount of meaning negotiation to that reported in other studies (e.g. Doughty and Pica 1986), although the quality of the negotiation was limited in a number of respects.[8]

Reporting the results

There are standardised procedures for reporting experimental studies (see the Publication Manual of the American Psychological Association). These concern how to present the literature review, the general statement of the research problem, the research questions/hypotheses, the design of the study, the results, the discussion of the results and the conclusion. The standardised procedures are intended to ensure that the results of the research are clear and that the conclusions based on them are valid.

In the first case, Fotos prepared a paper which she submitted as part of the requirements of a doctoral course she was taking. The paper conformed to the standardised procedures referred to above. Subsequently, she collaborated with the author in preparing the paper for submission to a refereed journal (*TESOL Quarterly*) where, after revision, it was eventually accepted for publication.

Task evaluation and task-based research compared

This detailed discussion of the procedures involved in carrying out a task evaluation and a task-based research study provide a basis for comparing the two types of enquiry. Table 9.1 provides an overall comparison. As this shows, there is an overall similarity in the two types of investigation with both involving the same types of activity concerning how to get started, identifying the focus of the investigation, planning the investigation, collecting and analysing data and preparing a report. However, differences are evident within each of these activities. These differences are discussed below.

Table 9.1   A comparison of task evaluation and task-based research

Stage	Task evaluation	Task-based research
Getting started	The evaluator determines what task to evaluate by identifying an innovative task or a familiar task that has aroused curiosity.	The researcher reviews the research literature to identify and define a research problem.
Focusing the investigation	The evaluator identifies the objectives of the task to be evaluated.	The researcher formulates research questions and hypotheses.
Planning the investigation	Non-intrusive, i.e. the evaluator adapts the evaluation to the classroom conditions.	Potentially intrusive, i.e. the researcher must ensure that the classroom conditions meet the requirements of the research design.
Data collection	Data collection procedures must be compatible with teaching.	Data collection procedures must ensure the data needed to answer the research questions.
Data analysis	The analyses must be sufficient to satisfy the personal needs of the teacher-evaluator, i.e. they can be subjective and qualitative.	The analyses must conform to publicly recognised ways of ensuring reliability and validity, e.g. they must be replicable and statistically sound.
Reporting the investigation	The report should be written in such a way as to be accessible to other teachers, e.g. it can be in narrative form.	The report must be written to conform to agreed conventions for research papers, i.e. 'terse accounts' are required.

One obvious difference concerns the nature of the starting point. In the case of task evaluations, the starting point involves the evaluator, usually a teacher, choosing a task that he or she wishes to evaluate. The choice is motivated by the need to investigate whether a particular task 'works' for a particular group of learners and it is, therefore, governed primarily by practical considerations. Thus Hoogwerf chose to investigate a grammar consciousness-raising task because she felt that this kind of task might help her deal with common errors in her college students' written work. In contrast, the starting point of task-based research is a theoretically directed problem. Fotos chose to investigate a grammar consciousness-raising task because she wanted to find out whether this kind of task provided a way of teaching grammar in the context of communicative language teaching. Fotos was concerned with trying to conduct research that would result in a *general* solution to a pedagogic problem – one that would be applicable, potentially at least, to situations other than that in which she was researching.

Following on from this essential difference, are a number of other differences. The task evaluator needs to consider the *objectives* of the task, because these will guide the information that will need to be collected. In contrast, the task-based researcher is concerned with formulating a *hypothesis*, derived from the research problem, which can be tested by investigating performance on a task. The task, therefore, constitutes an operationalisation of the treatment referred to in the hypothesis. Thus, where Hoogwerf's task had a pedagogic rationale, Fotos's task had a theoretical one. In both task evaluation and task-based research, however, objectives and hypotheses guide what is actually investigated.

Major differences arise in the planning stages of an evaluation/research study, particular if the research is experimental in nature.[9] The task evaluator must take the classroom as he or she finds it. Indeed, to attempt to 'fix' the classroom in some way (e.g. by giving instructions in the students' L1 when they are normally given in the L2) would invalidate the task evaluation, the purpose of which is to discover whether a task works in the *normal* classroom environment. In contrast, it is often necessary for the researcher to try to control or manipulate classroom variables, and failure to do so can imperil the research. Thus, in Fotos's study, the failure of the teacher in one of the sites to explain the task instructions in the subjects' L1, led to doubts about the validity of the results obtained. Sometimes, the need to control classroom variables may conflict with what is deemed to be desirable pedagogic practice, a problem that does not arise in task evaluations.

Linked to this is a more general difference. Task evaluations must occur in the context of everyday teaching. As such, they must not intrude unduly on teaching. This means that there are practical constraints on what information the evaluator can collect. As Hopkins (1985: 41) succinctly puts it: 'the teacher's primary job is to teach, and any research method should not interfere or disrupt the teaching commitment'. It is this 'teaching commitment' that makes it so difficult to conduct a learning-based evaluation. The teacher may feel that asking the students to complete the pre- and post-test typically required for a learning-based evaluation would consume too much time and perhaps create anxiety in the students. One of the praiseworthy features of Hoogwerf's evaluation is that she was able to obtain the information she needed for her learning-based evaluation without disturbing the pattern of her normal teaching. In contrast, experimental researchers such as Fotos feel obliged to use pre- and post-tests, and even ethnographic researchers need to ensure that they have adequate data for their purposes. The effects of collecting data for research purposes on the pedagogic climate of the classroom raise ethical issues that are rarely considered. In short, where evaluation seeks to be non-intrusive, research is necessarily intrusive.

A possible, but not necessary, difference exists with regard to how the data are analysed. I would like to argue that while it is desirable that the task evaluator carries out detailed and rigorous analyses of the information that has been collected, this is not strictly speaking necessary. A task evaluation is undertaken for what are essentially *personal* reasons (i.e. the evaluator wants to discover something about his or her own teaching), whereas research is carried out with the express purpose of making the results and conclusions public. Arguably, then, the task evaluator needs to carry out analyses in a way and to an extent that he or she feels are sufficient to perform the intended evaluation. The researcher, however, is obliged to conduct analyses that will ensure the reliability and validity of the study. Comparing Hoogwerf's and Fotos's papers, one of the most conspicuous differences exists with regard to the depth of detail of the analyses that were carried out. Hoogwerf is content to be qualitative and subjective, whereas Fotos is detailed and explicit, striving for objectivity.[10]

It is also possible to suggest that different criteria apply to the reporting of a task evaluation and a research study. In the case of a task evaluation, the key criterion is perhaps 'accessibility' (i.e. whether the evaluation is reported in a manner that other teachers can easily read and understand). Crookes (1993) suggests that action research (of which task evaluation is an example) needs to be presented in the form of 'teacher-oriented reports' that are discursive, subjective and anecdotal in style. In the case of a research study, however, it is necessary to provide what Clarke (1994) describes as 'terse accounts'. These follow the formal conventions for writing research papers required by academic journals. Indeed, if these conventions are flouted, the paper runs the risk of being rejected by editors of journals. However, these conventions are currently being challenged by critical research practice and alternative forms of research reporting have been proposed (see, for example, Canagarajah 1996) which are closer in format and style to the type of report Hoogwerf prepared.

In pointing out these differences it is important not to lose sight of the essential similarities between task evaluation and task-based research. Both involve empirical enquiry that requires systematic, self-conscious and rigorous reflection.

Conclusion

This chapter has examined some of the differences that exist between evaluation and SLA research, focusing on grammar consciousness-raising tasks. The purpose of identifying these differences has not been to demonstrate that evaluation and research are completely different activities – they are clearly similar in many respects – but rather to suggest that both constitute valid ways of investigating the classroom. I wish to conclude by pointing out how the two types of enquiry can mutually inform each other and by arguing that more attention needs to be paid to task evaluation as it provides a way in which teachers can investigate their own classrooms and construct a 'theory of action'.

Task evaluations and task-based research studies are best viewed as two different types of empirical enquiry into L2 classrooms. Each has the capacity to inform the other. Clarke (1994) has argued that SLA is of little value to teachers because it has typically excluded the classroom from consideration. This view is mistaken. Firstly, there has been a substantial amount of research in and of class-rooms (see Chaudron 1988 and Ellis 1990). Secondly, SLA research can serve as a useful *source* of ideas about teaching and of techniques for evaluating. Thus, task-based research can provide the teacher-evaluator with interesting tasks to evaluate. For example, Doughty (1991) developed an interesting computer-based task for raising learners' awareness of how relative clauses function in written texts. Doughty's study suggests that this kind of task is effective in promoting acquisition of grammatical structures. Teachers might like to try out this computer-based task and evaluate its effectiveness with their own students. A study of task-based SLA research may also assist teachers in planning task evaluations and in analysing data, particularly if they wish to employ quantitative techniques. However, teacher-evaluators should not feel the need to emulate researchers. As I have pointed out above, their primary duty is to teaching and the 'research' they carry out must be compatible with their teaching goals.

It might be felt that because task evaluators have no obligation to ensure the reliability and validity of their evaluations, their work has little to offer researchers. Researchers, it might be argued, should not pay attention to 'poor research'. Such a view is blinkered, however, particularly if researchers hope to see their research applied to the classroom. A recurring criticism of 'pure research' is that, because it is necessarily concerned with establishing what is *generally* true, its findings may not be relevant to particular teaching situations (see van Lier 1994b, for example). It follows that the findings of pure research cannot be directly applied, no matter how 'good' the research is. As Cronbach (1975: 125) puts it: 'When we give proper weight to local conditions, any generalization is a working hypothesis, not a conclusion.' It follows, therefore, that teachers need to investigate for themselves whether a generalisation is applicable to their own classrooms.

One way in which this can be accomplished is by evaluating tasks, as Foster (1993) illustrates. She observed that the bulk of research which has investigated communicative tasks has taken place under laboratory conditions and wondered whether similar results would be obtained under real classroom conditions. She carried out a small-scale study (in effect, an evaluation) of a number of tasks in a real classroom situation. Her findings were surprising. Contrary to the results reported in the task-based research, she found relatively few instances of meaning negotiation. Foster suggests that, in the context of the classroom she was investigating, the students viewed the tasks as 'fun' and, as a result, were not inclined to persist in solving communication problems when they arose. Foster's study indicates the importance of teachers testing out the results of research in their own classrooms and demonstrates how a task evaluation can accomplish this. Researchers as well as teachers can benefit from this symbiosis of research and evaluation. The findings of evaluations can be used to hone the theoretical frameworks that inform their research, thereby affording hypotheses for future study. For example, Foster's study suggests that task-based researchers need to pay more attention to learners' perceptions of what they are doing when they perform tasks, as these may influence their performance on them. Whereas researchers reify, abstracting away from the real-life complexity of classrooms, evaluators must struggle to take account of the curricular, methodological, social and personal factors out of which teaching acts are born (Prabhu 1992). It is for this reason that the enquiries of researchers and evaluators should be seen as complementary.

Irrespective of whether task evaluations have anything to offer the researcher, they are potentially of great value to the teacher. I would like to conclude by pointing out some of the advantages.

1. Task evaluation serves as a practical way of undertaking action research. Nunan (1990b) has pointed out that teachers often experience a number of difficulties with action research; for example, they are often unable to identify an investigatable 'problem' and they are frequently overly self-critical of their own teaching. Task evaluations may avoid both of these obstacles. The starting point is the identification of a 'task' rather than a 'problem', which teachers may find easier. Also, because the focus of the evaluation is a 'task', teachers may be less inclined to be too self-critical of their own teaching. Certainly Hoogwerf did not appear to experience either of these difficulties.

2. Clarke (1994) has argued persuasively that teachers need to keep their own counsel regarding what works and does not work in the classroom, rather than turn to researchers. While I would refute his contention that research has little to offer teachers, I would agree that teachers do need to ascertain for themselves what proposals are workable in their own classrooms. Task evaluation constitutes a means by which teachers can go beyond the kind of impressionistic adjudications they habitually make.

3. Teachers frequently have a fear of research. Wright (1992) notes that teachers feel that research is not part of their professional life and are often alienated by it and avoid it. Teachers may also be wary of evaluations that are conducted by outsiders. Task evaluation, however, constitutes a kind of insider research that threatens teachers less, if only because it encapsulates what they attempt to do informally in the course of their everyday teaching and because they remain in charge of whatever 'action' is to be undertaken as a result of the evaluation.

4. Dufon (1993) has observed that TESOL researchers have tended to be too concerned with mastering the technical aspects of research to have paid adequate attention to ethical aspects. I would argue that ethical problems are inherent in what researchers do because their work frequently requires them to interfere with normal teaching. In contrast, for a task evaluation to be trustworthy, it must be carried out within the context of the teacher's standard practice. Such an evaluation is, therefore, inherently ethical.

5. Task evaluations provide a means by which teachers can become 'reflective practitioners' (Schön 1983). Teachers, organise their tacit knowledge of teaching into 'theories of action' which can be 'in use' (i.e. are revealed in practice but cannot be articulated) or 'espoused' (i.e. are explicit and describable). Schön argues that theories of action are developed through 'reflection on action'. Task evaluation can serve as a means by which teachers can reflect on their action and, thereby, develop their theories of action and make them more explicit.

6. Task evaluations may also help to bolster teachers' own self-esteem and sense of professionalism. Hoogwerf's comments on her evaluation testify to this. She observes that the evaluation helped to reinforce her confidence in her ability to identify worthwhile tasks for her students to do, that an evaluation which follows a formal, systematic approach provides the back-up a teacher may need to influence future curricular decisions and that it might also help to convince other teachers that they should try out the task in their own classrooms.

Task evaluation, then, provides a means by which teachers can develop 'an understanding of the L2 classroom . . . as a culture in its own right' (Wright 1992: 192). One caveat is in order, however. A task evaluation, although not as demanding as a programme evaluation, is still time consuming. It adds to the work of busy teachers and is clearly not something that can be undertaken every day. Hopefully teachers, like Hoogwerf, will find the effort worth while.

Notes

1. Evaluations often have 'hidden agendas' (Alderson 1992). Also, there may be different perceptions among the stakeholders regarding the purpose of an evaluation. It might be argued that hidden agendas and different perceptions are characteristic of research, but it is probably true to say that they are less so, perhaps because research deals with 'subjects' rather than 'stakeholders' and is not committed to 'action'.
2. It has been pointed out that the disjunction between 'theory' and 'practice' is precisely what makes SLA of limited relevance to language pedagogy. Whereas SLA is concerned with the general, pedagogy (of which evaluation is a component element) is necessarily concerned with the particular. See van Lier (1994b) and Clarke (1994) for discussions of this important difference.
3. In fact, it may also prove useful if a similar sheet to that shown in Figure 9.2 is used for purposes of summarising the planning of the lesson/evaluation. Of course, the contents of such a planning sheet and of the subsequent record sheet may vary, as the teacher-evaluator may find it necessary to adapt the lesson and/or the evaluation procedures while the task is in progress. The planning and record sheets can themselves serve as useful data in an evaluation.
4. Ideally, the conclusions and recommendations derived from a task evaluation need to be made 'actionable'. Unfortunately, I have no way of knowing what effect Hoogwerf's task evaluation had on her subsequent teaching.
5. It is not intended to suggest that researchers invariably follow these stages in sequence. As Ary *et al.* (1990) point out, the stages overlap, with much moving back and forth from one stage to another.
6. In this respect, researching tasks is not so different from evaluating tasks. The 'objectives' of a task can be viewed as hypotheses regarding what behaviours learners will engage in while performing the task or what they will learn as a result of completing it. However, such 'objectives' are not formulated with reference to previous 'research' or to formal theory but rather based on teachers' practical experience of teaching.
7. Fotos and Ellis (1991) eliminated sentences in the pilot task that were unproblematic to the students and that, therefore, did not result in any negotiation of meaning.

8. The negotiations consisted of the subjects asking whether a sentence was correct or incorrect, asking for repetition of a sentence or part of a sentence or making a comprehension check. There was little extended negotiation and not much evidence of reformulated output.

9. The differences between evaluation and research are less evident in the case of interpretative classroom research, as one of the goals of this kind of research is to understand classrooms as they naturally function. However, the very fact that such research involves an outsider is likely to have at least some impact on classroom behaviour. So, too, are the means that are typically used to gather data in interpretative research (e.g. audio or video recording lessons).

10. In this respect, a task evaluation may differ from a project evaluation. Where the results of an evaluation are to be used to determine actions that are likely to affect others (as is the case in outsider project evaluations) there is obviously a need to ensure that the analyses carried out are reliable and valid. However, when an evaluation constitutes a form of action research (as is the case in task-based evaluations) the need for reliability and validity takes second place to utility. In a task-based evaluation the key question is: Does the evaluation yield insights that are of value to the teacher in his or her teaching?

10

Linking change and assessment

MICHAEL FULLAN

Evaluation of educational change and improved performance have had a rather troubled history. Either there has been little or no evaluation of educational innovations, or schemes have been put in place which are formalistic, yielding invalid data and/or of limited clarity about what should be done to move forward. In this Chapter I argue that we must cast the evaluation problem in more generic change concepts if we are to produce systems that have an in-built capacity to monitor and act on performance data. I do this in three ways: firstly, by raising five key ideas and insights about *change and the change process*; secondly, by focusing more deeply on the nature and impact of *collaborative work cultures*; and, thirdly, by reframing the relationship between *schools and their environments*.

Key change ideas

I have written elsewhere about systematic frameworks and factors affecting educational change (Fullan 1991, 1993). Here I would like to bring forward and highlight five key ideas which are very much associated with our capacity to understand the essence of change, and thus our ability to figure out the role of evaluation in the change process. These ideas are:

- There is no panacea or model of change.
- Change is a highly personal psychological process.
- Resistance and conflict are positively necessary.
- Improving relationships is the key to successful change.
- Emotion and hope are crucial motivators.

No panacea

The management of change business is huge and still rapidly growing. Leaders are desperate for solutions that work, and for that reason they are susceptible to fads. Evans (1996: 146–7) states it well in his characterisation of the life cycle of leadership theory:

1. It begins outside of education, developed by political scientists from studies of gifted historical figures or by management experts from studies of gifted business leaders (no one would ever think of basing a leadership model on studies of gifted school administrators!).
2. It gains favor in corporate America and comes to be a hot concept in management writing.
3. As it nears the apex of its influence, someone decides to apply it to education, even if it has little apparent relevance to schools.
4. It grows hot in educational circles as it begins to cool in the corporate world, where it is showing hitherto unnoticed weakness.
5. It is often misapplied in education, either through slavish rigidity (failing to modify the model to fit schools' unique characteristics) or false clarity (adopting the form of the innovation but not its true substance).
6. Well after it has lost its cachet among business leaders, it lingers on in vestigial form in schools and schools of education, until its popularity finally subsides there, too.

Or, as Micklethwait and Woolridge observe in their book on 'making sense of management gurus' (1997: 15), the advice is plentiful, but often contradictory:

For every theory dragging companies one way, there are two other theories dragging it in another. One moment, the gurus are preaching total-quality management – and the importance of checking quality and reducing defects; the next, they are insisting that what matters is speed (which means being a little less painstaking about checking quality). One moment, they are saying that what gives a company its edge is its corporate culture, the more distinctive the better; the next, they are ordering companies to become more 'multicultural' in order to be able to hold a mirror up to the rest of society. One moment, companies are urged to agree upon and then follow a single strong 'vision'; the next, they are being warned that they live in an 'age of uncertainty' where following any single vision can be suicidal. Most management theorists have not worked out whether it is important to be global or local, to be big or small, to be run in the interests of shareholders or stakeholders. Usually, they end up telling managers to do both.

An even more basic problem is that even the best proven ideas do not, indeed cannot, tell you how to get there, because that requires working in specific settings with their unique combination of factors and personalities that play themselves out in unpredictable ways. The first order of business, then, is to give up the search for the silver bullet, and to realise that one must work through problems on one's own, with guidance but no certainty from other sources. The uncertainty about how to get there is endemic in complex systems.

Change is personal

This is a theme that I have pursued over the past quarter of a century. I have said at the outset that the *meaning* of change on the part of each and every participant is the *sine qua non* of effective change, and that people must be engaged in a process of altering their behaviour (skills, practices) and beliefs (rationale, understanding) *vis-à-vis* new directions. It is only when individuals find themselves experiencing a process of redoing (behaviour) and rethinking (beliefs) that we can expect quality innovations to have their desired impact. From a strategy and an evaluation perspective, the focus must be on what conditions and processes motivate and sustain this kind of behaviour/beliefs deliberation.

Resistance and conflict are positively necessary

Leaders are urged to foster experimentation, but what if staff appear uninterested in trying new things? Performance appraisal schemes are based on the need for continuous growth, but what if they function to demotivate rather than stimulate learning? In order to have any chance of grappling with these dilemmas we must learn to appreciate that resistance and conflict can be positively essential for successful change. Gitlin and Margonis (1995: 386–7) examined teacher's reaction to new policies and concluded:

> We believe teachers' initial expressions of cynicism about reform should not automatically be viewed as obstructionist acts to overcome. Instead, time should be spent looking carefully at those resistant acts to see if they might embody a form of good sense – potential insights into the root causes of why the more things change the more they stay the same.

Similarly, homogeneous cultures, almost by definition, have less conflict than heterogeneous cultures. But the former is also more stagnant while the latter contains many more seeds of breakthrough. Let us use a hypothetical example which contrasts the old with a newer way of approaching potential differences of view. Assume that you are a principal who is strongly committed to the increased use of technology. The hypothetical old way of thinking would approach the problem along the following lines:

> I am sure that technology is one of the keys to the future for my students; parents support it. I know that some teachers favor it, but others are going to be Luddites. How can I get some teacher leaders to support it? What kind of external resources and expertise can I generate to provide support and pressure to move forward? Maybe I can secure a few transfers and new appointments. My whole approach is advocacy and co-optation into an agenda that I am sure is right. (Fullan 1997: 222)

In the new way:

> I am equally convinced that technology is critical, but I approach it differently. Cutting the story short, let's say that I am having a staff session in which I am about to show a video segment that portrays a highly successful technology-based school in action. Instead of showing it to make my case, I present it differently. I randomly ask one half of the staff to view the video with a 'positive lens' noting what might be in it for us; I ask the other half of the staff to view it 'negatively or critically' by identifying what might be problematic or potentially negative for us. If I am sincere, I have legitimized dissent. I have made it easy for staff to speak up about concerns (which would come out later anyway in more subtle and/or inaccessible ways). I listen carefully, suspending my own advocacy, because I know that some fundamental problems will be identified and that people's fears, real or imagined, will need to be examined carefully. This information may lead me to go back to the drawing board or to work with staff on some preconditions that would have to be addressed; or to proceed into action on a 'start small, think big' basis, or to abandon high-profile technology in favor of a different approach. (Fullan 1997: 222)

Thus, it is the counter-intuitive approach – legitimise dissent and make it easy to raise objections – that is most likely to uncover problems that will be necessary to address in rethinking and/or in moving in new directions. The realisation that resistance and conflict are essential for success raises whole new questions relative to the motivation for and assessment of performance.

Improving relationships is the key

This can be said succinctly. No amount of political advocacy or even technical support will generate success unless *relationships improve*. If I had to identify one and only one indicator of successful implementation it would be whether or not relationships among participants improved. To motivate change we must develop better relationships.

Emotion and hope

Educational change processes are an emotional roller coaster. Yet until very recently the role of emotions on change was not part of our change theories (see Fullan 1997). Later on I will return to the question that educators must learn 'to go deeper' in developing emotional intelligence in themselves and in their relationships (Goleman 1995) and must examine the role of hope, especially under conditions that do not call for it. Hope in this sense is unwarranted optimism. Connecting hope with the other four key ideas is part of the pathway to constructive change.

Collaborative work cultures

There have been at least two decades of research on the role of school cultures in educational reform. It starts with the observation that school cultures are traditionally *individualistic* in which teachers keep to themselves rather than work together – schools in which innovation fails to happen or does not spread; and in which problems persist behind classroom doors and school walls. It continues with the discovery that some schools are strongly collaborative. Teachers in these schools work together for the common good under conditions of shared trust and joint work and learning, focusing on solving problems and making continuous improvements (see Fullan and Hargreaves 1996).

Along the way we discovered that changes in school governance do not by themselves make a difference because they alter *structure* not *culture*. We and others found that restructuring, like site-based management and other role and organisational change, do not translate into cultural and classroom change that would impact teachers and students. We concluded that 'reculturing' must precede or at least lead 'restructuring'.

Newmann and Wehlage (1995) provide a concise confirmation of these findings in their study of over 800 schools engaged in school reform. Those schools that were more successful (defined as making a positive difference in student learning and performance) were characterised by greater internal organisational capacity to work and learn together, labelled by the authors as *Professional Communities*. These professional learning communities (or collaborative work cultures) worked better because they generated a school-wide sense of purpose, collaborative activity and collective responsibility for each other and for students' learning.

Professional community affected classroom performance which, in turn, affected student learning – all of which were dynamically developed as the school assessed its performance on an ongoing basis.

As noted above, one further critical finding in our work on the management of change in organisations, as referred to above, are the roles of diversity and conflict. Time and again we and others have found that conflict and differences are not only inevitable, but are an essential and valuable part of productive change processes (Fullan 1993, Maurer 1996). Effective leaders encourage differences of opinion, especially early in the change process, see resistance as something to be engaged in and learned from, and respect diversity. Collaborative work cultures simultaneously value the group and the individual. Skills of collaboration and skills of conflict management go hand in hand.

Collaborative work of the kind described in the case studies creates a culture, as Macdonald (1997) observes of 'lateral accountability', which 'puts more peer pressure and accountability on staff who may not have carried out their fair share, but it can also ease the burden on teachers who have worked hard in isolation, but who felt unable to help some students' (Newmann and Wehlage 1995: 31). In other words, the creation of collaborative cultures at the same time establishes evaluation dynamics (peers working with each other, focusing on performance) that is far more powerful than remote hierarchical schemes. This is not to say that external standards are unimportant, as we will see in the next section.

Schools and their environments

In our *What's Worth Fighting For* series, my colleague Andy Hargreaves and I have been analysing conditions inside and outside the school, and making action recommendations (Fullan 1997, Fullan and Hargreaves 1996, Hargreaves and Fullan, in press). In the previous section, I referred to *What's Worth Fighting For in Your School* (Fullan and Hargreaves 1996), in which we argued that the walls of the classroom are (and should come) tumbling down, metaphorically speaking. In *What's Worth Fighting For Out There*, we extend the analysis to say that the walls of the school are (and should come) tumbling down (Hargreaves and Fullan, 1998).

These days the 'out there' is 'in here', as school boundaries are more permeable and transparent, and as the matter of how schools are performing is much more visible. For that reason we suggest that teachers and principals must reframe the relationship with the outside including new approaches to parents and community, businesses, the media, state policies, universities and other agencies. In this chapter, I take only one of these components to illustrate this new line of thinking and action – namely: How should schools deal with state policies related to assessment of student learning?

It is crucial to understand that assessment of student achievement, to be effective, must have a subsequent impact on how the school and classroom are functioning. Assessment schemes must provide some degree of accountability to the public and political decision makers, but they must also serve as a tool for improvement. It is this latter role of 'assessment for learning' that I address here (see Earl and LeMahieu 1997).

Assessment systems for student learning must be both sound (the formal element) and organised for teacher sharing and learning. In the same way that weighing a pig does not make it fatter, testing *per se* does not affect student learning. As Linda Darling-Hammond (1995) so clearly observes, the purposes and uses of tests are just as important as their nature and content.

Darling-Hammond argues that assessment systems must focus on equity of learning as well as enhancing teaching and learning and that at least five conditions are necessary to make testing effective as a lever for school change: (a) they must report on and help us understand performance; (b) they must involve teachers in the process; (c) there must be room for choice; (d) they must be authentic and rich (i.e. get at how students think as well as how much they know); and (e) they must provide an opportunity for teachers to learn.

The value of tests, then, is to help track performance and to provide rich information that will help shape curriculum and teaching. Assessment systems in this sense should guide and lead local practice. Echoing the themes discussed earlier, Darling-Hammond says that assessment systems are not 'testing days' but need to be embedded in the curriculum as practised. They are, above all, a means for developing shared commitment and action for school-wide change focusing on more challenging goals.

This, of course, is a tall order. In most change efforts, we find that the evaluation and enquiry habit necessary for reform are the last and most difficult aspects to be addressed (Walter and Duncan Gordon Charitable Foundation 1995). Thus, one of the most challenging changes required is to create mechanisms (such as School Quality Reviews) and to embed norms of school-wide enquiry, reflection and corresponding actions in relation to indicators of performance.

Testing will not make a difference until large numbers of teachers engage in this process together. As Earl and LeMahieu (1997: 162–3) put it:

> The notion that assessment is part of learning is deeply rooted in a constructivist theory that learning is a process of taking in information, interpreting it, connecting it to existing knowledge or beliefs, and, if necessary, reorganizing understanding to accommodate that information (Shepard 1997). If people learn by constructing their own understanding from their experiences, assessment is not only part of learning, it is the critical component that allows the learners and their teachers to check their understanding against the views of others, and against the collective wisdom of the culture as it has been recorded in the knowledge, theories, models, formulas, solutions, and stories that make up the curriculum and the disciplines. The alternative is for learners to be passive and uncritical recipients of disconnected (and often conflicting ideas), without the skills to challenge or judge for themselves.

This means that teacher development must include new accountability skills and habits that enable teachers to:

- look closely and deeply at student work
- develop shared notions of quality in students' performances or products
- determine what constitutes adequate evidence of quality, and ultimately

■ reflect upon the learning experiences that can produce the desired performances.

(Earl and LeMahieu 1997: 165)

I hope it is clear that teacher appraisal and development and student learning and development must go hand in hand. Collaborative cultures embed teacher learning into the very culture of the organisation. Appraisal policies are one means of buttressing development, but they must be integrated with interactive cultures. Otherwise they will have only a perfunctory presence.

Teacher and student learning require both intra-school reform (namely, collaborative work cultures) and new orientations to the external policy system. It is revealing to note that Newmann and Wehlage (1995) found that successful schools incorporated both internal and external capacities. With respect to the external they state (1995: 4):

> We found that external agencies helped schools to focus on student learning and to enhance organizational capacity through three strategies: setting standards for learning of high intellectual quality; providing sustained, schoolwide staff development; and using deregulation to increase school autonomy.

At the same time, external assessment regulations present a problem for teachers as the tests are often superficially interpreted and used punitively. Our advice in *What's Worth Fighting For Out There*, is that educators must do precisely the opposite to what they feel like doing. Instead of retreating and otherwise being defensive, they are better to become more proficient in assessment practices, and to enter the fray. Consistent with recent change insights, it is more effective, albeit counter-intuitive, to 'move towards the danger' and to engage in the debate and dialogue. This way educators are more likely to learn to hold their own. In any case, assessment is here to stay and there is no way to avoid it.

Conclusion

As long as change and evaluation are detached from each other we cannot mobilise the data and motivation to make improvements. The key to evaluations that make a difference involves creating work conditions – collaborative cultures – that build in lateral accountability through day-to-day interaction focusing on teacher and student work and performance.

At the same time, external standards and frameworks of pressure and support must be established. On the one side, policy frameworks are needed that focus on the qualifications and capacities of teachers as well as the performance of students. On the other side, schools need to embrace external frameworks and associated forms of support and professional development. In short, until the profession of teaching changes in fundamental ways, evaluation will never have its intended impact.

11

Eavesdropping on debates in
language education and
learning

ELLIOT STERN

Why build bridges?

To be an evaluator in Great Britain today inevitably requires the
building of many bridges across many disciplinary divides. I first
encountered language teachers with an interest in evaluation at
an early gathering of the UK Evaluation Society. Until that time I
had not realised that there was such a strong interest in evaluation
within that professional group.

Over the last few years the criss-cross of bridges (or, to be
truthful, sometimes rope-ladders) that now links different parts
of the UK evaluation community has come to include language
teachers, among others, for the first time. Bridge building is justified – and it has to be justified if only because of the time it takes
– because so many of the approaches, dilemmas, methodologies
and theories of evaluation appear to be common across divides of
discipline or fields of application. For example, in Part I of this
book concerned with innovation and evaluation – a preoccupation of most evaluators – the authors approach innovation from a
particular but by no means unique perspective. This, then, is the
view of someone crossing the bridge from one side of a divide: an
evaluator eavesdropping on debates within language and education.

The relatedness of evaluation to innovation

In most evaluation traditions, innovation and evaluation are closely
related (see, in particular, Fullan, Chapter 10 in this volume).

263

Although evaluators sometimes address ongoing or established programmes (or projects or organisations or policies . . .) it is more common to focus on some planned change (see Karavas-Doukas in Chapter 2). What constitutes innovation can be problematic (see below), but far more problematic is the proper relationship between innovation and evaluation. In some fields and disciplines the relationship between the two is so intimate as to make them indistinguishable. In software engineering, for example, evaluation is at the heart of the development process necessary to ensure that reliable 'bug free' products are produced. Regional planning and crime prevention are two other domains where the relationship is close. In most fields, however – education, health promotion, local development, international development, to name but a few – there is at least a tension between an integrated and more separated vision of evaluation and innovation. By separation I refer to some distance between those who innovate and those who evaluate. Evaluators then see themselves as outside rather than within an innovation process. Those who manage innovation are also less likely to incorporate evaluation (formally) into their own management practice (but see Anderson, Chapter 7 in this volume). An integrated vision, on the other hand, does not even maintain a division between the role of manager of innovation and the role of evaluator. Professionals self-evaluate as part of the way they fulfil their own roles.

Evaluation purposes

The ways evaluation and innovation do and do not intersect follow from the different purposes of evaluation and the nature of the field or domain within which innovation and evaluation occurs.

Celia Roberts (Chapter 3), in passing (and citing Gipps), makes a distinction between assessment as 'accountable' and 'educational'. I tend to distinguish three main 'purposes' of evaluation driven respectively by notions of *accountability, management* and *learning.* Some of the contributors in this volume clearly eschew an 'accountability' purpose for evaluation. Holliday (Chapter 8), for example, does this most explicitly when he refers to the 'tendency for aid agencies to exercise "hyperrational" controls on aid projects' and 'increased demands . . . for more sophisticated management approaches, especially within the areas of evaluation and innovation'. However, similar sentiments are expressed by other authors. Roberts adopts a 'cultural and ethnographic perspective [which] problematises . . . approaches to evaluation which focus on measurement-based outcomes . . .', and Kiely (Chapter 4), concerned as he is with teachers' and tutors' practice, speaks of 'action research', 'ethnographic approaches', 'reflective practice' and 'participant evaluation'.

All then are concerned with managing and learning from innovation. Roberts does so with the 'illuminative' perspective formed by ethnographers, Holliday with similar methodological interests but also with a strong 'critical' voice, and Kiely with an eye on learning for practitioners. Particular understandings of the relationship between innovation and evaluation are partly a question of values, and authors in this volume are fairly explicit about their own value stance. But they are also not unrelated to the dynamics of the domain itself – for example, the role of professional educationalists and how this is regulated. Applied linguistics, and, within this, English language education, places practitioners in a position where they need to negotiate their own roles and are able to exercise a high degree of autonomy. However, it is also clear from chapters in this volume that the notion of the autonomous professional, dominant throughout education in the 1970s, is not going unchallenged in language teaching today. Integrating innovation management and evaluation will probably only be possible in this field if, somewhere, there are evaluators who follow a more independent path: who ask questions about outcomes and effectiveness however difficult it is to come up with credible answers.

An arbitrary selection

Scanning chapters in search of insights that might be helpful in other evaluation contexts, I find no shortage of material. Selecting from such a rich *smörgasbord* is not easy: Kiely's perspective on implementation, Holliday's reflections on the 'object' of study and Roberts's attempt to problematise innovation and position theory in relation to method are all to some extent arbitrarily chosen. However, this selection does raise questions and even occasionally highlights new 'ways of seeing' that I have found thought-provoking and will probably interest others who also evaluate innovative processes.

Professional tensions and the object of study

Adrian Holliday is an advocate for the 'young academic tradition' of applied linguistics in the face of the 'dominant non-academic culture of English language teaching'. Though, more significantly, he recognises the 'tensions' between these two traditions. From an evaluator's standpoint the interest in what might otherwise be seen as a spat between those who engage in and those who study English language education, is that Holliday pins his case to an argument about the 'primary object of study'. Evaluators also need to keep their eyes on the 'object', in their case the object of evaluation, and the choice thereof is never as simple as it seems. Holliday's argument in this regard follows a logic with which many evaluators will be familiar. He understands English language education in a particular way: as a domain in which language is a significant constituent of culture. Appropriate methodologies such as discourse analysis and ethnography then follow and are used to show how, even in the classroom, the more practical or skills-based ELT interplays with the more knowledge-based professional cultures of applied linguistics. Holliday carries this further: being reflexive 'about one's own involvement and effect . . . is necessary for knowing how and what to evaluate and how and what to innovate'.

Along the same lines, Holliday uses notions such as the 'technologisation of discourse' which he associates with ELT, to understand broader changes in British education 'where quality assurance activity has made all academics focus on [the definition of the] skills, competences and learning objectives . . .'. This makes a great deal of sense in evaluation terms. I would argue that an important criterion in the choice of an object of evaluation must be in terms of its encapsulation at an accessible level of analysis of more global or generalisable processes. Holliday's 'discoursal and micro-cultural relationships within institutions' matches the bill and for me reinforces an important message about the relationship between evaluation and innovation. If evaluators are to make a contribution to understanding innovation, perhaps the single most important decision they have to make is in their choice of an object of evaluation that can illuminate the dynamics of contemporary innovation processes. Roberts explicitly makes the same point regarding the 'good' case study and 'to show how general principles . . . manifest themselves in some given set of particular circumstances'.

Innovation, method and theory

Celia Roberts, like Holliday, emphasises the interconnections of culture and language learning. Her case study of 'intercultural communication' centres around 'language learners as ethnographers' even though she also recognises the limitations of ethnography which were 'never developed for evaluative purposes'. Roberts, in line with her ethnographic stance, confronts head-on a key question for this section and probably for this volume: What *is* innovation? She contrasts the way innovation is understood in different European countries: 'there are contested views about what counts as innovation, even within countries relatively geographically close'. Anyone who has worked with European Union (EU) programmes will recognise such contestation. For some EU countries, innovation is importing another's 'good practice'; for some only dramatic change justifies the label 'innovative'; while, for still others in Europe, such step-level changes are by definition *not* innovative. The self-defining of innovation may well be the only valid approach, though it will make those who seek some normative or even comparative basis for evaluation uneasy. It remains true that unless evaluators problematise innovation in some way they cannot hope to understand, let alone contribute to, the innovation process.

Celia Roberts, in her evaluation of ethnographic case studies, comments that 'we aimed to place the content and methods of the project in symbiotic relationship to the evaluative methods'. Roberts sees ethnographic methods as related to the nature of language learning and teaching within an inter-cultural milieu. While close to Holliday's position, though for quite practical ends (e.g. 'to examine the benefits and interconnections between the preparatory and returning experiences in the UK institution and period abroad') she is also concerned with theory. For Roberts, cultural and social theory is necessary for ethnographic methods to be valid and to lead to understandings that are 'generalisable' rather than 'anecdotal'. This also is a preoccupation for many evaluators. In many domains it is easy for sophisticated methods to be applied atheoretically and for sophisticated theory to be elaborated in isolation from any method. It is rare for both theory and method to be adequately combined. At other times I have argued for the need for different types of theory to be taken on board by evaluators. Minimally this needs to include theories of the domain (e.g. what are the dynamics shaping language education today?), theories of innovation (e.g. what is the nature and definition of innovation and are there levers that are redirecting contemporary systems?) and theories of evaluation (e.g. how do different evaluation purposes meet the needs of different stakeholders and how are assessments made of the value of an innovative scheme?).

I would argue that all these types of theory are present within this volume. However, integrating different theoretical strands is likely to be no easier in language education than in other evaluative fields of endeavour. And integrating theory and method in the evaluation of innovation always seems just beyond the horizon. These chapters offer a glimpse over this horizon from a very particular vantage point, enabling some further triangulation of *terra incognita* – some points of reference for evaluators to plot on their maps when planning future expeditions.

Bibliography

ADELMAN, C. 1996 Anything goes: evaluation and relativism. *Evaluation* **2** (3): 291–306.

ADELMAN, C. and ALEXANDER, R. 1987 The integrity of evaluation. In MURPHY, R. and TORRANCE, H. (eds) *Evaluating education: issues and methods.* London: Harper & Rowe, pp. 294–310.

AGAR, M. 1980 *The professional stranger: an informal introduction to ethnography.* New York: Academic Press.

AGAR, M. 1987 *Independents declared: the dilemma of independent trucking.* Washington DC: Smithsonian Institute.

AGAR, M. 1994 *Language shock: understanding the culture of conversation.* New York: William Morrow & Co.

AHMED, A.S. and DONNAN, H. 1994 Islam in the age of postmodernity. In AHMED, A.S. and DONNAN, H. (eds) *Islam, globalisation and postmodernity.* London: Routledge, pp. 1–20.

AITCHISON, H. 1993 Women and management training in 1990s. In OUSTEN, J. (ed.) *Women in Education Management.* London: Longman.

AKŞIT, T. 1996 *ELT teachers' perception of a teacher appraisal scheme: a case study.* Unpublished MA Thesis, Ankara.

ALDERSON, J.C. 1992 Guidelines for the evaluation of language education. In ALDERSON, J.C. and BERETTA, A. (eds).

ALDERSON, J.C. and BERETTA, A. (eds) 1992 *Evaluating second language education.* Cambridge: Cambridge University Press.

ALDERSON, J.C. and SCOTT, M. 1992 Insiders, outsiders and participatory evaluation. In ALDERSON, J.C. and BERETTA, A. (eds) *Evaluating second language education.* Cambridge: Cambridge University Press, pp. 25–57.

ALLWRIGHT, R.L. 1982 *Communicative curricula in language teaching.* Paper presented at the international conference on language science and the teaching of languages and literatures, Bari, Italy.

ALLWRIGHT, R.L. 1988 *Observation in the language classroom.* London: Longman.

ANIVAN, S. (ed.) 1991 *Issues in language programme evaluation in the 1990's.* Anthology Series 27. Singapore: RELC.

ARY, D., JACOBS, L. and RAZAVIEH, A. 1990 *Introduction to research in education,* 4th edition. Fort Worth: Harcourt, Brace, Jovanovich College Publishers.

ASAD, T. and DIXON, J. 1984 Translating Europe's others. In BARKER, F., HULME, P., IVERSEN, M. and LOXLEY, D. (eds) *Europe and its others,* Vol. 1. Colchester: University of Essex.

ASPINWALL, K., SIMMINS, T., WILKINSON, J.F. and McAULAY, J.M. 1992 *Managing evaluation in education.* London: Routledge.

ATKINSON, P. 1992 *Understanding ethnographic texts.* London: Sage.

AZIZ, A.A. 1987 Strategies for communication between teachers and pupils. Implications for classroom teaching strategies. In DAS, B.K. (ed.) *Patterns of classroom interaction in Southeast Asia.* Singapore: SEAMEO Regional Language Centre.

BAILEY, K. and NUNAN, D. (eds) 1996 *Voices from the language classroom.* Cambridge: Cambridge University Press.

BALES, R.F. 1950 *Interaction process analysis: a method for the study of smallgroups.* Cambridge: Addison-Wesley.

BALL, S. 1994 *Education reform: a critical and post-structural approach.* Buckingham: Open University Press.

BAUMANN, G. 1996 *Contesting culture.* Cambridge: Cambridge University Press.

BAMMAN, R. and SHERZER, J. (eds) 1989 *Explorations in the ethnography of speaking.* Cambridge: Cambridge University Press.

BAZERGAN, E. 1995 Project based review in Indonesia: an account of an on-going evaluation project. *ELT Management,* No. 17 (the Newsletter of the Management Special Interest Group of IATEFL).

BELBIN, M. 1981 *Management teams: why they succeed or fail.* London: Heinemann.

BENNETT, N., CRAWFORD, M. and RICHES, C. (eds) 1992 *Managing change in education.* Milton Keynes: The Open University.

BENNIS, W. and SHEPARD, H. 1956 A theory of group development. *Human Relations* IX.

BERETTA, A. 1990a Implementation of the Bangalore project. *Applied Linguistics* **11** (4): 321–37.

BERETTA, A. 1990 Who should evaluate L2 programmes? In C. BRUMFIT and R. MITCHELL (eds) *Research in the language classroom.* Basingstoke: Modern English Publications/The British Council (ELT Docs 133), pp. 156–60.

BERETTA, A. 1992 Evaluation of language education: an overview. In ALDERSON, J.C. and BERETTA, A. (eds), pp. 5–24.

BERNSTEIN, B. 1991 On the classification and framing of educational knowledge. In YOUNG, M.F.D. (ed.) *Knowledge and control.* London: Collier-Macmillan, pp.47–69.

BIRDWHISTELL, R. 1970 *Kinesics and context.* Philadelphia: University of Pennsylvania Press.

BIRNBAUM, J. and ENNIG, J. 1991 Case study. In FLOOD, J., JENSEN, J., LAPP, D. and SQUIRE, J. (eds) *Handbook of research on teaching the English language arts.* New York: Macmillan.

BLUE, G. and GRUNDY, P. 1996 Team evaluation of language teaching and language courses. *English Language Teaching Journal* **50** (3): 244–53.

BOWERS, R. 1986 *Appropriate methodology.* Unpublished paper presented in dialogue with H.G. WIDDOWSON, Dunford House Conference, The British Council.

BRAMLEY, P. 1996 *Evaluating training effectiveness.* London: McGraw-Hill.

BREEN, M. 1983 Open discussion on Andrews S. Communicative language teaching – some implications for teacher education. In JOHNSON, K. and PORTER, D. (eds) *Perspectives in communicative language teaching.* London: Academic Press.

BREEN, M. 1991 Understanding the language teacher. In PHILLIPSON, R., KELLERMAN, E., SELINKER, L., SHARWOOD SMITH, M. and SWAIN, M. (eds) *Foreign/second language pedagogy research.* Clevedon, Philadelphia: Multilingual Matters.

BREEN, M., CANDLIN, C., DAM, L. and GABRIELSEN, G. 1989 The evolution of a teacher training programme. In JOHNSON, R.K. (ed.) *The second language curriculum.* Cambridge: Cambridge University Press.

BRINDLEY, G. 1989 The role of needs analysis in adult ESL programme design. In JOHNSON, R.K. (ed.) *The second language curriculum.* Cambridge: Cambridge University Press.

BRINDLEY, G. and HOOD, S. 1990 Curriculum innovation in adult ESL. In BRINDLEY, G. (ed.) *The second language curriculum in action.* Sydney, Australia: NCELTR.

BRITTEN, D. and O'DWYER, J. 1995 Self-evaluation in in-service teacher training. In REA-DICKINS, P. and LWAITAMA, A. (eds) *Evaluation for development in English language teaching.* Review of ELT, Vol. 3, No. 3. Basingstoke: Modern English Publications/The British Council, pp. 87–106.

BROCK, M.N. 1994 Reflections on change: implementing the process approach in Japan. *RELC Journal* **25** (2): 51–70.

BROGGER, F. 1992 *Culture, language, text: culture studies within the study of English as a foreign language.* Oslo: Scandinavian University Press.

BROWN, J.D. 1990 The use of multiple t-tests in language research, *TESOL Quarterly* **24**: 770–5.

BROWN, J.D. 1994 *The elements of language curriculum: a systematic approach to programme development.* Boston: Heinle & Heinle.

BROWN, S. 1980 Key issues in the implementation of innovations in schools. *Curriculum* **1** (1): 32–9.

BROWN, S. and McINTYRE, D. 1978 Factors influencing teacher responses to curricular innovations. *Research Intelligence* **4** (1): 19–23.

BRUMFIT, C. and MITCHELL, R. (eds) 1990 *Research in the language classroom.* ELT Documents 133. Modern English Publications.

BULLOUGH, J. and WEBBER, R. (eds) 1996 *Accountability in Governmental and NGO Projects and Programmes.* Dunford Seminar Report 1996. Manchester: The British Council.

BURGESS, R.G. (ed.) 1993 *Educational research and evaluation for policy and practice.* London: Falmer Press.

BURNS, A. 1990 Focus on language in the communicative classroom. In BRINDLEY, G. (ed.) *The second language curriculum in action.* Sydney, Australia: NCELTR.

BUSEL 1993 *Teacher profile explanatory booklet.* Unpublished. University of Bilkent.

BUSEL 1995 *The teacher appraisal scheme handbook.* Unpublished. University of Bilkent.

BUTTJES, D. and BYRAM, M. (eds) 1991 *Mediating languages and cultures.* Clevedon: Multilingual Matters.

BYRAM, M. 1989 *Cultural studies in foreign language education.* Clevedon: Multilingual Matters.

BYRAM, M. 1997 *Assessing and teacher's intercultural communicative competence.* Clevedon: Multilingual Matters.

BYRAM, M. and MORGAN, C. 1994 *Teaching-and-learning, language-culture.* Clevedon: Multilingual Matters.

CALDWELL, B.J. and SPINKS, J.M. 1988 *The self-managing school.* London: Falmer Press.

CAMERON, D., FRAZER, E., HARVEY, P., RAMPTON, B. and RICHARDSON, K. 1992 *Researching language: issues of power and method.* London: Routledge.

CANAGARAJAH, A.S. 1993 Critical ethnography of a Sri Lankan classroom: ambiguities in opposition to reproduction through ESOL. *TESOL Quarterly* **27** (4): 601–26.

CANAGARAJAH, A.S. 1996 From critical research practice to critical research reporting. *TESOL Quarterly* **30**: 321–30.

CANDLIN, C. and MURPHY, D. 1987 *Language learning tasks,* Oxford: Pergamon.

CARR, W. and KEMMIS, S. 1985 *Becoming critical: knowing through research.* Victoria: Deakin University Press.

CHAMBERS, F. 1996 Project frameworks – are they accountable enough? In BULLOUGH, J. and WEBBER, R. (eds), pp. 24–40.

CHAMBERS, F. 1997 Seeking consensus in coursebook evaluation. *ELT Journal* **51** (1): 29–35.

CHAUDRON, C. 1988 *Second language classrooms: research on teaching and learning.* Cambridge: Cambridge University Press.

CHELIMSKY, E. 1997 The coming transformations in evaluation. In CHELIMSKY, E. and SHADISH, W.R. (eds), pp. 1–26.

CHELIMSKY, E. and SHADISH, W.R. (eds) 1997 *Evaluation for the 21st Century.* USA: Sage.

CHRISTOPHER, L. and SMITH, L. 1991 *Negotiation training through gaming.* London: Kogan Page.

CLARK, C.M. and PETERSON, P.L. 1986 Teachers' thought processes. In WITTROCK, M.C. (ed.) *Handbook of research on teaching.* London: Macmillan.

CLARK, J.L. 1987 *Curriculum renewal in school foreign language learning.* Oxford: Oxford University Press.

CLARKE, M. 1994 The dysfunctions of the theory/practice discourse. *TESOL Quarterly* **28**: 9–26.

CLIFFORD, J. and MARCUS, G. 1986 *Writing culture: the poetics and politics of ethnography.* Berkeley: University of California Press.

COLEMAN, H. 1996a Autonomy and ideology in the English language classroom. In COLEMAN, H. (ed.) *Society and the language classroom.* Cambridge: Cambridge University Press.

COLEMAN, J. 1996b *Studying languages: a survey of British and European students.* London: Centre for Information on Language Teaching.

COLEMAN, H. 1997 Undergraduate ELT, where have we been and where are we going? In COLEMAN, H., SOEDRADJAT, T. and WESTAWAY, G. (eds) *Teaching English to university undergraduates in the Indonesian context: issues and developments.* Bandung: ITB Press and Leeds University School of Education.

CRACKNELL, B.E. 1996 Evaluating development aid: strengths and weaknesses. *Evaluation* **21** (1): 23–33.

CRANE, D. 1994 Introduction: the challenge of the sociology of culture to sociology as discipline. In CRANE, D. (ed.) *The sociology of culture.* Oxford: Blackwell, pp. 1–19.

CROCKER, T. 1994 Endpiece. *The Journal for Teachers of English in Indonesia.* Pilot Edition: 27–8.

CRONBACH, L. 1975 Beyond the two disciplines of scientific psychology. *American Psychologist* **30**: 116–27.

CROOKES, G. 1993 Action research and second language teachers: going beyond teacher research. *Applied Linguistics* **14**: 130–44.

CROOKES, G. and GASS, S. (eds) 1993a *Tasks and language learning: integrating theory and practice.* Clevedon: Multilingual Matters.

CROOKES, G. and GASS, S. (eds) 1993b *Tasks in a pedagogical context: integrating theory and practice.* Clevedon: Multilingual Matters.

CUBAN, L. 1988 A fundamental puzzle of school reform. *Phi Delta Kappa* **70** (5): 341–4.

CUMMING, A. 1993 Teachers' curriculum planning and accommodations of innovation: case studies of adult ESL instruction. *TESL Canada Journal* **11** (1): 30–52.

CUMMING, A. and MACKAY, R. 1994 Evaluating school policies for antiracist education. *ORBIT,* **25** (2): 34–46.

DALIN, P. and ROLFF, H.G. 1993 *Changing the school culture.* London: Cassell.

DARLING-HAMMOND, L. 1995 *Effects of assessment choices on teaching and equity.* Toronto Canada: The Learning Consortium International Conferences on Evaluation.

DENDRINOS, B. 1985a *Report on the ELT project in Greece.* Athens: OEDB.

DENDRINOS, B. 1985b *The ELT guide.* Athens: OEDB.

DENHAM, P.A. 1997 Eight autumns in Hanoi. In KENNY, B. and SAVAGE, W. (eds), pp. 193–207.

DENZIN, N.K. 1988 *The research act: a theoretical introduction to sociological methods,* 3rd edition. Englewood Cliffs, New Jersey: Prentice-Hall.

DES 1983 *Teaching quality.* London: HMSO.

DES 1985a *Better schools: evaluation and appraisal conference proceedings.* DES.

DES 1985b *Quality in schools: evaluation and appraisal.* London: HMSO.

DES 1989a *Developments in the appraisal of teachers.* HMI/DES.

DES 1989b *School teacher appraisal: a national framework.* London: HMSO.

DICKINSON, L. 1987 *Self-instruction in language learning.* Cambridge: Cambridge University Press.

DOUGHTY, C. 1991 Second language instruction does make a difference: evidence from an empirical study on SL relativization. *Studies in Second Language Acquisition* **13**: 431–69.

DOUGHTY, C. and PICA, T. 1986 Information gap tasks: do they facilitate second language acquisition? *TESOL Quarterly* **20**: 305–25.

DOYLE, W. and PONDER, G.A. 1977 The practicality ethic in teacher decision-making. *Interchange* **8** (3): 1–12.

DUFON, M. 1993 Ethics in TESOL research. *TESOL Quarterly* **27**: 157–60.

EARL, L. and LEMAHIEU, P. 1997 Rethinking assessment and accountability. In HARGREAVES, A. (ed.) *Rethinking educational change with heart and minds.* Alexandria, VA: Association for Supervision and Curriculum Development, pp. 149–68.

EASEN, P. 1985 *Making school centred INSET work.* Milton Keynes: The Open University/Croom Helm.

EDWARDS, R. 1991 The politics of meeting learner needs: power, subject, subjection. *Studies in the Education of Adults* **23** (1): 85–97.

EDWARDS, R. and USHER, R. 1994 Disciplining the subject: the power of competence. *Studies in the Education of Adults* **26** (1): 1–14.

EHRLICH, S., AVERY, P. and YORIO, C. 1989 Discourse structure and the negotiation of comprehensible input. *Studies in Second Language Acquisition* **11**: 397–414.

EISNER, E. 1985 *The art of educational evaluation.* Lewes: Falmer Press.

ELLEN, R. 1984 *Ethnographic research: a guide to general conduct.* London: Academic Press.

ELLIOTT, J. 1994 *Action research for educational change.* Milton Keynes: Open University Press (1st edition 1991).

ELLIS, G. 1996 How culturally appropriate is the communicative approach? *ELT Journal* **50** (3): 213–18.

ELLIS, R. 1987 Interlanguage variability in narrative discourse: style shifting in the use of the past tense. *Studies in Second Language Acquisition* **9**: 1–20.

ELLIS, R. 1988 Coursework task, MA in ELT. Ealing College of Higher Education.

ELLIS, R. 1990 *Instructed second language acquisition.* Oxford: Blackwell.

ELLIS, R. 1991 Grammar teaching – practice or consciousness-raising? In ELLIS, R. *Second language acquisition and language pedagogy.* Clevedon: Multilingual Matters.

ELLIS, R. 1993 Second language acquisition and the structural syllabus. *TESOL Quarterly* **27**: 91–113.

ELLIS, R. 1994 *The study of second language acquisition.* Oxford: Oxford University Press.

ELLIS, R. 1995 Does it 'work'? Evaluating tasks. University of Luton, *MATSDA Journal* **2**: 19–21.

ELLIS, R. 1996 The empirical evaluation of language teaching materials. *ELT Journal* **51** (1): 36–42.

ELLIS, R. 1997 Evaluating communicative tasks. In TOMLINSON, B. (ed.) *Materials development in L2 teaching.* Cambridge: Cambridge University Press.

ELLIS, R., TANAKA, Y. and YAMAZAKI, A. 1994 Classroom interaction, comprehension, and the acquisition of L2 word meanings. *Language Learning* **44**: 449–91.

ERICKSON, F. 1977 Some approaches to inquiry in school/community ethnography. *Anthropology and Education Quarterly* **8** (3): 58–69.

EVANS, A. and TOMLINSON, J. 1989 *Teacher appraisal: a nationwide approach.* London: Jessica Kingsley.

EVANS, C. 1988 *Language people: the experience of teaching and learning modern languages in British universities.* Milton Keynes: Open University Press.

EVANS, R. 1996 *The human side of school change.* San Francisco, CA: Jossey-Bass.

EVERARD, K.B. and MORRIS, G. 1996 *Effective school management,* 3rd edition. London: Paul Chapman (1st edition 1985; 2nd edition 1992).

FAIRCLOUGH, N. 1989 *Language and power.* London: Longman.

FAIRCLOUGH, N. 1995 *Critical discourse analysis: the critical study of language.* London: Longman.

FALCHIKOV, N. 1991 Group process analysis: self and peer assessment of working together in a group. In BROWN, S. and DOVE, P. (eds) *SCED Paper* **63**: 15–25.

FETTERMAN, D.M. 1997 Empowerment, evaluation and accreditation in higher education. In CHEMLINSKY, E. and SHADISH (eds) *Evaluation for the 21st century.* London: Sage.

FIDLER, B. 1989 Staff appraisal – theory, concepts and experience in other organizations and problems of adaptation to education. In RICHES, C. and MORGAN, C. (eds).

FITZ-GIBBON, C.T. 1992 Performance indicators and examination results, Scottish Office Education Department. *Interchange No 11.*

FITZ-GIBBON, C.T. 1996 *Monitoring education: indicators, quality and effectiveness.* London: Cassell.

FLETCHER, C. 1993 *Appraisal.* London: IPM.

FOSTER, PAULINE 1993 Discoursal outcomes of small group work in an EFL classroom: a look at the interaction of non-native speakers. *Thames Valley University Working Papers in English Language Teaching* **2**: 1–32.

FOTOS, S. and ELLIS, R. 1991 Communicating about grammar: a task-based approach. *TESOL Quarterly* **25**: 605–28.

FREED, B.F. (ed.) 1995 *Second language acquisition in a study abroad context.* Amsterdam/Philadelphia: John Benjamins.

FULLAN, M. 1982 *The meaning of educational change.* Ontario: The Ontario Institute for Studies in Education Press.

FULLAN, M.G. 1991 *The new meaning of educational change.* London: Cassell.

FULLAN, M. 1992 *Successful school improvement.* Buckingham: Open University Press.

FULLAN, M. 1993 *Change forces.* London: Falmer Press.

FULLAN, M. 1997 Emotion and hope: constructive concepts for complex times. In HARGREAVES, A. (ed.) *Rethinking educational change with heart and minds.* Alexandria, VA: Association for Supervision and Curriculum Development, pp. 216–33.

FULLAN, M. and HARGREAVES, A. 1996 *What's worth fighting for in your school.* New York: Teachers College Press; ON: Ontario Public Schools Teachers' Federation.

FULLAN, M. and PARK, P. 1981 *Curriculum implementation.* Toronto: Ontario Institute for Studies in Education.

FULLAN, M. and POMFRET, A. 1977 Research on curriculum and instruction implementation. *Review of Educational Research* **47** (1): 335–97.

FULLAN, M. and STEIGELBAUER, S. 1991 *The new meaning of educational change.* London: Cassell.

FURNHAM, A. and BOCHNER, S. 1986 *Culture shock.* London: Routledge.

GAL, S. 1989 Language and political economy. *Annual Review of Anthropology* **18**: 345–67.

GASS, S. and VARONIS, M. 1994 Input, interaction, and second language production. *Studies in Second Language Acquisition* **18**: 283–302.

GEERTZ, C. 1973 *The interpretation of cultures.* New York: Basic Books.

GIPPS, C. 1994 *Beyond testing: towards a theory of educational assessment.* London: Falmer Press.

GITLIN, A. and MARGONIS, F. 1995 The political aspects of reform. *American Journal of Education* **103**: 377–405.

GLASS, G. and WORTHEN, N. 1971 Evaluation and research: similarities and differences. *Curriculum Theory Network*, Fall: 149–65.

GOLEMAN, D. 1995 *Emotional intelligence.* New York: Bantam Books.

GOSLING, L. and EDWARDS, M. 1995 Toolkits: a practical guide to assessment, monitoring, review and evaluation. London: Save the Children.

GREEN, J. and BLOOME, D. 1997 Ethnography and ethnographers of and in education: a situated perspective. In FLOOD, J., HEATH, S.B. and LAPP, D. (eds) 1997 *Handbook of research on teaching literacy through the communicative visual arts.* New York: IRA Simon Schuster Macmillan.

GREEN, K. and SANDERS, M. 1990 *The teacher appraisal book.* London: Mary Glasgow Publications.

GREENWOOD, J. 1985 Bangalore revisited: a reluctant complaint. *English Language Teaching Journal* **39** (4): 268–73.

GROSS, N., GIAQUINTA, J. and BERNSTEIN, M. 1971 *Implementing organisational innovations: a sociological analysis of planned educational change.* New York: Basic Books.

GROTJAHN, R. 1987 On the methodological basis of introspective methods. In FAERCH, C. and KASPAR, G. (eds) *Introspection in second language studies.* Clevedon: Multilingual Matters, pp. 54–81.

GROTJAHN, R. 1991 The research programme subjective theories. *Studies in Second Language Acquisition* **13** (2): 187–214.

GUBA, E.C. and LINCOLN, Y.S. 1981 *Effective evaluation.* San Francisco: Jossey-Bass.

GUBA, E.G. and LINCOLN, Y.S. 1989 *Fourth generation evaluation.* Newbury Park: Sage.

GUMPERZ, J. 1982 *Discourse strategies.* Cambridge: Cambridge University Press.

GUMPERZ, J. and HYMES, D. (eds) 1972 *Directions in sociolinguistics: the ethnography of communication.* New York: Holt, Rinehart & Winston.

GUMPERZ, J. and LEVINSON, S. (eds) 1996 *Rethinking linguistic relativity.* Cambridge: Cambridge University Press.

HALL, D. 1997 Why projects fail. In KENNY, B. and SAVAGE, W. (eds), pp. 258–67.

HAMILTON, J. 1996 *Inspiring innovations in language teaching.* Clevedon: Multilingual Matters.

HAMMERSLEY, M. 1992 *What's wrong with ethnography?* London: Routledge.

HAMMERSLEY, M. and ATKINSON, P. 1983 *Ethnography: principles in practice.* London: Tavistock Publications.

HANDY, C. 1993 *Understanding Organizations.* London: Penguin.

HANDY, C. and AITKEN, R. 1986 *Understanding schools as organisations.* Harmondsworth: Penguin Books Ltd.

HARGREAVES, A. 1994 *Changing Teachers, Changing Times.* London: Cassell.

HARGREAVES, A. and FULLAN, M. 1998 *What's worth fighting for out there.* New York: Teachers College Press, Buckingham, UK: Open University Press.

HARRISON, I. 1996a Look who's talking now: listening to voices in curriculum renewal. In BAILEY, K.M. and NUNAN, D. (eds) *Voices from the language classroom.* Cambridge: Cambridge University Press.

HARRISON, M. 1996b Accountability from the donor perspective. In BULLOUGH, J. and WEBBER, R. (eds), pp. 8–13.

HATCH, E. and LAZARATON, A. 1991 *The research manual: design and statistics for applied linguistics*. New York: Newbury House/Harper Collins.

HATTON, N. and SMITH, D. 1995 Reflection in teacher education: towards definition and implementation. *Teaching and Teacher Education* **11** (1): 33–49.

HEATH, S.B. 1993 *Ways with words*. Cambridge: Cambridge University Press.

HEDGE, T. 1987 The deskilled language teacher: a casualty of inservice training. *Triangle* **6**: 99–110. The British Council/Goethe Institut/Aupelf/Didier Erudition, Paris.

HEDGE, T. 1994 Course handout, Diploma in ELT. Centre for English Language Teacher Education, University of Warwick.

HEIDEMANN, T. 1996 Innovation policy in Denmark. Unpublished report for the observatory on innovation in education. Haderslev, Denmark: The Royal Danish School of Educational Studies.

HERZBERG, F., MAUSNER, B. and SYNDERMAN, B. 1959 *The motivation to work*. New York: Wiley.

HOFSTEDE, G. 1980 *Culture's consequences: international differences in work-related values*. Beverly Hills: Sage Publications.

HOFSTEDE, G. 1991 *Cultures and organizations*. London: McGraw-Hill.

HOLEC, H. 1982 Aspects of autonomy in foreign language learning. Oxford: Pergamon Press.

HOLLIDAY, A.R. 1992a Tissue rejection and informal orders in ELT projects: collecting the right information. *Applied Linguistics* **13** (4): 403–24.

HOLLIDAY, A.R. 1992b Intercompetence: sources of conflict between local and expatriate ELT personnel. *System* **20** (2).

HOLLIDAY, A.R. 1994a *Appropriate methodology and social context*. Cambridge: Cambridge University Press.

HOLLIDAY, A.R. 1994b Student culture and English language education: an international context. *Language, Culture and Curriculum* **7** (2).

HOLLIDAY, A.R. 1995a Evaluation as cultural negotiation. *Second PRODESS Colloquium: Evaluation in Planning and Managing Language Education Projects*, 26–28 March. Manchester: The British Council, pp. 6–11.

HOLLIDAY, A.R. 1995b Handing over the project: an exercise in restraint. *System* **23** (1): 57–68.

HOLLIDAY, A.R. 1996a Developing a sociological imagination: expanding ethnography in international English language education. *Applied Linguistics* **17** (2): 234–55.

HOLLIDAY, A.R. 1996b *Cultural accommodation in an 'ESL' curriculum project*. Unpublished paper, Canterbury Christ Church College.

HOLLIDAY, A.R. 1997 The politics of participation in international English language education. *System* **25** (3).

HOLLIDAY, A.R. (forthcoming) Six lessons: cultural continuity in communicative language teaching. *Language Teaching Research* 1/3: 212–38.

HOLLY, P. and WHITEHEAD, D. 1986 Collaborative action research. *Class-room Action Research Network Bulletin*, Vol. 7. Cambridge: Cambridge Institute of Education.

HOOGWERF, P. 1995 *Evaluation of a grammar CR task*. Unpublished M.Ed course paper, Temple University, Japan.

HOPKINS, D. 1985 *A teacher's guide to classroom research*. Milton Keynes: Open University Press.

HOPKINS, D. 1986 *In-service training and educational development. An international survey*. Croom Helm.

HOPKINS, D. 1989 *Evaluation for school development*. Milton Keynes: Open University Press.

HOPKINS, D., AINSCOW, M. and WEST, M. 1994 *School improvement in an era of social change*. London: Cassell.

HUBERMAN, M. and MILES, M. 1984 *Innovations up close*. New York: Plenum.

HURST, P. 1983 Implementing educational change: a critical review of the literature. *EDC Occasional Papers 5*. University of London Institute of Education.

HUTCHINSON, T. and WATERS, A. 1984 How communicative is ESP? *English Language Teaching Journal* **38** (2): 108–13.

HYMES, D. 1980 Qualitative/quantitative research methodologies in education: a linguistic perspective. In HYMES, D. *Language in education: ethnolinguistics essays*. Washington: Centre for Applied Linguistics, pp. 62–87.

JACOB, G.P. 1991 The mediators: providing access to texts in English in a semi-urban Maharashtrian college community. *PENN Working Papers in Educational Linguistics* 7/1. University of Pennsylvania Graduate School of Education, pp. 1–14.

JACOB, G.P. 1996. *The curriculum development survey co-ordinator*. Unpublished paper, Department of English, University of Pune, India.

JACQUES, D. 1991 *Learning in groups*. London: Kogan Page (1st edition published in 1984).

JOHNSON, D. and JOHNSON, F. 1987 *Joining together: group theory and group skills*. New Jersey: Prentice Hall.

JOHNSON, G. and SCHOLES, K. 1993 *Exploring corporate strategy*. London: Prentice Hall.

JONES, K. 1991 *Icebreakers*. London: Kogan Page.

JORDAN, S. 1993 *It's not my job*. Unpublished ethnographic study. London: Thames Valley University.

JOSHI, S. (ed.) 1994 *Rethinking English: essays in literature, language, history*. Delhi: Oxford University Press.

JURASEK, R. 1995 Using ethnography to bridge the gap between study abroad and the on-campus language and culture curriculum. In KRAMSCH, C. (ed.) *Redefining the boundaries of language study*. Boston: Heinle & Heinle.

KANTER, R.M. 1983 *The change masters: corporate entrepreneurs at work.* New York: Counterpoint.

KARAVAS, E. 1993 *English language teachers in the Greek secondary school: a study of their classroom practices and their attitudes towards methodological and materials innovation.* Unpublished PhD Dissertation, Centre for English Language Teacher Education, University of Warwick.

KARAVAS-DOUKAS, E. 1995a Teacher identified factors affecting the implementation of an EFL innovation in Greek public secondary schools. *Language, Culture and Curriculum* **8** (3): 53–68.

KARAVAS-DOUKAS, E. 1995b Understanding the gap between teachers' theories and their classroom practices: An investigation of teachers' attitudes towards error correction and their classroom error correcting behaviour. *English Language Teacher Education and Development* **1** (1): 1–19.

KARAVAS-DOUKAS, E. 1996a Evaluating the implementation of an EFL innovation in Greek public secondary schools. *Issues in Applied Linguistics: Evaluation Perspectives* **1** (1): 49–71.

KARAVAS-DOUKAS, E. 1996b Using attitude scales to investigate teachers' attitudes to the communicative approach. *ELT Journal* **50** (3): 187–98.

KELCHTERMANS, G. 1996 *National report on Belgium.* Unpublished report for European observatory on innovation in education. University of Leuven, Leuven, Belgium.

KELLY, P. 1980 From innovation to adaptability; the changing perspective of curriculum development. In GALTON, M. (ed.) *Curriculum change: the lessons of a decade.* Leicester: Leicester University Press.

KEMMIS, S. and MCTAGGERT, R. (eds) 1988 *The action research planner.* Geelong: Deakin University Press.

KENNEDY, C. 1987 Innovating for a change: teacher development and innovation: *ELT Journal* **41** (3): 163–70.

KENNEDY, C. 1988 Evaluation of the management of change in ELT projects. *Applied Linguistics* **9** (4): 329–42.

KENNEDY, C. 1993 Teacher attitudes and change implementation. *PRODESS Colloquium: Managing Change and Development ELT in ECE.* Manchester: The British Council.

KENNEDY, C. 1996 Teacher roles in curriculum reform. *English Language Teacher Education and Development* **2** (1): 77–89.

KENNEDY, D. 1996 The role of the foreign teacher as agent of change and implications for teacher education programmes in Chinese teacher training colleges. *English Language Teacher Education and Development* **2** (1): 52–65.

KENNY, B. and SAVAGE, W. (eds) 1997 *Language and development: teachers in a changing world.* New York: Addison Wesley Longman.

KIELY, R. 1998 Book Review of PAWSON, R. and TILLEY, N. Realistic Evaluation. London: Sage. In *Language Teaching Research* 2/1: 83–6.

KIELY, R., MURPHY, D. and REA-DICKINS, P. (eds) 1993 *Managing change and development in ELT in East and Central Europe.* Manchester: The British Council.

KIELY, R., MURPHY, D., REA-DICKINS, P. and REID, M. (Reviewers) 1994 *Guidelines for evaluation practice.* Manchester: The British Council.

KIELY, R., MURPHY, D., REA-DICKINS, P. and REID, M. (eds) 1995 *Evaluation in planning and managing language education projects.* Manchester: The British Council.

KING, J.A., LYONS MORRIS, L. and FITZ-GIBBON, C.T. 1987 *How to assess program implementation.* London: Sage.

KNUTSON, J. and BITZ, I. 1991 *Project management: how to plan and manage successful projects.* New York: AMACOM.

KOLB, D. 1984 *Experiential learning.* Englewood Cliffs, New Jersey: Prentice Hall.

KRAMSCH, C. 1993 *Context and culture in language teaching.* Oxford: Oxford University Press.

KUHN, T.S. 1970 *The structure of scientific revolutions.* Reprinted and enlarged. Chicago: University of Chicago Press.

KUSHNER, S. 1997 Consumers and heroes: a critical review of some recent writings of Michael Scriven. *Evaluation* **3** (3): 363–74.

KYRIACOU, C. 1989 Teacher stress and burnout: an international review. In RICHES, C. and MORGAN, C. (eds).

LAKOFF, G. and JOHNSON, M. 1980 *Metaphors we live by.* Chicago: University of Chicago Press.

LAMB, M. 1995 The consequences of INSET. *ELT Journal* **49** (1): 72–80.

LANGE, D. 1990 A blueprint for a teacher development program. In RICHARDS, J. and NUNAN, D. (eds) *Second language teacher education.* Cambridge: Cambridge University Press, pp. 245–68.

LARSEN-FREEMAN, D. 1983 Training teachers or educating a teacher. In ALATIS, J.E., STERN, H.H. and STREVENS, P. (eds) *Georgetown University round table acquisition research.* Georgetown University Press.

LAWRENCE, L. 1990 *Language in education: an evaluation of the teaching of structure in Zambian grade 8 classes.* Unpublished PhD thesis. Lusaka: University of Zambia.

LEADER, D. and MURPHY, E. 1996 *Observatory of innovation in European education: national report, Ireland.* Unpublished report for European observatory on innovation in education. Dublin: Marino Institute of Education.

LEAP 1991 *Appraisal in schools.* London: BBC.

LEGUTKE, M. and THOMAS, H. 1992 *Process and experience in the language classroom.* Harlow: Longman.

LEWIN, K. 1993 Defining the Education and Development Agenda: six issues. *Oxford Studies in Comparative Education,* **3** (2): 68–79 Triangle Books, Oxford.

LINCOLN, Y. and GUBA, E. 1985 *Naturalistic inquiry.* Newbury Park: Sage.

LONG, M.H. 1980 *Input, interaction and second language acquisition* Unpublished PhD dissertation. University of California at Los Angeles.

LONG, M. 1983 Native and non-native speaker conversation and the negotiation of comprehensible input. In CLARKE, M. and HANDSCOMBE, J. (eds) 1983 *On TESOL' 82*. Washington, D.C.: TESOL.

LONG, M.H. 1984 Process and product in ESL programme evaluation. *TESOL Quarterly* **18** (3): 409–25.

LONG, M. 1985 A role for instruction in second language acquisition: task-based language teaching. In HYLTENSTAM, K. and PIENEMANN, M. (eds) *Modelling and assessing second language acquisition*. Clevedon: Multilingual Matters.

LONG, M. 1989 *Task, group, and task-group interactions*. University of Hawaii Working Papers in ESL, **8**: 1–26.

LONG, M. 1990 Second language classroom research and teacher education. In BRUMFIT, C. and MITCHELL, R. (eds) *Research in the language classroom*. ELT Documents 133: Modern English Publications.

LOSCHKY, L. 1994 Comprehensible input and second language acquisition: what is the relationship? *Studies in Second Language Acquisition* **16**: 303–24.

LOW, L., DUFFIELD, J., BROWN, S. and JOHNSTONE, R. 1993 *Evaluating foreign languages in primary schools*. Scottish Centre for Information on Language Teaching, University of Stirling.

LYNCH, B. 1992 Evaluating a programme inside and out. In ALDERSON, J.C. and BERETTA, A. (eds) *Evaluating second language education*. Cambridge: Cambridge University Press, pp. 61–96.

LYNCH, B. 1996 *Language programme evaluation: theory and practice*. Cambridge: Cambridge University Press.

MACDONALD, B. 1971 The evaluation of the humanities curriculum project: a holistic approach. *Theory and Practice* **10**: 163–7.

MACDONALD, B. 1976 Evaluation and the control of education. In TAWNEY, D. (ed.) *Curriculum evaluation today*. London: Macmillan (cited in Hopkins, 1989: 205).

MACDONALD, B. 1987 Evaluation and the control of education. In MURPHY, R. and TORRANCE, H. (eds) *Evaluating education: issues and methods*. London: Harper & Rowe.

MACDONALD, B. and RUDDUCK, J. 1971 Curriculum research and development projects: barriers to success. *British Journal of Educational Psychology* **41** (2): 148–54.

MACDONALD, J. 1997 *Redesigning schools*. New York: Teachers College Press.

MACKAY, R. 1991 How program personnel can help maximize the utility of language program evaluations in. In ANIVAN, S. (ed.) *Issues in language programme evaluation in the 1990s*. Anthology Series **27**: 60–71. Singapore: Regional Language Centre.

MACKAY, R. 1993 Programme Evaluation as a management tool for both accountability and improvement. *ELT Management*, No. 12, (the Newsletter of the Management Special Interest Group of IATEFL).

MACKAY, R. 1994 Undertaking ESL/EFL programme review for account-ability and improvement. *English Language Teaching Journal* **48** (2): 142–9.

MACKAY, R., WELLESLEY, S. and BAZERGAN, E. 1995 Participatory evalua-tion. *English Language Teaching Journal* **49** (4): 308–17.

MACKAY, R., WELLESLEY, S. and BAZERGAN, E. 1996 Promoting participa-tory evaluation. *ELT Journal* **49** (4).

MALINOWSKI, B. 1923 The problem of meaning in primitive languages. In OGDEN, C.K. and RICHARDS, I.A. *The meaning of meaning.* London: Routledge and Kegan Paul.

MARKEE, N. 1993 The diffusion of innovation in language teaching. *An-nual Review of Applied Linguistics* **13**: 229–43.

MARKEE, N. 1997 *Managing curricular innovation.* Cambridge: Cambridge University Press.

MARPAUNG, M.P. and KIRK, T. 1997 Sustaining a project. In KENNY, B. and SAVAGE, W. (eds), pp. 241–57.

MARSH, C.J. 1986 Curriculum implementation: an analysis of Australian research studies 1973–1983. *Curriculum Perspectives* **6** (1): 11–22.

MARSH, H.W. 1987 Students' evaluations of university teaching: research findings, methodological issues and directions for future research. *International Journal of Educational Research* **11** (3): 257–387.

MAURER, R. 1996 *Beyond the wall of resistance.* Austin, TX: Bard Books.

McCLELLAND, D.C. 1961 *The achieving society.* New York: Free Press.

McGREGOR, D. 1960 *The human side of enterprise.* New York: McGraw-Hill.

McNIFF, J. 1988 *Action research: principles and practice.* Houndmills: Macmillan Education.

MEHAN, H. 1979 *Learning lessons.* Harvard: Harvard University Press.

MELDE, W. 1987 *Zur Integration von Landeskunde und Kommunikation im Fremdsprachenunterricht.* Tubingen: Gunther Narr Verlag.

MICKLETHWAIT, J. and WOOLRIDGE, A. 1997 *The witch doctors: making sense of management gurus.* New York: Times Books, Random House.

MILLMAN, J. and DARLING-HAMMOND, L. (eds) 1990 *Teacher evaluation.* London: Sage.

MITCHELL, R. 1984 Case study. In ELLEN, R. *Ethnographic research: a guide to general conduct.* London: Academic Press.

MITCHELL, R. 1988 *Communicative language teaching in practice.* London: CILT.

MITCHELL, R. 1990 Evaluation of second language teaching projects and programmes. *Language, Culture and Curriculum* **3** (1): 3–17.

MITCHELL, R. 1992 The 'independent' evaluation of bilingual primary education. In ALDERSON, J.C. and BERETTA, A. (eds), pp. 100–40.

MORGAN, G. 1989 *Riding the waves of change.* London: Sage.

MORRIS, P. 1985 Teachers' perceptions of the barriers to the implemen-tation of a pedagogic innovation: a southeast Asian case study. *Interna-tional Review of Education* **31**: 3–18.

MURPHY, D. 1993 Evaluating language learning tasks in the classroom. In CROOKES, G. and GASS, S. (eds) *Tasks and language learning: integrating theory and practice.* Clevedon: Multilingual Matters.

MURPHY, D.F. 1995 Developing theory and practice in evaluation. In REA-DICKINS, P. and LWAITAMA, A.F. (eds), pp. 10–28.

MURPHY, D.F. 1996 The evaluator's apprentices: learning to do evaluation. *Evaluation* **2** (3): 321–28.

MURPHY, R. and TORRANCE, H. (eds) 1987 *Evaluating education: issues and methods.* London: Harper & Rowe.

NEVO, D. 1986 Conceptualisation of educational evaluation. In HOUSE, E. (ed.) *New directions in educational evaluation.* Lewes: Falmer Press.

NEWMANN, F. and WEHLAGE, G. 1995 *Successful school restructuring.* Madison, WI: Centre on Organization and Restructuring of Schools.

NEWTON, C. and TARRANT, T. 1992 *Managing change in schools.* London: Routledge.

NORRIS, N. 1993 *Understanding educational evaluation.* London: Kogan Page.

NUNAN, D. 1985 The role of the national curriculum resource centre within the adult migrant education programme. *Prospect Journal* **1** (1).

NUNAN, D. 1987 Communicative language teaching: making it work. *ELT Journal* **41** (2): 136–45.

NUNAN, D. 1989a A client centred approach to teacher development. *ELT Journal* **43** (2): 111–18.

NUNAN, D. 1989b *Understanding language classrooms: a guide for teacher-initiated action.* New York: Prentice Hall International.

NUNAN, D. 1989c *Designing tasks for the communicative classroom.* Cambridge: Cambridge University Press.

NUNAN, D. 1990a The language teacher as decision-maker: a case study. In BRINDLEY, G. (ed.) *The second language curriculum in action.* Sydney, Australia: NCELTR.

NUNAN, D. 1990b The teacher as researcher. In BRUMFIT, C. and MITCHELL, R. (eds) *Research in the language classroom.* ELT Documents 133: Modern English Publications.

NUNAN, D. and LAMB, C. 1996 *The self-directed teacher – managing the learning process.* Cambridge: Cambridge University Press.

OCHS, E. and SCHIEFFELIN, B. 1983 *Acquiring conversational competence.* London: Routledge & Kegan Paul.

OLSON, J. 1981 Teacher influence in the classroom. *Instructional Science* **10**: 259–75.

OPINION 1997 Keep the bright sparks burning. *The Times Higher Education Supplement,* 31 January, p. 11.

PACEK, D. 1996 Lessons to be learnt from negative evaluation. *ELT Journal* **50** (4): 335–43.

PAJARES, M.F. 1992 Teachers' beliefs and educational research: cleaning up a messy construct. *Journal of Educational Research* **62** (3): 307–32.

PARISH, R. and ARRENDS, R. 1983 Why innovative programs are discontinued. *Educational Leadership* **40** (4): 62–5.

PARKER, G. and ROUXVILLE, A. (eds) 1995 *The year abroad: preparation, monitoring and evaluation.* London: Association of French Language Studies in association with the Centre for Information on Language Teaching.

PARLETT, M. 1984 The new evaluation. In MCCORMICK, R. (ed.) *Calling education to account.* Milton Keynes: The Open University, pp. 185–91.

PARLETT, M. and HAMILTON, D. 1976 Evaluation as illumination: a new approach to the study of innovative programmes. In GLASS, G.V. (ed.) *Evaluation Studies Review Annual,* Vol. 1: 140–157. Beverly Hills, California: Sage.

PARLETT, M. and HAMILTON, D. 1977 Evaluation as illumination: a new approach to the study of innovative programmes. In HAMILTON, D. (ed.) *Beyond the numbers game.* London: Macmillan.

PATTON, M.Q. 1980 *Qualitative evaluation methods,* Beverly Hills: Sage.

PAWSON, R. 1996 Three steps to constructivist heaven. *Evaluation* **2** (2): 213–19.

PAWSON, R. and TILLEY, N. 1997 *Realistic evaluation.* London: Sage.

PENNER, J. 1995 Change and conflict: introduction of the communicative approach in China. *TESL Canada Journal* **12** (2): 1–17.

PENNINGTON, M.C. 1995 The teacher change cycle TESOL Quarterly **29**: 4705–31.

PENNINGTON, M.C. and YOUNG, A.L. 1989 Approaches to faculty evaluation for ESL. *TESOL Quarterly* **23** (4): 619–46.

PENNYCOOK, A. 1989 The concept of method, interested knowledge, and the politics of language teaching. *TESOL Quarterly* **23** (4): 589–618.

PENNYCOOK, A. 1994a *The cultural politics of English as an international language.* London: Longman.

PENNYCOOK, A. 1994b Incommensurable discourses? *Applied Linguistics* **15** (2): 1–24.

PETERS, R.S. 1966 *Ethics and education.* London: Allen & Unwin.

PETERS, T. and WATERMAN, R. 1982 *In search of excellence: lessons from America's best run companies.* New York: Harper & Rowe.

PHILLIPSON, R. 1992 *Linguistic imperialism.* Oxford: Oxford University Press.

PICA, T. and DOUGHTY, C. 1985 The role of group work in classroom second language acquisition. *Studies in Second Language Acquisition* **7**: 233–48.

PICA, T., KANAGY, R. and FALODUN, J. 1993 Choosing and using communication tasks for second language instruction. In CROOKES, G. and GASS, S. (eds) *Tasks and language learning: integrating theory and practice.* Clevedon: Multilingual Matters.

PICA, T., YOUNG, R. and DOUGHTY, C. 1987 The impact of interaction on comprehension. *TESOL Quarterly* **21**: 737–58.

POSTER, C. and POSTER, D. 1991 *Teacher appraisal.* London: Routledge.

PRABHU, N.S. 1992 The dynamics of the language lesson. *TESOL Quarterly* **26**: 225–41.

RAMANI, E. 1990 Theorizing from the classroom. In ROSSNER, R. and BOLITHO, R. (eds) *Currents of change in ELT.* Oxford: Oxford University Press, pp. 196–208.

RAMPTON, B. 1994 Politics and change in research in applied linguistics. *Applied Linguistics* **16** (2): 233–56.

RAMPTON, B. 1997 Retuning in applied linguistics. Special Issue of *International Journal of Applied Linguistics* **7** (1): 3–25.

RANDELL, G. 1994 Employee appraisal. In SISSON, K. (ed.).

REA-DICKINS, P. 1992 *The politics of evaluation: focus on the external evaluator.* Paper presented at the 26th Annual TESOL Conference, Vancouver.

REA-DICKINS, P. 1994 Evaluation and English language teaching. (State of the art article.) *Language Teaching* **27** (2): 71–91.

REA-DICKINS, P. 1995 Obtaining, Disseminating and Using Baseline Data in Project Evaluations. In *Evaluation in Planning and Managing Language Education Projects.* Manchester: The British Council.

REA-DICKINS, P. (forthcoming) Investigating Roles for Evaluation in EAL Contexts. In LEUNG, C. and TOSI, A. (eds) *Rethinking Language Education.* London: CILT.

REA-DICKINS, P. and GERMAINE, K. 1992 *Evaluation.* Oxford: Oxford University Press.

REA-DICKINS, P. and LWAITAMA, A.F. 1995 (eds) *Evaluation for development in English language teaching. Review of ELT,* Vol. 3, No. 3. Basingstoke: Modern English Publications/The British Council/Macmillan.

REA-DICKINS, P. and POTTER, M. 1994 Introduction in *Managing Change and Development in ELT in East and Central Europe.* Manchester: The British Council, pp. 1–4.

REYNOLDS, D. and CUTTANCE, P. 1992 *School effectiveness research, policy and practice.* London: Cassell.

RICHARDS, J. 1990 Preface to *Second language teacher education* (with Nunan, D.) Cambridge: Cambridge University Press.

RICHARDS, J., PLATT, J. and WEBER, H. 1985 *Longman dictionary of applied linguistics.* London: Longman.

RICHARDS, J. and LOCKHART, C. 1994 *Reflective teaching in second language classrooms.* Cambridge: Cambridge University Press.

RICHES, C. and MORGAN, C. (eds) 1989 *Human resource management in education.* Milton Keynes: Open University Press.

ROBERTS, C. and TEASDALE, J. 1996 *National report: England and Wales.* Unpublished report for the European observatory on innovation in education. London: Thames Valley University.

ROGERS, G. and BADHAM, L. 1992 *Evaluation in schools.* London: Routledge.

SACKS, H. and SCHEGLOFF, E. 1974 Opening up closings. In TURNER, R. (ed.) *Ethnomethodology.* Harmondsworth: Penguin, pp. 233–64.

SANDERS, J.R. *et al.* 1994 *The program evaluation standards.* London: Sage Publications.

SANJEK, R. (ed.) 1990 *Fieldnotes: the makings of anthropology.* Ithaca and London: Cornell University Press.

SARASON, S.B. 1971 *The culture of the school and the problem of change.* Boston: Allyn & Bacon.

SARASON, S.B. 1990 *The predictable failure of educational reform.* San Francisco: Jossey-Bass.

SAWWAN, M.K.H.H. 1984 *The communicative teaching of English as a foreign language to secondary school students in Kuwait.* Unpublished PhD Thesis. Cardiff: University of Wales.

SCHÖN, D.A. 1983 *The reflective practitioner: how professionals think in action.* New York: Basic Books.

SCHÖN, D.A. 1987 *Educating the reflective practitioner.* San Francisco: Jossey-Bass.

SCHUDSON, M. 1994 Culture and the integration of national societies. In CRANE, D. (ed.) *The sociology of culture.* Oxford: Blackwell, pp. 21–43.

SCOLLON, R. and SCOLLON, S. 1994 *Intercultural communication.* Oxford: Blackwell.

SCRIVEN, M. 1967 The methodology of Evaluation. In *Perspectives of curriculum evaluation.* Aera Monograph Series on Curriculum Evaluation, 1: 39–83. Rand McNally & Company.

SCRIVEN, M. 1996 The theory behind practical evaluation. *Evaluation* 2 (4): 393–404.

SHARPE, K. 1993 Catechistic teaching style in French primary education: analysis of a grammar lesson with seven-year olds. *Comparative Education* 28 (3): 249–68.

SHARPE, K. 1995 *The Protestant ethic and the spirit of Catholicism: ideological and institutional constraints on system change in English and French primary schooling.* Paper presented at the European Conference on Educational Research, University of Bath.

SHEPARD, L. 1997 Rethinking assessment and accountability. In HARGREAVES, A. (ed.) *Rethinking educational changes with heart and mind.* Alexandria, VA: Association for Supervision and Curriculum Development, pp. 149–68.

SIMMONS, H. and ELLIOTT, J. (eds) 1989 *Rethinking appraisal and assessment.* Milton Keynes: Open University Press.

SIMPSON, J. 1996 Of flux and functional fixedness: towards an educational role for EAP. *Research News* No. 8, (the Newsletter of the IATEFL Research Special Interest Group, pp. 15–21).

SISSON, K. (ed.) 1994 *Personnel management.* Oxford: Blackwell.

SKEHAN, P. 1996 A framework for the implementation of task-based instruction. *Applied Linguistics* 16: 542–65.

SLIMANI, A. 1989 The role of topicalization in classroom language learning. *System* 17: 223–34.

SMITH, N.L. 1991 Evaluation reflections: the context of reflection in cross-cultural evaluation. *Studies in Educational Evaluation* **17**: 3–21.

SMYTH, J. 1991 *Teachers as collaborative learners.* Milton Keynes: Open University Press.

SOED 1992 *Using Performance Indicators in Secondary School Self-Evaluation.* Scottish Office Education Department Edinburgh.

SPINDLER, G. (ed.) 1983 *Education and anthropology.* Stanford, California: Stanford University Press.

SPRADLEY, J.P. 1979 *The ethnographic interview.* New York: Holt, Rinehart & Winston.

STAKE, R.E. 1975 *Evaluating the arts in education: a responsive approach.* Columbus, Ohio: Charles E. Merrill.

STAKE, R. 1995 *The art of case study research.* Thousand Oaks: Sage.

STENHOUSE, L. 1975 *An introduction to curriculum research and development.* London: Heinemann Educational Books.

STERN, C. and KEISLAR, E.R. 1977 Teacher attitudes and attitude change. *Journal of Research and Development in Education* **10** (2): 63–76.

STREET, B. 1993 Culture is a verb. In GRADDOL, D., BYRAM, M. and THOMPSON, L. (eds) *Language and culture.* Clevedon: Multilingual Matters.

SWALES, J. 1989 Service English programme design and opportunity cost. In JOHNSON, R.K. (ed.) *The second language curriculum.* Cambridge: Cambridge University Press, pp. 79–90.

The British Council/Thames Valley University, *PRODESS News.*

TIRRI, K. 1996 *National report, Finland.* Unpublished report for the European observatory on innovation in education, University of Helsinki, Finland.

TORRINGTON, D. 1991 *Management face to face.* London: Prentice Hall.

TRETHOWAN, D. 1987 *Appraisal and target setting.* London: Paul Chapman.

TRETHOWAN, D. 1991 *Managing with appraisal.* London: Paul Chapman.

TUCKMAN, B.W. and JENSEN, M.A.C. 1977 Stages of small group development. *Group and Organisational Studies* **2** (4).

TUDOR, I. 1993 Teacher roles in the learner-centred classroom. *TESOL Quarterly* **47** (1): 22–31.

TURNER, G. and CLIFT, P. 1988 *Studies in teacher appraisal.* London: Falmer Press.

TYLER, R. 1986 Changing concepts of educational evaluation. *International Journal of Educational Research* **10** (1): 1–113.

TYLER, S. 1986 Post-modern ethnography: from document of the occult to occult document. In CLIFFORD, J. and MARCUS, G. *Writing culture: the poetics and politics of ethnography.* Berkeley: University of California Press.

UNDO 1992 United Nations Development Programme: *Human development report.* New York: UNDO.

URBAN, G. 1991 *A discourse-centred approach to culture: native South American myths and rituals.* Austin, Texas: Austin University Press.

USHER, R. and EDWARDS, R. 1994 *Postmodernism and education: different voices, different worlds.* London: Routledge.

VAN EK, J.A. 1986 *Objectives for foreign language learning* Vol. 1: *Scope.* Strasbourg: Council of Europe.

VAN LIER, L. 1988 *The classroom and the language learner.* London: Longman.

VAN LIER, L. 1994a *Educational linguistics: field and project.* Paper presented at Georgetown University Round Table, 1994, Washington, D.C.

VAN LIER, L. 1994b Some features of a theory of practice. *TESOL Journal* **4**: 6–10.

VERSPOOR, A. 1989 *Pathways to change. Improving the quality of education in developing countries.* Washington D.C.: The World Bank.

VROOM, V.H. 1964 *Work and motivation.* New York: Wiley.

WAGNER, J. 1991 Innovation in foreign language teaching. In PHILLIPSON, R. *et al.* (eds) *Foreign/second language pedagogy research.* Clevedon: Multilingual Matters.

WALLACE, M.J. 1991 *Training foreign language teachers.* Cambridge: Cambridge University Press.

WALSH, J., HAMMOND, J., BRINDLEY, G. and NUNAN, D. 1990 *Evaluation of the Metropolitan East Disadvantaged Schools Program Professional Development Program for Primary Teachers, Focusing on Teaching Factual Writing.* Macquarie University: National Centre for English Language Teaching and Research.

WALTER AND DUNCAN GORDON CHARITABLE FOUNDATION 1995 *The seeds of change: the Manitoba school improvement program.* Toronto, Canada: The Watler and Duncan Gordon Charitable Foundation.

WAUGH, R.F. and PUNCH, K.F. 1987 Teacher receptivity to systemwide change in the implementation stage. *Review of Educational Research* **57** (3): 237–54.

WEIR, C. 1996 Evaluating English language programmes and projects. In BULLOUGH, J. and WEBBER, R. (eds), pp. 14–23.

WEIR, C. and ROBERTS, J. 1991 Evaluating a teacher training project in difficult circumstances. In ANIVAN, S. (ed.), pp. 91–109.

WEIR, C. and ROBERTS, J. 1994 *Evaluation in ELT.* Oxford: Blackwell.

WEISS, C. 1972 *Evaluation research: methods of assessing program effectiveness.* Englewood Cliffs, NJ: Prentice Hall.

WELLESLEY, S. 1993 Project based review in practice. *ELT Management: the Newsletter of the Management Special Interest Group of IATEFL* No. 13, October.

WENDEN, A. 1991 *Learner strategies for learner autonomy.* New Jersey: Prentice Hall.

WEST, M. and BOLLINGTON, R. 1990 *Teacher appraisal.* London: David Fulton.

WHITE, R.V. 1987 Managing innovation. *ELT Journal* **11** (3): 211–18.

WHITE, R.V. 1988 *The ELT curriculum.* Oxford: Blackwell.

WHITE, R., MARTYN, M., STIMSON, M. and HODGE, R. 1991 *Management in English language teaching.* Cambridge: Cambridge University Press.

WILSON, D.G. 1992 *A strategy of change.* London: Routledge.

WILSON, S.N. and GUDMUNSDOTTIR, S. 1987 What is this a case of: exploring some conceptual issues in case study. *Education and Urban Society* **20** (1): 42–54.

WINTER, R. 1989 Problems in teacher appraisal: an action research solution. In SIMMONS, H. and ELLIOTT, J. (eds) *Rethinking appraisal and assessment.* Milton Keynes: Open University Press.

WOOLARD, K. 1989 *Double talk: bilingualism and the politics of ethnicity in Catalonia.* California: Stanford University Press.

WRIGHT, T. 1987 *The roles of teachers and learners.* Oxford: Oxford University Press.

WRIGHT, T. 1992 Classroom research and teacher education: towards a collaborative approach. In FLOWERDEW, J., BROCK, M. and HSIA, S. (eds) *Perspectives on second language teacher education.* Hong Kong: City Polytechnic of Hong Kong.

YIN, R.K. 1984 *Case study research: design and methods.* Beverly Hills: Sage.

YOUNG, R. and LEE, S. 1987 EFL curriculum innovation and teachers' attitudes. In LORD, R. and CHENG, H.N.L. (eds) *Language education in Hong Kong.* Hong Kong: The Chinese University Press.

ZAHARLICK, A. and GREEN, J. 1991 Ethnographic research. In FLOOD, J. *et al.* (eds) *Handbook of research on teaching the English language arts.* New York: Macmillan.

ZARATE, G. 1986 *Enseigner une culture étrangère.* Paris: Hachette, Collection F.

Index

accountability, 3–5, 10, 13, 17, 23,
  164, 176, 191
  lateral, 262
  purposes, 264
  skills, 260–1
action
  plan, 18, 39, 128, 182
  research, 147, 150
  theory of, 116, 133–4, 190, 229, 233,
    250
applied linguistics, 81, 189, 195–201,
  203, 209
appraisal, 134, 159–86, 255
  authority, 165–6
  challenges, 184
  criteria, 167–8
  functions, 161
  implementation, 173–6
  in education, 162–3, 261
  opportunity cost, 170, 178
  purposes, 163
  rewards, 185
  self-, 136
  tensions, 178–80
assessment, 74, 191, 253, 259–61
  external, 261
  learner, 259
  practices, 261
  state policies, 259
  systems, 259–60
associations, 4–5
attitude clarification, 33, 37
attitudes, 134
autonomous professional, 265
awareness-building, 139–41

baseline evaluation, 88
bridge building, 15–17, 46, 189, 192,
  214, 263

case study, 24, 26, 33, 37, 39–40,
  61–73, 86–98, 143–6, 171–83,
  206–8, 256
centre-periphery argument, 205
centre-periphery paradigm, 213
change, 26, 31, 253
  agents, 38, 50
  counter-intuitive approach, 256
  differences of view, 256
  educational, 190–1, 253–7
  managing, 48–50, 190
  process, 48, 190
  school-wide, 260
  sustainable, 36
classroom archaeology, 208
classroom materials, 29, 30, 32, 45,
  46
collaboration, 148
collaborative culture, 260–1
commitment criterion, 133
commodification of social processes,
  205
communication, 16, 36, 39, 43
  intercultural, 51
  support, 39–40
communicative
  approach, 28, 39, 41, 44–5, 49, 81
  language teaching, 42–50
  practices, 51
consensus, 8
constructivist, 18, 260
context-free, 205–6
cosmopolitan, 215–16
Council of Europe, 42
criteria for self-evaluation, 134
critical framework, 133
culture, 256
  academic, 195, 203, 204
  collectionist, 195, 204–5, 207–8

integrationist, 195, 204, 207–8
professional, 200, 203, 205, 210, 217
school, 257–8
cultural learning, 72
cultural theory, 52
culturism, 212–16, 218

democracy, 147–8
descriptors, 142
design features, 6–7, 9
dialogic pedagogy, 135–6
discipline
  boundaries, 197–8
  English language teaching, 201–2
discourse, 189, 201–18
  and evaluation, 203, 216–18
  and imperialism, 209–12
  and innovation, 203, 216–18
  critical discourse analysis, 196
  dominant, 197, 201–6, 210, 215
  marketisation, 211
  of English language teaching, 216
  technologisation, 211
diversity and conflict, 258
domains, 15, 17
dynamic innovation processes, 266

eavesdropping, 263
educational context, 40, 48–9
educational reform, 32, 38
educational status, 202
emotional intelligence, 257
empiricist paradigm, 8
empowerment, 148–9
English for academic purposes (EAP),
  79, 81, 87, 103
English language teaching (ELT), 13,
  99, 195, 200, 201, 208–9
ethnocentricity, 203–6, 218
ethnographic evaluation, 66–73, 75,
  80
ethnography, 18, 51–60, 197, 201, 209
  holistic, 57
  relativist, 58, 75
European Union, 267
evaluation
  changing nature, 11–12
  complexity, 23
  criteria, 111, 146, 266
  curriculum, 26
  development processes, 264
  developmental, 13–14, 16, 18, 132,
    139–43, 146–7
  domains, 264–5

dynamics, 258
formative, 13, 87, 149, 164
functions, 13–14, 17
goal-free, 12
illuminative, 14, 74, 149
impact, 11, 128–9
innovation, 16, 192, 216, 261–2
instruments, 141
intersections, 264
macro, 6, 223–4
management, 14, 17, 209, 216
methodology, 11–12, 14, 220–1
micro, 9, 18
naturalistic, 12
participatory, 8–11, 111, 126, 147
planning, 231
programme, 4
purposes, 13, 78, 84, 229, 264–5
quality, 180, 185
second language acquisition, 220–3
self, 131, 134, 136, 143, 149, 178
student, 164
studies, 5–11
summative, 87
theory, 83
trends, 4–11
utilization-focused, 12

false clarity, 33, 46
feasibility, 83
fiscal responsibility, 13
formative evaluation, 90, 97, 101
framework, 14, 18

geopolitical, 25
global cultural conflict, 217
government, 25
Greece, 23, 25–8, 42–3, 48
group
  functions, 142, 156–7
  management, 136–9, 141, 147,
    152–8
  performance checklist, 142, 144–6
  phases, 138–9
  procedures, 141–2
  work, 135–6, 138

hegemonic, 203, 213, 215
hope, 257
hyperrational controls, 200, 264

ideological influence, 203
imperialism, 205–6
implementation, 29–30, 31, 33

innovation, 23, 25, 267–8
  administrative support, 40
  and evaluation, 192
  clarity, 33–5
  compatibility, 40–2, 48
  implementation, 29–30, 39, 43–9
  overload, 38
  peer support, 40
  process, 28
  resistance, 27, 41, 159, 178, 255–6
institutional policy, 102–3
instrumental environments, 40
instrumentalism, 205
integration, 16
intercultural, 23
international publishing, 202
interviews, 47

judgemental, 10, 13

knowledge, 14–17, 18, 19, 37, 49
  cultural, 73–4
  experiential, 14
  taken-for-granted, 203

language
  awareness, 85, 91–5
  centres, 117–19
  education, 3
  learning, 70–1
  modern, 64–5
  programme theory, 103
  teaching, 199
leadership, 40, 255, 258
leadership theory, 254
learner
  -centred, 81, 103, 207, 210, 218
  needs, 91
  self reflection, 74
learning cycle, 14
life-long learners, 38

management
  agenda, 103
  culture, 114, 169
  data, 101
  English language teaching, 195, 199,
    264
  evaluation, 203, 264
  group, 91–8, 136–9, 141–6, 152–8,
  gurus, 254
  innovation, 203, 264
  of a language centre, 122
  of appraisal, 160, 177

of motivation, 165–6
  of reward, 165–6
  of task, 141
  of time, 141
  performance, 170–1, 181, 183
measurement-based outcomes, 265
methodology, 266, 267
  ethnographic, 52–7
modern languages, 64–5
motivation, 166, 178–9, 255, 261
multidimensional, 24, 28
multiple methods, 8

new wave evaluations, 15
nominal group technique, 87, 90

object of evaluation, 266
observation, 39
ODA, 10, 13
  schedule, 43, 45
  teaching, 101, 161, 175
ownership, 13, 36

painful unclarity, 34
panacea and change, 254
paradigm shift, 11
pedagogy, 88, 98, 100, 204
performance data, 253
performance indicators (PIs), 118–20,
    260
  constraints, 121–2
  criteria, 120–1
  transferability, 121–2
personal constructs, 134, 136
polemic style, 209
policy shaping, 6–7
positivist, 18
post-modern sensitivities, 217
pragmatic, 18
process evaluation, 80
process review, 142
PRODESS, 10
professional, 82, 265–6
  development, 84–5, 265–6
  self-evaluation, 264
professional communities, 258
professionalism, 210, 211, 216
programme, 86
  -based review, 111–15, 125
  documentation, 83
  effectiveness, 24
  evaluation, 4, 78, 84, 98–100
  logic, 115–17
  logic model, 116

nature of, 83, 122
personnel, 113, 123
training, 35, 36
project evaluation, 66–8
projectitis, 49
publications, 3, 4

qualitative approach, 99
quality, 81, 260
    evaluation, 82–5
questionnaire, 24, 29, 44

reculturing, 257
reductionism, 214
reflexive ethnographic process, 209
reflexivity, 60, 71
reification of culture, 212–13
reified terminologies, 203
relationship, 201, 203, 257, 264
    micro-cultural, 217
    professional-academic, 203–4
reliability, 83–4
research, 19, 189–90, 220–3, 235–43,
    257–8
    methodology, 86, 237–43
retrospective, 6, 34
rich information, 260

school, 258–9
    boundaries, 259
    cultures, 257–8, 261
    quality reviews, 260
second language acquisition (SLA),
    80, 220–3
self-directed learning, 137
self-perception inventory, 142, 146,
    156–8
site-based management, 257
small-scale evaluations, 8
staff development, 65
    evaluation, 68
stakeholders, 5–8, 13, 14–15, 18, 24,
    83, 112–13, 126, 130, 189, 191
student
    achievement, 259
    agenda, 95
    needs, 88–9
    role perception, 101–2
    self-assessment, 88–9

studies, 5
subject boundaries, 204
successful change, 255, 257
summative evaluation, 97
sustainability, 122, 124, 261
sustainable change, 36
    and involvement, 14, 168, 257–62
systematic, 17
systematic frameworks, 253

task, 224, 226–8
    -based, 135, 244
    consciousness-raising, 142–3, 220,
        234, 239–42
    evaluation, 224–6, 228–35, 243–7
    functions, 142, 156–7
    learning-based, 229, 233
    research, 235–43, 248
    response-based, 229, 233
    student-based, 229, 232
teacher
    appraisal, 159–86
    as professionals, 166, 206
    attitudes and beliefs, 31–3, 37, 134,
        207–8, 255
    development, 132, 148, 161, 167,
        182, 259–60
    diaries, 141, 153
    education, 35–9, 80, 133,
        reflective, 133–4, 147, 250
    roles, 43, 45–6, 93–5
teaching English as a foreign language
    (TEFL), 196, 208
teams, 138, 140
tension, 85
terms of reference, 10, 15
testing, 260
tests, 259–60
Thatcherite legacy, 200, 205
track performance, 260
tradition, 12, 15
triangulation, 74, 268

UK evaluation community, 263
UK Evaluation Society, 263

validity, 84
value for money (VFM), 3, 10